Main Currents in Twentieth-Century Literary Criticism

Main Currents in Twentieth-Century Literary Criticism

A Critical Study

by

Yiannis Stamiris
)))

The Whitston Publishing Company
Troy, New York
1986

Library of Congress Catalog Card Number 82-50402

ISBN 0-87875-254-4

Printed in the United States of America

To Manuella

CONTENTS

TEN

ELEVEN

ACKNOWLEDGEMENTS

BASIC BOOKS, INC. PUBLISHERS for excerpts from *Structural Anthropology* by Claude Levi-Strauss. Translated from the French by Claire Jacobson and Brooke Grundfest Schoepf, (c) 1963 by Basic Books, Inc. Publishers, New York. Reprinted with permission.

THE CONTINUUM PUBLISHING CORPORATION for excerpts from *Truth and Method* by Hans Georg Gadamer. English translation copyright (c) 1975 by Sheed and Ward Ltd., published in 1975 by The Seabury Press. Reprinted with permission by The Continuum Publishing Corporation.

DOUBLEDAY AND COMPANY, INC. for excerpts from *The Social Construction of Reality* by Peter Berger and Thomas Luckmann. Reprinted with permission.

EDITIONS GALLIMARD for excerpts from *Marxisme et sciences humaines* by Lucien Goldmann. Reprinted with permission.

FARRAR, STRAUSS AND GIROUX, INC. for excerpts from *S/Z* by Roland Barthes. Translated by Richard Miller, published in 1974 by Hill and Wang. Reprinted with permission by Farrar, Strauss and Giroux, Inc. For excerpts from *On Racine* by Roland Barthes, published in 1964 by Hill and Wang. Reprinted with permission by Farrar, Strauss and Giroux, Inc.

GEORGE BRAZILLER, INC. for excerpts from *Saint Genet* by Jean-Paul Sartre, published in 1971 by the New American Library. Reprinted with permission by George Braziller, Inc.

GROSSET AND DUNLAP for excerpts from *Writer and Critic and Other Essays* by Georg Lukacs. Edited and translated by A. D. Kahn. Reprinted with permission.

edited by L. Matejka and K. Pomorska. Reprinted with permission.

METHUEN AND CO., LTD. for excerpts from *The Sacred Wood* by T. S. Eliot. Reprinted with permission.

MOUTON AND CO., for excerpts from *Russian Formalism: History-Doctrine* (2nd ed.) by Victor Erlich. Reprinted with permission.

NEW LEFT BOOKS for excerpts from *Critique of Dialectical Reason* by Jean-Paul Sartre, translated by Alan Sheridan-Smith, edited by Jonathan Ree. Reprinted with permission. For excerpts from *Between Existentialism and Marxism* by Jean-Paul Sartre. Translated by John Matthews. Reprinted with permission.

NORTHWESTERN UNIVERSITY PRESS for excerpts from *Adventures of the Dialectic* by Maurice Merleau-Ponty, translated by J. Bien. Reprinted with permission. For excerpts from *Critical Essays* by Roland Barthes, translated by Richard Howard. Reprinted with permission. For excerpts from *Outline of a Jungian Aesthetics* by Morris Philipson. Reprinted with permission.

OXFORD UNIVERSITY PRESS for excerpts from *The Critique of Judgment* by Immanuel Kant, translated by J. C. Meredity. Reprinted with permission.

PETER OWEN LTD, PUBLISHERS for excerpts from *Course in General Linguistics* by Ferdinand de Saussure, translated by Wade Baskin. Reprinted with permission.

PHILOSOPHICAL LIBRARY, INC. for excerpts from *Being and Nothingness* by Jean-Paul Sartre, translated by H. E. Barnes, published in 1975 by the Washington Square Press. Reprinted with permission of the Philosophical Library, Inc. For excerpts from *Encyclopedia of Philosophy* by G. W. F. Hegel, translated by Gustav Emil Mueller. Reprinted with permission.

PRINCETON UNIVERSITY PRESS for excerpts from *The*

Aesthetics of Gyorgy Lukacs by Bela Kiralyfalvi. Reprinted with permission. For excerpts from *The Prison-House of Language* by Fredric Jameson. Reprinted with permission. For excerpts from *The Collected Works of C. G. Jung,* translated by R. F. C. Hull, Bollingen Series XX, vol. 9, I, *The Archetypes and the Collective Unconscious,* copyright (c) 1959, 1969 by Princeton University Press. Reprinted with permission.

PROGRESS PUBLISHERS for excerpts from *Fundamental Problems of Marxism* by George Plekhanov. Reprinted with permission.

RANDOM HOUSE, INC. for excerpts from *Search for a Method* by Jean-Paul Sartre, translated by Hazel E. Barnes. Reprinted with permission. For excerpts from *Poems and Essays* by John Crowe Ransom. Reprinted with permission. For excerpts from *Grundrisse: Foundations of the Critique of Political Economy* by Karl Marx, translated with a foreword by Penquin Books in association with New Left Books. Reprinted with permission of Random House, Inc.

ROUTLEDGE AND KEGAN PAUL LTD. for excerpts from *The Critical Twilight* by John Fekete. Reprinted with permission. For excerpts from *Coleridge on Imagination,* (3rd ed.) by I. A. Richards. Reprinted with permission. For excerpts from *The Hidden God* by Lucien Goldmann, translated by P. Thody. Copyright for the U.S.A. Humanities Press. Reprinted with permission of Routledge and Kegan Paul, Ltd.

SCOTTISH ACADEMIC PRESS for excerpts from *Russian Formalism,* edited by Stephen Bann and John Bowlt. Reprinted with permission.

TAVISTOCK PUBLICATIONS for excerpts from *Towards a Sociology of the Novel* by Lucien Goldmann. Reprinted with permission.

TELOS PRESS for excerpts from *Marx and Engels on Literature and Art,* edited by Lee Baxandall and Stephan Morawski. Reprinted with permission.

THE UNIVERSITY OF CHICAGO PRESS for excerpts

from *The Savage Mind* by Claude Levi-Strauss, copyright (c) 1962 by Librarie Plon. English translation copyright (c) 1966 by George Weidenfeld and Nicolson Ltd. Reprinted with permission of The University of Chicago Press.

THE UNIVERSITY OF MICHIGAN PRESS for excerpts from *Literature and Revolution* by Leon Trotsky. Translated by Rose Strunsky. Reprinted with permission.

THE UNIVERSITY OF NEBRASKA PRESS, for excerpts from *Russian Formalist Criticism*, translated with an introduction by Lee T. Lemon. Copyright (c) 1965 by The University of Nebraska Press. Reprinted with permission.

YALE UNIVERSITY PRESS for excerpts from *A History of Modern Criticism: 1750-1950*, IV by Rene Wellek. Reprinted with permission.

PREFACE

This critical presentation of the main twentieth century approaches to literature is not a history of criticism or of literary critics. It is an exposition of some of the most promising paths that literary criticism has marked for the study of literary creations and of the problems of literature in general.

Literary criticism is a problematic concept. Its meaning varies and it may appear in a number of contexts: impressionistic, relativistic, interpretative, textual, linguistic, biographical, historical, comparative, ethical, judicial, etc. This last type reveals the original meaning of the term criticism, which is *evaluation* and *judgment*. The typology and differentiation of literary criticism according to its particular perspective is based on the numerous angles from which literary works can be viewed (i.e. historical, psychological, sociological, etc.) This systematization, together with its striving for generalizations, indicates that literary criticism is a scientific endeavor—as this term is usually employed in the social sciences. At the same time, individual critical works might contain certain artistic properties to the extent that some of them (e.g. Sartre's *Saint Genet)* resemble literary creations.

In general, the products of literary criticism are neither exclusively 'scientific' nor 'purely' artistic because both elements often co-exist, although one or the other may occasionally predominate. Literary criticism then should be considered both as scientific and artistic in nature, aiming, on the one hand, at the description, interpretation and evaluation of literary works, and on the other, at the establishment of principles and the construction of theories which are applicable to these works. The fact that this definition is linked with the literary work alone does not mean that the latter's creator and other significant factors directly and/or indirectly related to it are excluded by the term as it is employed here. Its wider meaning, however, cannot be confined to a restricted definition; it will appear as this concept will be used in the eleven chapters of this book.

The first chapter discusses those nineteenth century ideas of Taine, Marx and Engels which have provided the foundations of the sociology of literature and of dialectical criticism. The second, is devoted to an examination of the content-oriented sociological approach to literature developed by Georg Plekhanov. The third chapter is an account of Lucien Goldmann's genetic structuralist method which offers a new alternative to the sociology of literature. Hence, Lukacs' dialectical criticism is examined as an approach to literary production full of possibilities. The discussion of Freud's and Jung's psychoanalytic criticism which follows, with its concern for the creative subject, adds another dimension to the study of literature. The field of operation of Russian formalism is the subject matter of the sixth chapter, while the seventh explores the fundamentals of American new criticism with special reference to the work of John Crowe Ransom. One major representative of French structuralism, Roland Barthes, is presented in the eighth chapter, after an introduction to the Kantian and linguistic basis of this approach to literature as well as to some ideas developed by Claude Levi-Strauss. The ninth chapter examines some aspects of phenomenological criticism, and the tenth deals with the hermeneutic philosophy of Hans-Georg Gadamer, as it relates to literature. The final chapter is a comprehensive account of the literary criticism of Jean-Paul Sartre.

The reader is warned not to expect a comparison between the various approaches to literature included here or between their respective theories. This is because these diverse approaches and theories are the outcome of varied epistemological and philosophical orientations. The same approaches and theories do not only pose different questions; they even ask similar questions with dissimilar meanings. The lack, therefore, of a common ground on which they could be compared makes them incommensurable. Certainly, literary criticism is after specific *facts*. Yet even when different aesthetic theories are after the same facts, they interpret and evaluate them according to their own special rules, which in turn affect the nature of these facts. The latter then are not 'objective' but relative to the frame of reference of each particular theory; properly speaking, they are not verifiable. Critical theories, therefore, cannot be evaluated by comparison, each one of them providing its own criteria of validation. The ultimate criterion, then, is not the 'scientific' verifiability of the conclusions which an aesthetic theory arrives at, but the fulfilment of the objectives it purports to achieve, the adequacy of its methods and its relative self-sufficiency. In the final analysis, any literary theory or aesthetics or poetics is a system of rules and principles which makes consistent the accounts of concrete literary works. In this sense, the variety of approaches and theories enriches our capability to deal with literature and all factors related to it.

Yiannis Stamiris
Athens, Greece

ONE

TAINE, MARX AND ENGELS:
FROM POSITIVISM TO DIALECTICS

1. *Taine: Foundations of the Sociology of Literature*

The so-called sociological approach to literature regards literary works not as individual but as clearly social phenomena. Broadly speaking, the sociology of literature can take two directions.[1] The first focuses on the work itself, seeing it more or less as a 'mirror-image' of the society which gave rise to it. The conception of the literary text as a mirror has been greatly abused, but we will discuss this problem later on. At this point, we should stress that for the sociologist, literature is viewed primarily as having documentary value. This can range from the crude idea that everything in literature is a photocopy of real life, to the refined assertion that "information about reality has been presented to and by the human species in the form of narrative fiction. . . . In one sense, everything is fiction; in another, fiction is reality."[2] In this kind of approach to literature, sociology becomes intertwined with the study of history, anthropology, religion, etc.

The second direction focuses essentially on literature as a mode of production, mainly examining the situation of the producer (writer), the owner of the means of reproduction and distribution (publisher), and the situation of the market (reading public). In a technical sense, this is a more genuine sociological approach which tries to throw light on the relationship between the writer and the publisher within the framework of the capitalist market. The French sociologist, Robert Escarpit, has done some pioneering work in this direction,[3] and he is considered the leading expert in this field. We should mention of course that Sartre's essay "For whom does one write?" explores the socio-historical relationship between the writer and his patron (i.e. an aristocrat or a publisher), and also between the writer and his public.[4]   The character of this last relationship is also explored in the framework of what is labelled the sociology of taste.[5]

In this chapter, we will only discuss the first direction which sociology takes, because we are not concerned at this moment with the writer as producer and with the literary work as a marketable product.

It was the Italian philosopher Giambattista Vico who first expressed the idea of the relationship between literature and its social environment,[6] and he is regarded as the founder of the historical* approach.[7]   After Vico, Johan Gottfried Herder had a very strong feeling for history and he demanded of the literary critic that he enter "the spirit of the piece itself" and to consider that "the most indispensable explanation especially of a poet is the explanation of the customs of his age and nation."[8] Herder also spoke about the influence of the geographical environment on literary production.

A little younger than Herder, Madame de Staël laid the cornerstone of a sociological approach to literature in her book *De la litérature considerée dans les rapports avec les institutions sociales* (1800), in which—however unsystematically—she discusses the influence of social institutions, climate and specific geographical features on literary works.   It is a rather unsuccessful book, but Madame de Staël tried to demonstrate the "influence of religion, manners and laws on literature, and what the influence is of literature on religion, manners and laws."[9]   Important to Madame de Staël's theory is the notion of *national character* which can be located and identified in the literary expression of each nation.   She claims for example that the literature of Northern Europe reflects the "passionate sadness of the inhabitants of a foggy climate", while the literature of the South is rich in "images of freshness, limpid streams, and the shade protecting us from the burning rays of the sun."[10]

The way Vico, Herder and de Staël express their views on literature might seem unsophisticated today, (especially in the cases of Herder and de Staël), permeated by the crude mechanical materialism of the seventeenth and eighteenth centuries.   Yet one cannot deny the importance of some of

---

*By historical here is meant the approach which views literature from a social, economic and political point of view.

their ideas and the lasting influence which they still exercise on literary criticism. These ideas were further refined and enriched in the nineteenth century and thus the foundations of the sociology of literature were laid down, directly by Hippolyte Taine, the French positivist thinker on the one hand, and indirectly, by Marx and Engels on the other.

Taine concluded his study on Balzac with the following sentence: "Balzac is the greatest storehouse of documents on human nature that we possess."[11] It was not only Balzac's literary production that Taine thought of as a treasurehouse of documents. His view of Balzac's work epitomizes his stand towards literature in general which he regards as the most trustworthy record of the past. Properly analyzed, literature can reveal the secrets of the nature of a particular people at a specific time, within the framework of a unique geographical area. Above all, these literary records can reveal the "special psychology" of a people which determines, for example, their aesthetic judgment and which is itself determined by the concrete geographical surroundings in which these people live. Taine writes:

> The great achievements of painting in Flanders in the seventeenth century, of poetry in England in the sixteenth century, of music in Germany in the eighteenth century, can be traced to the presence of certain germs, of certain psychological conditions. It is the law of human regulation for which history must now search: It is their special psychology of each special formation which must be got at. . . . If a document is rich, and we know how to interpret it, we shall find in it the psychology of a particular soul, often that of an age and sometimes that of a race. In this respect a great poem, a good novel, the confession of a superior man are more instructive than a mass of historians and histories.[12]

These assertions were quite influential even on Marxists. Plekhanov, for example, accepting many of Taine's ideas, quotes some passages from this book *A Tour Through the Pyrenées,* which refer to the role of environment in the shaping of men's psychology in general and of their aesthetic taste in particular.[13] But let us examine in some detail Taine's literary criticism.

The key words in Taine's theory of literature are *Race,*

Milieu and *Moment.* In the introduction to his study of English literature he develops his ideas and makes clear his positivistic orientation as he tries to approach literature the way the natural sciences approach their objects of investigation. The elements of Race, Milieu and Moment are related to each other. In each particular case, however, (i.e. in a specific literary work) one is more predominantly manifested than the others.

For Taine, one human race is distinct from another on the basis of certain innate as well as physical characteristics, the basic patterns of which cannot be disregarded even if a given race is scattered throughout the world. In his mind, these special characteristics of a race are acquired "from the climate, from the soil, the food, and the great events that it underwent at its origin."[14]   Taine also maintains that although the racial characteristics of people once acquired do not change, no matter how much the conditions of life and climate change, the *national* characteristics of the same people are quite different in nature from the *racial* ones, and they change, since among other things they are also determined by the historical process.

Obviously, Taine's theory of race is simplistic (all people of the same race regardless of whether they are poor or hungry or rich, and regardless of the nature of their work, have the same racial characteristics), naively eternal (not affected by time), and evidently useless for the approach of a really great literary work; above all, it facilitates the development of racist theory.[15]

Taine's notion of milieu is the most basic concept of his theory, and a unique example of the way mechanical determinism thinks. Milieu appears to be a multivalent notion, its basis being climate and geography. Taine himself explains the meaning of the term milieu by simply rephrasing Madame de Staël's ideas on the subject. To understand how milieu could determine almost everything without any chance of liberating oneself from its casual influence, Taine tells us in his *Philosophie de l' Art* in reference to Holland:

> It might well be said that in this country water makes grass, grass makes cattle, cattle makes cheese, butter and meat; and all these, with beer, make the inhabitant. Indeed, out of this physical organization, saturated with moisture, spring the phlegmatic temperament, the regular habits, the tranquil mind and nerves, the capacity for taking life easily and prudently, the unbroken content-

ment, the love of well being, and consequently, the reign
of cleanliness and the perfection of comfort. [16]

The point one can make here is not to judge Taine—the
narrowness of his thinking and its intellectual basis are too
obvious to make comment necessary—but to observe that ideas
of similar nature were to be expressed decades after his death
(in psychology, as we will see later on, by Freud and also in
the work of Lombroso—the constitution of a man's body and
spirit determines his behavior; in the fatalistic philosophy of
Nietzsche—the will to power; in vulgar materialism, etc.). At
any rate, for Taine, milieu determines literature, and by employing this notion, together with the notions of race and moment,
almost nothing remains inexplicable in the sphere of literary
production.

Moment, the third key-word in his theory, is also a multivalent concept, and Wellek suggests that it can mean "the age,
the *Zeitgeist*" or even the literary tradition.[17] Moment, however, is distinct from both race and milieu because it is the only
one which implies change. At the same time, like race and
milieu, it is an obscure, ill-defined term.

It is fair to mention that Taine himself, becoming progressively aware of the gaps in his theory of literature, somehow
tried to remedy them. For example, he correctly noticed the
adaptability of literary production to its actual—not potential—
public. He also gave some thought to the importance of the
special psychology of the writer, his creative faculty, etc. But
Taine's unsystematic attempts to correct his crude positivism
and mechanistic materialism were in vain, because he never really
saw the literary work as something distinct and in many respects
autonomous. Nevertheless, he remained influential in the subsequent development of the sociology of literature, a part of
which still regards literary works merely as documents.

These brief comments are not intended to invalidate Taine's
contribution to literary criticism, and if some of his faults
alone are emphasized, this is because we simply want to underline a number of positions which other literary critics—of whom
we shall speak later—tried to avoid. Within this framework, we
can agree with Albert Guerard, that "Taine himself may be
antiquated: his method is still with us. It does not tell the
whole truth, not perhaps the essential truth: but the truth it
tells is far from negligible."[18]

2. *Marx and Engels: Foundations of Dialectical Criticism.*

a. *Marx, Engels and Literature*

Writings about the influence of Marx and Engels on literary criticism are so numerous that even a cursory look at them can be an undertaking in itself. These writings can be tentatively classified into two broad categories. First, those which aim basically at attacking Marx and Engels on the basis of their sporadic and occasional comments on specific literary works and authors, while the doctrine of economic determinism is always associated with these comments. One representative of this tendency for example is Peter Demetz, who concludes his study *Marx, Engels and the Poets* by stating that he himself "attempted to show that Marx and Engels arrived at their explanations of literary phenomena by way of oblique, personal and often diverging paths."[19]   Another follower of this tendency is Rene Wellek, who, like Demetz concludes by making three points: first, that Marx and Engels can by no means be considered theoreticians of literary works; second, that economic determinism is the main characteristic of their scattered comments; and third, that their crude deterministic explanations of literature become somewhat milder in the "late" Engels who recognizes some degree of autonomy to the superstructure.[20]

The second category of writings on the same subject is exemplified by Mikhail Lifshitz in his pioneering study *The Philosophy of Art of Karl Marx*, written more than forty years ago.   Concretely, instead of trying just to isolate comments made by Marx and Engels on particular occasions or merely to relate these comments to aspects of the Marxian system or its historical consequences presented in their crudest form (economic determinism, Stalinism, etc.)—a practice often adopted by many scholars openly hostile to Marxism—Lifshitz places the whole issue in its proper framework by trying "to analyze Marx's aesthetic judgment as an element within his general theoretical development." This way, instead of taking Marx's statements on literary matters at their face value and deriving general inferences from them, he is able "to trace some crucial aesthetic themes in Marx's work in terms of their integral relations to the developing totality of his thought."[21]

To begin with, it is correct to say that neither Marx nor

Engels ever engaged systematically in the development of a theory of literature, yet it is equally correct that aesthetic problems are an integral part of Marx's overall conception of history.[22] Specifically, genuine artistic activity is for Marx—among other things—a form of human labor which in the case of capitalist society is even identical to productive labor: "A writer is a productive laborer not insofar as he produces ideas, but insofar as he enriches the publisher who publishes his work."[23] In this sense, the use of the term Marxist aesthetics means, as Lukács points out, not something "radically new" (where for example some of the most basic aesthetic questions are concerned, i.e. the relation between an artistic creation and its external reality), but a body of ideas which "merely raises onto the highest level of awareness what has always been the central point of theory and practice for the great artists of the past."[24]

It would be factually untrue to refer to Marxist aesthetics as something revolutionarily different from classical aesthetic theories, as some advocates of the vulgar version of socialist realism would have us believe.[25] The ultimate Marxist contribution to aesthetics is that "Marxism searches for the material roots of each phenomenon, regards them in their historical connections and movement, ascertains the laws of such movement and demonstrates their development from root to flower . . . ."[26]

To avoid misconceptions and faulty judgments a distinction should be made—for analytic purposes only—between the actual statements of Marx and Engels in reference to specific works and authors *and* their very general formulations concerning the relationship between the material and ideological production of men (especially the overquoted passages from the 'Preface' and *The German Ideology*) as well as their more particular remarks, which we shall talk about shortly, concerning art and literature and their relation to man.

A second distinction should be made between these particular statements and general principles and 'Marxist aesthetics' as it is constantly developing on the basis of the unfolding totality of Marxian ideas. Thus, while a number of Marxist theoreticians have sometimes misinterpreted Marx's and Engel's circumstantial utterances, one should refrain from making general inferences deriving just from this fact and avoid the example of Peter Demetz who emphatically points out that according to "orthodox functionaries" Marx and Engels developed a complete aesthetics comparable to Hegel's detailed theorizing on the subject.

In general, one should be aware of the nature and direction of Marx's and Engels' commentaries which, despite the fact that they are outside the main framework of their major studies, have affected in one way or another the ideas expressed by subsequent Marxists. One might suggest, then, that the full significance—both actual and potential—of the Marxian problematic for the development of a well-defined aesthetics (the construction of which was attempted by Lukács, as we shall see in another chapter), can be seen in terms of four general levels. First, the *epistemological* level, which lays down the foundation of a specific theory of knowledge; second, the *philosophical* level especially in relation to the problem of the value of artistic and literary products; third, the *theoretical* level, where the phenomena of artistic creation in general and literary creation in particular can be accounted for; and finally, the *methodological* level where a particular method is developed for the approach to literary works.

The discussion of the various implications of Marxian ideas as a whole and above all of Marxian logic on questions concerning literature will be taken up in the last section of this chapter. As for the concrete statements mentioned earlier made by Marx and Engels, we do not consider it necessary to present them here in detail, first because they have been discussed by other studies,[27] and second because notwithstanding their importance we can accept Lukács' assertion that "The generalized principles of Marxist Aesthetics and literary history are to be found in the doctrines of historical materialism."[28]

Here, we should only refer to major themes[29] touched upon by Marx's and Engels' remarks on men's life in general and art and literature in particular, commenting on those which are not dealt with in other chapters of this study. Further, we shall see how certain of these themes, in combination with Marx's emphasis on the primacy of the material over the ideological activity of society on the one hand, and his viewing of art and literature not as individual but as social products on the other, resulted in a markedly different *sociological* approach to literature than that for example of Taine. Specifically, Plekhanov and Goldmann will be presented separately as two major contributors to this approach—each one following a different strategy. Also, the literary criticism of Lukács, reaching beyond the limitations of a merely sociological treatment of literature, despite his strong interest in the latter's social aspects, will be examined in a subsequent chapter.

b. *Major Themes of Marx's and Engels' Aesthetic Thought*

The first theme concerns the origin of artistic production, which is attributed to man's ability to expand his productive field beyond the sphere of his immediate needs. Marx writes in *The Economic and Philosophic Manuscripts of 1844*:

> an animal only produces what it immediately needs for itself or its young. It produces one-sidedly, while man produces universally. It produces only under the dominion of immediate physical needs, while man produces even when he is free from physical need and only truly produces in freedom therefrom. An animal produces only itself, while man reproduces the whole of nature. . . . Man, therefore, also forms things in accordance with the laws of beauty. . . .[30]

The basic source of artistic production is human labor, which having "a form that is exclusively characteristic of man" is a purposeful activity carried on not instinctively but according to plans conceived in man's *imagination*.[31] The conception and execution of artistic plans is not instinctual either, therefore, a developed aesthetic sensibility is to be found not in the natural individual but in *social* man. Aesthetic sensibility, then, is an historical product, an outcome of the *social* process. This was very clear in Marx's mind: "the *senses* of the social man are *other* senses than those of the non-social man."[32] As Mészáros puts it, these senses become "refined" and "humanized" in society. But as the latter unfolds and expands, the former increase in "number," "richness" and "complexity," despite their constant dehumanization inflicted upon them by capitalist alienation: thus, the urgent necessity of their emancipation.[33]

The human need which resulted in the pursuit of artistic works had two dimensions: one material (i.e. control and use of nature), the other spiritual (i.e. magic). Thus, initially, "Art was a magic tool and it served man in mastering nature and developing social relationships."[34]   The consolidation of artistic endeavor as a distinct productive activity and its evolution along-side the overall production of men became possible first by *labor*, and second by *language*, "the two most essential stimuli," according to Engels, "under the influence of which the brain of the ape gradually changed into that of a man."[35]   Consequently, one can say together with Engels not just that labor in general "created man himself,"[36] but, in our particular case, that art, man's most liberated activity from mundane considerations, created in turn and is still creating man.   Everything said about art applies to literature, being the artistic expression through language of man's awareness of himself in society and nature.

The second theme refers to the relation between art and the problem of human alienation.   But, one may ask, how is it possible that the very products of man's freedom can be estranged from himself?   And to what extent does this specific estrangement affect the essence of human life?   As Marx argues, it is in the nature of the capitalist system of private property to condemn humans to an existence shackled by the chains of alienation.   Under this system, the members of a human group are not colleagues in a collective enterprise—the enterprise of the forming of a community of co-operating equals—but rivals competing in a struggle of exploitation of one by another.   One of the forms that this exploitation takes—in the commodity-producing society—is the creation of artificial needs, the satisfaction of which requires further sacrifices, laborious efforts and privations, resulting in the subjection of individuals to a multitude of "alien" powers that engulf them.   As these powers multiply "every new product represents a new *potency* of mutual swindling and mutual plundering."   Consequently, "Man becomes ever poorer as man. . . ."[37]

Under capitalism, the plethora of ever-increasing needs is the facade of one fundamental need: the pressing need for money.   Not that money was not desirable before the advent of capitalism, but the difference now is that for the first time in its history money is endowed with the possibility of taking the form of capital, and consequently of ruling over all the other powers, material, spiritual, moral, etc. of the capitalist society.   However, for money to be accumulated—at least at the level of the individual—a second rule, together with that of exploitation, reigns supreme: "the denial of life and of all human needs. . . ."[38]

Are we then faced under capitalism with the absurd contradiction of the annihilation of man's ultimate treasure, his own life, for the sake of money? One answer seems to be in the affirmative and it is illuminating to see with what words Marx describes this improbable yet very real phenomenon:

> The less you eat, drink and read books; the less you go
> to the theatre, the dance hall, the public-house; the less
> you think, love, theorize, sing, paint, fence, etc. the
> more you *save*—the *greater* becomes your treasure which
> neither moths nor dust will devour—your *capital*. The
> less you *are*, the more you *have*; the less you express
> your own life, the greater is your *alienated* life—the
> greater is the store of your estranged being. Everything
> which the political economist* takes from you in life
> and in humanity, he replaces for you in *money* and in
> *wealth*; and all the things which you cannot do, your
> money can do. It can eat and drink, go to the dance
> hall and the theatre; it can travel, it can appropriate art,
> learning, the treasures of the past, political power—all
> this it *can* appropriate for you—it can buy all this for
> you: it is the true endowment. Yet being all this, it is
> *inclined* to do nothing but create itself, buy itself; for
> everything else is after all its servant. And when I have
> the master I have the servant and do not need his servant.
> All passions and all activity must therefore be submerged
> in avarice. . . .[39]

Here, Marx indicates that he is not unaware of the fact that the capitalists, once their purse is full and profits are finding their way in, do not deprive themselves of the pleasures and luxuries of life; on the contrary the automatic satisfaction of every need that appears as such in their minds may cause them feelings of boredom. What Marx stresses is the trend indicating that the pleasure of the capitalist "is only a side-issue—recuperation—something subordinated to production: at the same time it is a calculated and therefore, itself an *economical* pleasure."[40] In other words, not only the exploited

---

*The *capitalist* political economist.

but also the exploiters, not only the thirsty for riches and money but even those who are wealthy often adopt the denial, not the enjoyment of life. To paraphrase Marx, the more they have, the less they are: their own alienation is a fact of their gilded life.

Marx arrives at the conclusion that in contrast to pre-capitalist economic formations, and especially to "the childlike world of the ancients" which in its treatment of artistic production "appears to be superior," capitalism is "hostile to intellectual production such as art and poetry."[41] To grasp the objective basis justifying this qualitative comparison between two distant worlds, however, we must proceed to a third theme concerning the relation between art and the process of production and consumption.

The chief purpose of capitalism is profit-making realized in the process of the marketing of commodities: the mass production of commodities then is capitalism's foremost prerequisite. Marx states: "that which determines the magnitude of the value of any article is the amount of labor socially necessary, or the labor time socially necessary for its production . . . nothing can have value without being an object of utility."[42] Now let us pose the question: Does Marx include art and literature here? Or, to put it another way, does Marx view artistic and literary works as ordinary marketable commodities, i.e. utensils, cloths, etc. producible by the rationalized capitalist factories, which after following the path of the so-called *circulation of commodities* can be used as mere objects of utility?

The answer is clearly in the negative for three main reasons: a) Works of art and literature are unique, that is, created once and for all. We can only reproduce as many *copies* of them as we like (copies of Hemingway's *The Old Man and the Sea*, Picasso's *Guernica*, etc.) or we can *perform* them infinitely (dances, musical pieces, etc.) On the contrary, when a Detroit plant produces cars, it brings out of its assembly line distinct individual units, no matter how great their resemblance to each other is. Thus, as Walter Benjamin states in his famous essay "The Work of Art in the Age of Mechanical Reproduction," "Even the most perfect reproduction of a work of art is lacking one element: its presence in time and space, its unique existence at the place where it happens to be."[43] b) Since works of art cannot be produced on a mass scale like every-day commodities, their commodity-like circulation in the market is not possible, except in the form of their copies or performances.* Of course, certain works of art, i.e. paintings, can be bought and sold (i.e. take a commodity form).   However, the act of their exchange for money represents a half circle, i.e. it can be repeated but not completed because the money collected for a given art-work cannot be used as capital for the continuation of production of other *same* works.   c) The meaning of the utility of a work of art or literature does not coincide with the meaning of the utility of a regular commodity. The utility of the former, properly defined, has an aesthetic core peculiar to works of art. Therefore, although there is a mode of consumption pertaining to artistic works and absolutely necessary for the continuation of artistic production, nevertheless it is essentially different from the mode of consumption of commodities, i.e. foodstuffs.

István Mészáros, discussing the position of art-works in commodity producing (and consuming) societies, emphasizes the disadvantage of the former in comparison to ordinary commodities.   This disadvantage consists in art's alienation from society as a whole and it is attributed to the lack of that kind of consumer demand which would make artistic production indispensable to society's normal, i.e. unalienated, life. After quoting Marx as maintaining that *"consumption creates the drive for production,"* and demonstrating that these two sister-processes have individual as well as social aspects, Mészáros focuses on the problems which art faces under capitalism, always considered from Marx's point of view. Hence, he makes five essential points which can substantiate our previous remarks (a), (b) and (c): An artistic creation is not "consumed" as a mere *"object of utility;"* the ownership of an artistic work and its aesthetic enjoyment are not related; works of art do not alter the objects which they depict; aesthetic enjoyment is not necessitated by men's essential needs but by needs of another kind; even though an art-work remains unchanged in the course of its consumption "its aesthetic substance is constantly recreated."[4]

The important fact indicated here is that the privatization of works of art and the lack of the proper motivation for their creative and not just utilitarian consumption result in their

---

*The case of cinematographic art is outside the framework of this study. It is subsequent to Marx's time and it is too complicated to be considered here.

ultimate reduction to commercial objects, that is, to commodities. Therefore, capitalism alienates art from all, the artist
included. To meet this problem, the elevation of the aesthetic
sensibility of society is required and this is another theme which
seems to concern Marx.[45] However, as both Marx and Engels
suggest, the ideal of a disalienated art, or the production and
consumption of works of art in a process wherein all people
will be prepared to participate accordingly, is linked with another
ideal which, to the extent that it is not a utopia, has the potential
of contributing to the enrichment of man's artistic (freed) life:
the ideal of a truly communist society.[46]

As we have already mentioned, another theme, namely that
of the value of artistic and literary products, will be discussed in
the course of our examination of the philosophical level of the
Marxist construction. Other themes touched upon by Marx and
Engels are the class values expressed in literary works[47] and
so-called tendentious literature: the practice by which the
writer's own opinions, values, political beliefs, etc, are *openly*
exposed in his writings.

Engels, for instance, was very much against such a propa-
gandistic literary practice, viewing it as demonstrating lack
of talent.[48] This, he makes very clear in two of his letters:
one to Minna Kautsky and another to Margaret Harkness. Engels
is fully aware of the artists' inclination to express their ideology
through their works—he refers specifically to some of the greatest
poets and writers, e.g. Aeschylus, Aristophanes, Dante, Cer-
vantes, etc. He argues nevertheless that the exercise of such a
right on the part of the artist should always comply with certain
artistic requirements.[49]

The most important of the remaining themes is related
to the issue of realism in literature: the backbone of Marxian
aesthetics. Yet we shall deal with this in the chapter devoted
to the literary criticism of Lukács. Here we can only warn that
Engels' remark on realism made in the above-mentioned letter
to Margaret Harkness should not be taken as revealing the Marxist position on the subject. It would be erroneous to assume that
realism is a dogmatic recipe,[50] based solely on Engels' statement
that "Realism . . . implies, besides truth of detail, the truthful
reproduction of typical characters under typical circumstances."[51] As will be shown later, the Marxist concept of
realism is much more general and suggestive than that.

These themes—and a few more—are indeed overexamined,

overused and overdebated by Marxists and non-Marxists alike. As far as the former are concerned, some try to remain close to the Marxian theoretical system to the best of their ability; some others try to make a synthesis by introducing elements, ideas and insights from outside the body of Marxian thinking.[52] What is distinctive about the attempts toward a Marxist criticism is their emphasis on a *sociological* approach to literary works, specifically on the socio-historical and cultural conditions which surround (are extrinsic to) such works. In turn, as has been indicated, the primary subject of the Marxist oriented sociological investigation is the *ideology* expressed in literary works,[53] ultimately conditioned itself by the material life of society (i.e. productive forces and relations of production). This point, however, introduces a problem requiring more attention: historical materialism's treatment of art and literature.

c. *Historical Materialism and Literary Criticism*

The general observation one can make in relation to the sociological approach is that the spirit of Marxian guidelines is often misunderstood and/or distorted, resulting in vulgar materialist literary criticism, i.e. that based on economic determinism. This happens because the highly complicated relationships between ideas, feelings, attitudes, judgments, desires, expectations, etc.—particularly when they are expressed in an artistic manner—and the material life of society are not viewed in the light of a complex network of mediations (not of course for their complete explanation, which seems to be inaccessible at the present state of our knowledge, but for an approximate elucidation of them) but are accounted for mechanically as direct one-to-one relations between the economic base and the artistic/literary superstructure.

The vulgar materialist pretends ignorance of or appears to be indifferent to Marx's own warning: "As regards art, it is well known that some of its peaks by no means correspond to the general development of society; nor do they therefore to the material substructure, the skeleton as it were of its organization. For example the Greeks compared with modern (nations) or else Shakespeare."[54] What the vulgar materialist seems to repeat in parrot fashion, sometimes alongside those who are hostile to

Marxism, is the celebrated paragraph from the 'Preface'[55] which the latter never fail to quote in evidence of Marx's adherence to economic reductionism. In order to do away with such abuses of the essence of Marx's writings let us elaborate on these two statements, which are by no means contradictory.

A close reading suggests that each one of these pronouncements refers to a *different* subject, and it is nonsense to invoke a divided or perplexed Marx, at one point subscribing to the relative autonomy of the artistic mode of production and at another maintaining its immediate, continuous causation and control by the economic base. The excerpt from the preface correlates dialectically—not mechanically—"the mode of production of material life" with "the general process of . . . intellectual life. . . ," that is, *only* with the *general* pattern of the *ideological content* of artistic and literary products. As for the excerpt from the introduction, it appears to refer exclusively to some exceptional cases of *artistic excellence* attained by certain works, or ultimately to the *individual talents** which were proven able to achieve it.

The society's state of overall development—primarily its material substructure—ultimately conditions, or better still, it is the precondition for artistic production; artistic excellence however does not necessarily correspond to it. Certainly, a given social formation might contribute positively or negatively to the manifestation of the creative craftsmanship of an individual talent; it might also offer or not offer the adequate all-embracing climate necessary for it to reach a maximum performance. Yet, no matter how advanced its state of general development, in no case can any social formation create a superb artistic talent, produce a great literary piece, or qualitatively surpass the artistic production of another formation with less advanced state of general development *by the mere supremacy of its material base.*

---

*Talent here refers neither to an inborn, natural ability, after the manner of the Romantics, nor to a divinely entrusted mental endowment. It is rather meant to be a special skill acquired in the formative process of an individual's personality as a result of the dialectical interaction between numerous objective (socio-cultural, biographic, material, etc.) and subjective elements of various kinds.

The distortion of the spirit of historical materialism has also resulted in rigid dogmas, like for example the Stalinist version of socialist realism, which reduce literature to a mere piece of machinery in the hands of a rigid party. In relation to this we can say that Lenin's principle of "party literature" was understood not as having a tactical political purpose, but was rather exploited as a principle with universal theoretical validity.[56]

It appears that it was in anticipation of the grave consequences of such distortions that Trotsky warned that "The domain of art is not one in which the party is called upon to command", explaining to the dogmatists that "the dictatorship of the proletariat is not an organization for the production of the culture of the new society, but a revolutionary and military system struggling for it."[57]

There is no point in engaging here in the history of the various forms which sociological Marxist criticism has taken under various conditions in the course of its development.[58] A discussion of Plekhanov's work will be sufficient to indicate not only some of the positive elements of this traditional sociological approach to literature influenced by Marxism but also some of its vulnerable aspects and limitations. Here we should take a close look at Marxism and literary criticism in terms of the four interrelated levels mentioned earlier: the epistemological, the philosophical, the theoretical and the methodological. Our starting point, however, should be a brief consideration of what might be called a Marxist ontology, which Lukács set forth to work out.

Lukács maintains[59] that in contrast to idealist philosophies which stress the primacy of consciousness over being (for subjective idealism, i.e. Kant, *human* consciousness produces being, whereas for objective idealism, i.e. Hegel, this consciousness is superior to that which is human: absolute mind), Marx developed his materialist conception of history on the ontological basis of the primacy of being over thinking. At the same time Marx rejected, in his first thesis on Feuerbach, the latter's "ontological and epistemological dualism" which is characteristic of his materialist philosophy, and transcended it in terms of the mediating role of "practice."[60]

Marx, in his third thesis on Feuerbach states that "The materialist doctrine concerning the changing of circumstances and upbringing forgets that circumstances are changed by men and that it is essential to educate the educator himself."[61] Thus, the idea of the *unity* between subject and object, being and thinking was firmly placed on its dialectical basis. As a result, the interpretation of history was enlightened and Feuerbach's materialism was transcended. Consequently, while Feuerbach was referring to "human essence" ("art, religion, philosophy, and science are but the manifestation or revelation of genuine human essence," which could only be found "in community, in man's unity with man"),[62] Marx's stand on this in his sixth thesis was a significant step in a concrete direction: "Feuerbach resolves the religious essence into the human essence. But the human essence is no abstraction inherent in each single individual. In its reality it is the ensemble of the social relations."[63]

At the level of epistemology, Marx's system holds a distinct position which can be precisely defined if, accepting Lukács' proposition, we take into account that "every epistemological question and answer depends on how the philosopher conceives the relationship between being and the mind."[64] Further, in opposition to non-dialectical idealist philosophies which regard reality as static, Marx adopted Hegel's account of reality as dynamic in nature.

According to Marxist epistemology, then, reality is not unchangeable, given and eternal. It changes constantly and in this change man's practical and theoretical activity plays an essential role; hence, reality is historical. It is in this sense that man's mental and manual activity is regarded by Marxism as a liberating force, because while it is the product of historical circumstances, it is at the same time the creative power which changes these circumstances in the realm of society and the natural realm as well.

It is equally nonsensical to attribute to Marxism a mechanical materialism, a rigid causality, to criticize it as the doctrine of absolute necessity and to praise it as the planner of absolute freedom. In Marxism there can be no absolutes and permanencies, and as we shall see shortly, relativism is also excluded; there is only struggle and change which, while following a certain pattern, are not given but are always being shaped by man's conscious activity. Here is a quotation from *The German Ideology:* "the sensuous world . . . is not a thing given direct from all eternity, ever the same, but the product of industry and the state of society; and, indeed in the sense that it is a historical product, the result of the activity of a whole succession of generations, each standing on the shoulders of the preceding one, developing its industry and its intercourse, modifying its social organization according to the changed needs."[65]

There are at least three aspects of Marxist epistemology which can immediately affect literary criticism. The first, derives from its declaration that the world is objective and knowable. This implies that objective knowledge, and consequently an objective approach to literary phenomena is possible. Therefore, the adherence to the idea of the primacy of being over thinking or of content over form (we shall refer to their *dialectical unity* in a moment) makes an objective literary criticism both feasible and necessary.

This, however, leads us to the second aspect of Marxist epistemology because an objective approach to literary production presupposes that the latter is seen not in isolation or as the arbitrary product of distorted i.e. irrational minds, even the minds of geniuses, but as the fruit of conscious human activity. Hence, we have Lukács' attempt towards the development of a *rational* Marxist epistemology in contradistinction to those philosophies which focus on that reality which they consider as the product of the *irrational* mind (i.e. intuitive philosophies: Dilthey, Bergson, Husserl, Neitzsche, etc.).[66] Lukács himself regards intuition and the unconscious as parts of the rational and conscious, and as he attributes primary importance to conscious and purposeful human activity he opposes Freud's theory as a misleading exaggeration.[67]

The third aspect concerns the dynamic relationship between man's theoretical and practical activity, on the one hand, and socio-historical motion, on the other. Thus, Marxist epistemology does not favor a dogmatic and deterministic literary criticism—as it has often been claimed—but a literary criticism which itself contributes to the making of history, while it is in turn historically conditioned. As Bela Kiralyfalvi observes in his short report of Lukács' epistemology, one should remember that in Marxism "practice provides the criterion for theoretical truth."[68] Also, according to Lukács, the dialectical unity of the two is presupposed since as he states, "in materialist dialectical theory even the most abstract categories are reflections in thought of objective reality."[69]

On the philosophical level, Marxism takes an attitude towards art and literature which—being part of the whole Marxist world-view—regards literary works, in the words of István Mészáros, as having meaning and representing value "only insofar as there is a human need that finds fulfilment in the creation and enjoyment of works of art."[70] To borrow again the terms of political economy, we can say that in Marx's world-view both the process of artistic production and the process of artistic consumption are utterly human activities, obliged to embrace the whole of society and not a small privileged part of it, because, after all, production without consumption is meaningless.

This relation between production and consumption should not be understood—especially in the case of art and literature—as utilitarian, but as something enriching the quality of human life and relations. Thus, in art—to the extent that it involves those human activities which are nearer the realm of freedom and farther from mundane considerations—the words of Marx appear to hold true and it seems useful to quote from the *Grundrisse* at some length to elucidate this:

> The human being is in the most literal sense a ζῷον πολιτικόν . . . an animal which can individuate itself only in the midst of society. Production by an isolated individual outside society . . . is as much of an absurdity as is the development of language without individuals living *together* and talking to each other . . . . The product only obtains its 'last finish' in consumption. A railway on which no trains run, hence which is not used up, not consumed, is a railway only δυνάμει and not in reality. Without production no consumption; but also, without consumption, no production; since production would then be purposeless. . . . Production not only supplies a material for a need, but it also supplies a need for the material. . . . The need which consumption feels for the object is created by the perception of it. *The object of art—like every other product—creates a public which is sensitive to art and enjoys beauty. Production thus not only creates an object for the subject, but also a subject for the object.*[71]
>
> (My italics)

As with Aristotle, Marx's philosophical system then is anthropocentric. And man, as already emphasized, is not conceived as an abstract, isolated individual, but always in community with other men, since it is due to his social relationships that his creative activities acquire a meaning by taking aim at a purpose. No product can have any meaning or value if it does not satisfy a human need; and almost all human needs—except basic biological ones—are created as man demonstrates his capacity to fulfil them (production), a dialectical process which is best exemplified in artistic production.

From a philosophical point of view, Marxism does not regard artistic and literary products as valuable because they simply possess an abstract beauty, but they are valuable—as are all other products of human labor—because they create and at the same time satisfy certain human needs, thus making human beings more demanding in an endless process in which they themselves set higher and higher standards of their demands. In other words, in the Marxist anthropocentric system the value of artistic and literary production is inseparably related to its contribution to the general qualitative development of human society.

On the theoretical level, literature is seen as one of the superstructures, which does not necessarily imply the "reflection, the imitation or the reproduction of the reality of the base in the superstructure in a more or less direct way,"[72] as Raymond Williams suggests, provided that a literary theory is not developed by an adherent of economic determinism but by a dialectician like Lukács—as we shall see in the relevant chapter.

Marx outlines in a number of his works the overall theoretical framework of the relationship between the artistic and other modes of production, and also the relationship between artistic production and society.[73] However, the level of generality of his theoretical statements, their incompleteness and their unsystematic nature have often resulted not only in deterministic abuses of a mechanistic type on the part of vulgar materialism, but also in superficial rejections of Marx's theoretical reference to ideas in general by ill-informed critics of his work.[74]

Here, of course, we do not intend to engage in controversy with either. It should suffice for the present to mention that the application of Marx's theoretical guidelines to literature can result in varied approaches: in a strictly extrinsic approach, for example, when the main elements of literary works are primarily explained by reference to corresponding elements of the economic base according to the principle of causality, or in an approach which does not neglect to view literary works too as autonomous aesthetic entities, and the literary critic as mediating between a work and its interpretation.

For the Marxist literary critic, the problem is both *what* theory to develop in each specific case—on the basis of the overall Marxian theoretical perspective—and at the same time *how* to use it. By these preliminary clarifications we do not mean to hide the "poor results"[75] arising from the "application" of some of Marx's ideas by a number of Marxists. On the contrary, we want to point out that since Marx did not develop a methodical aesthetics, his theoretical contribution in this area should not be referred to as a specific theory of art and literature.

On the methodological level, certain principles[76] constitute the basis of historical materialism, which, according to Lukács, is primarily a *method*[77] by the use of which, in his words, "we can penetrate beneath the surface and perceive the profound historical forces which in reality control events."[78] But how can a method the principal concern of which is to provide the conceptual, logical and research procedures adequate for the study of "social formations or economic formations of society,"[79] also be used for example for the study of literature?

This is a legitimate question, and it might seem untenable at first glance to try to approach Kafka's *The Trial* with a methodology based on the same principles that are used to study the contemporary forms of imperialism. And the use of this method will seem irrelevant as long as artistic and literary production is not seen as the result of conscious human activity which derives from and deals with that "human essence" which is the fruit of the "ensemble of human relations."

Lukács points out that for Marx and Engels social phenomena and events cannot be understood apart from the general framework of the "total historical process."[80] By the same token, while these two thinkers never denied the "relative autonomy" of artistic and literary products, they nevertheless regarded this autonomy as not "arising exclusively from a peculiar inner dialectic," because the development of such works "is determined by the movement of the history of social production as a whole; changes and developments are to be explained in a truly scientific manner only in relation to this base."[81]

In the aesthetics constructed by Lukács himself, this inter-connection between artistic/literary production and "total historical process" is not to be understood as a cause/effect relationship, but as the findings of a methodological enterprise which aims to encompass what Henri Lefebvre refers to as "total content,"[82] on the one hand, and the various forms which this content can take, on the other. This discussion, however, leads us right into the heart of Marxism: the *materialist dialectic*.

d. *Aspects of the Dialectical Marxist Outlook*

We can state from the outset that the Marxian system—considered from the point of view of the particular levels mentioned earlier—can provide the general principles for an objective literary criticism on the basis of the direction given by Aristotelian aesthetics, according to which the poet is an imitator *and* a creator. The question now is if this kind of objective criticism implies a positivistic step towards scientism, in view of the claim often made that Marx's own position demonstrates his preference for empirical facts and the scientific method, which in turn unites the socio-cultural with the natural sciences.[83] An answer to this question will clarify the Marxist standpoint in relation to the issue of subjectivity versus objectivity as it can shape literary criticism, and in relation to the nature of art and literature, that is, in regard to the question of whether or not art and literature are directly conditioned by the objective factors of life.

Both the positivistic tendencies within Marxism, and the issue of subjectivity versus objectivity in its black-and-white form, can be transcended on the basis of the Lukácsean category of *dialectical totality*.[84] In this sense, Marxism can be given credit because as a system of thought and action it contains within itself the seeds of its own emancipation from the tyranny of facts and the constraints of scientism. If one wishes, therefore, to single out the fundamental improvement of Marx's system over already established aesthetic ideas, one should refer to its dialectical nature.

It is the dialectical flexibility of the Marxian materialist approach bequeathed by Hegel which opens up new possibilities in the area of literary criticism. For this reason, let us leave aside the materialist element at present, and make a brief reference to the essential characteristics of the dialectical way of thinking and viewing reality, characteristics which make it radically different, more adequate and richer than the formal way of viewing society.[85]

To begin with, we should be reminded that formal logic is built upon the so-called 'law of identity', according to which a thing (either mental or material) is always equal or identical with itself. Here, we are not concerned of course, with the innumerable implications of this law for man's attitude towards the world, since for the specific purpose of this study it will be sufficient to examine some of the implications of this law for literary criticism.

Concretely, any theory of art and literature which remains within the framework of formal logic, should by definition try to establish the identity of the various aspects of literary works, for example, in a determinate, absolute and final way. Hence, once the 'ises' of a given literary work have been established, its total picture composed and painted by literary criticism will be fixed and more or less rigid. Thus, according to the law of identity, literary criticism should establish definite facts—by subjective and/or by objective criteria—and then present its report on a given work in an irrevocable and permanent way.

It is possible that different attempts by various literary critics, despite their common adherence to the same imperatives of formal logic, might produce different pictures, explanations, etc., of one and the same work. In other words, they might establish different identities at different times. What is out of the question, however, is for such criticism to recognize the coexistence of more than one identity in a work simultaneously. That is, formal logic, no matter in which area of human activity is employed (art, politics, philosophy, etc.) provides us only—when it does so—with conclusions of an either/or type.

This kind of logic, of course, is indispensable. Without some capability on the part of the critic to locate, recognize and identify certain stable properties in a piece of literature, no meaningful approach to that work would be possible, no theory could be constructed, and no relationship could be established. "All that is real is rational," is Hegel's famous proposition, which seems to mark—from the point of view of the realm of human thought and action which exclusively concerns us here[86]

—the line separating knowledge from ignorance, rationality from irrationality, an ordered from a chaotic life. Thus, as far as the need for the establishment of identities is concerned, the reasoning of formal logic is absolutely essential.

Human reality, however, cannot be fully understood as a mere *is* (or many ises) established on a black-and-white basis; human reality is much richer and more complex than this. Socio-historical phenomena and thought processes seem to be full of contradictions—but we will return to this in a moment.

Another characteristic of formal logic which should not escape our attention here, is the principle according to which the thinking subject is separated from the object of his investigation. Should a literary critic, for example, focus on his object (i.e. a novel, a poem, etc.) with the assumption that it is something completely isolated, independent and irrelevant to him, he himself remains in the darkness, unaware of and uninterested in his own relationship to his object, or on another level, indifferent to his own position in society and history.

This incapability of formal logic to reflect upon itself—that is, the incapability of an individual adherent to it to see himself *both* as subject and object, together with his incapability to go beyond the absoluteness and rigidity of the law of identity—marks the upper limit of this logic, which even though valid and useful, is so only up to a certain point. The upper limit of formal logic which prevents it from grasping human reality as a *whole* was superseded by another logic, namely, *dialectics*, which while retaining the propositions of formal logic as true and valuable (within certain limits), nevertheless transcends them and reaches a higher plane.

The basic law of dialectical logic incorporates the main law of formal logic (the law of identity) accepting thus that a human phenomenon *is* equal and identical with itself, at the same time, however, maintaining that the *same* phenomenon *is not* equal and identical with itself. Both the *is* of a phenomenon and its *opposite* co-exist in the form of an unfolding dialectical totality.

Dialectical logic is based on a revolutionary new law, the 'law of the unity of opposites,' according to which everything bears its own contradiction within itself, resulting ultimately in the transformation of a thing into something else. Hegel writes: "Everything is opposite. Neither in heaven, nor on earth, neither in the world of mind, nor of nature is there anywhere such an abstract 'either or' as common sense thought maintains. All that is, is concrete, with difference and opposition within itself." And he continues:

> Contradiction, above all things, is what moves the
> world. . . . Wherever there is movement, wherever there
> source of all knowledge which is truly scientific. . . .
> actual world, there dialectic is at work. It is also the
> source of all knowledge which is truly scientific. . . .
> Dialectics gives expression to a law which is felt in all
> grades of consciousness and in general experience. Every-
> thing that surrounds us may be viewed as an instance of
> dialectic. We are aware that everything finite, instead of
> being inflexible and ultimate, is rather changeable and
> transient; and this is exactly what we mean by the di-
> alectic of the finite, by which the finite, as implicitly
> other than it is, is forced to surrender its own immediate
> or natural being, and to turn suddenly into its
> opposite.[87]

The parts of this excerpt which refer to nature do not concern us here. What interests us is that Hegel's dialectical logic expresses a fundamental law of the whole range of phenomena pertaining to the realm of man's thought and activity, that is, to human history: in this realm, everything is temporary, changeable; nothing is permanent.[88] This change and eventual passing away of everything which once existed is called the 'negation' of the latter, which in turn will be negated itself, according to the law of 'negation of the negation.'

As far as the content of this law is concerned, a distinction is made between 'metaphysical' and 'dialectical' negation. The first, is idealist, transcended and negative in the sense that it results in the complete destruction of the old, and hence in the rejection of continuity and development. The second, adopted by Marxist dialectics, views the new in intrinsic connection with the old that has been negated, and in this sense, dialectical negation is positive and constructive, although a "return" to the old is simply "apparent." Only the positive properties are preserved while those which do not correspond to concrete reality any longer are left out. All in all, even the remaining elements of the old are transformed by the new on a higher level, and thus, even though connection and repetition are included, dialectical negation results in development.[89]

But if negation of the negation is a law of all historical reality, how can we ever establish firm knowledge over an event or phenomenon since this is bound to pass away, to be negated, and to be transformed into a new quality which again will itself be negated, and so on and so forth? "All that is real is rational" is the famous Hegelian proposition as we mentioned earlier. This proposition implies that within certain limits stable relationships can be established among events and phenomena and meaningful conclusions can be drawn. In other words, the acquisition of knowledge is possible, which means that man can achieve 'truth.'

From a Marxist point of view, this truth is not only objective (i.e. independent of man) but also dialectical: it is neither *absolute* nor merely *relative*, but both absolute and relative at the same time. It is absolute to the extent that it contains elements of exact and permanent knowledge about a given reality. And it is relative to the extent that due to the finiteness and historicity of men (i.e. of historical individuals and generations) the truth they can arrive at cannot cover the entire knowledge about reality, that is, they cannot produce complete knowledge over the *whole* range of socio-cultural events and phenomena. Men are not and will never be able to focus on the whole of historical process since it is always in the becoming, in the making, revealing only to us its temporary existences, its immediate beings, destined to be dialectically negated in an endless process of negations.[90]

This is the reason why the dialectician Hegel completed his initial proposition with its opposite: "All that is rational is real." This proposition, which is the dialectical negation of the previous one, is but an expression of the passing away and transformation of historical events and phenomena. The specific meaning of this statement is that it is on the basis of the reality (here reality means necessity, which in turn means the complete correspondence between *appearance* and *essence*) of an event, phenomenon, thought-process, etc. that stable knowledge can be established over it. If an event, phenomenon, etc, is unreal, unnecessary, without a concrete foundation, an empty appearance and not an appearance united with and corresponding to an underlying essence, then it is irrational.

At this point, let us refer to some of the consequences of dialectics for literary criticism. To begin with, what literary criticism may legitimately view as permanent, and in a sense, as the objective limit of the possible reinterpretations of a literary work, is the historically conditioned and established relationship between it and all reality which gave rise to it on the basis of the expression of this relationship (or the lack of it) in the work itself. Everything else, and especially the critic's perception of this relationship, is temporary, relative, subject to change. The investigator's knowledge of the reality which has resulted in a given work is constantly increasing, while never complete, and his own perception of it is an existential relation formed, de-formed and re-formed with time and conditions.

The rules, criteria and special interests of literary criticism are unceasingly, so to speak, updated in order for it to be at any given place and time real and rational. Moreover, literary criticism must be able to reflect upon itself and its own relationship with the object of its investigation by uniting within itself two opposite, although equally important, elements: one 'conservative' and the other 'revolutionary.' The former, as Engels points out in his *Ludwig Feuerbach*, "recognizes that definite stages of knowledge and society are justified for their time and circumstances," and the latter, " reveals the transitory character of everything and in everything."[9] [1]

On this basis, a truly objective* (not objective in the sense which this term takes as a positivist and/or vulgar materialist concept) literary criticism must be *dialectical.* Only dialectical criticism is endowed with such properties as to be able to take into account the all-expanding totality of the principal features of a reality in their interaction with each other, as well as the place of these features and the place of the totality of their reality within the process of history, which includes both the relative and permanent elements of literary creations.

In other words, only dialectical literary criticism can understand the structure and movement of a totality by means of an understanding of its mediations. And since this literary criticism is dialectical *and* materialist—in the Marxian sense of the term—its primary aim should be the grasping of concrete totality

---

*That is, self-aware of its own subjective aspects while striving to take into account all the elements (i.e. both particular and universal) of a work's reality in their interrelationship.

through the grasping of its concrete mediations, if some serious problems, which Lukács himself faced in his pre-Marxist years, are to be avoided.[92]   That is, a genuine dialectical materialist literary criticism must initiate any literary investigation by focusing on "the fact that the crucial intermediary link of all human phenomena is man's 'practico-critical activity', with its ultimate reference—a reference 'in the last analysis'—to the sphere of economics. . . ."[93]

Such literary criticism, however, should also strive to maintain the golden mean between its conservative and its revolutionary sides, between its capability to establish immediate knowledge and its awareness of the transient character of this knowledge and its supposed validity.   The inability on the part of literary criticism to keep the balance between the establishment of well-defined and definite knowledge, and the recognition that the necessity for this knowledge is itself subject to change in time, can result in the dominance of one side at the expense of the other.

Taking as our point of reference the (historically conditioned) average life-time of an individual (reader, critic or writer) —time unit control—we can say that elements of reality as well as elements of our understanding of it do change, but the fundamental characteristics of one's world (both subjective and objective) and life (personal conduct in that world) remain, at any event, real to one, and consequently, rational. Changes do occur—sometimes even revolutionary ones—because man's historical life moves endlessly, but we can detect the expression of such changes in literary works, for example, as creation in a human (limited) sense, i.e. creation on the basis of things known (understandable), not in a theological sense, that is, as abstract creation on the basis of things unknown and, as such, incomprehensible.

We can focus our attention now on another responsibility of dialectical literary criticism: to reveal both the identity and non-identity of literary works and also the interrelationship between the two, that is, the specific kind of unity they form together. This is of crucial importance because it is only in relationship to its opposite that a phenomenon, human action, thought-process, etc., takes on particular meaning and full significance. It is only by virtue of the proletariat, for example, that the bourgeoisie is the ruling class.

In a truly dialectical literary work, i.e. one based on the

premises of dialectics, the unity of opposites, namely, the unity of *ises* and *are nots* should be properly exposed as far as this is allowed by the artistic means and techniques available. But even if this does not explicitly happen—and this is the usual case—it is the prime task of a genuine dialectical literary criticism to reveal and illuminate these opposites in their unity, because such dynamic relationships of counteropposing elements are not mere mental (artistic) constructs but the expression of actively existing reality. The expression of the condition of concrete reality and its parts, either evident or hidden, cannot but be present in a literary work simply because the latter as a product of the creative power of the human mind cannot be composed of meaningful paragraphs and sentences, stanzas and lines, unless their construction is somehow based on a depiction and, above all, a comparison of aspects of reality in their existence or becoming. Only comparison can produce any kind of understanding, interpretation, evaluation, etc.

Often, one major *is* of a literary work, for example a work's philosophical outlook, is by virtue of its reality—from the writer's point of view—the evident, dominant outlook of the work; but it is equally true that its opposite outlook is somewhere there too, in the background, waiting for the opportunity to come itself to the foreground. The fact that the opposite of a dominant element is usually latent, does not mean that it is passive; any *is not* is as active, though not as successfully, as its opposite *is*. Any literary criticism which fails to throw light both on the identity and the non-identity of a literary work, as to disclose the kind of unity these two active opposites form, would be incomplete.

For the dialectical literary critic, however, to preserve a balance between the conservative and the revolutionary aspects of literary criticism, and also a balance between the extent to which the identity and non-identity of literary works should be dealt with, he must be able to determine how far to go in each direction, that is, where to put the limits and boundaries of each side. This cannot be done on the basis of the critic's personal judgment alone, since, as we have already indicated, he himself as a dialectical materialist investigator is well aware of the fact that the conservative and revolutionary aspects of literary criticism on the one hand, and the identity and non-identity of literary works on the other, are but the expression of concrete reality in the constitution of which, he too participates through his praxis while he is simultaneously and in many respects its outcome.

The rounded understanding of the unfolding totality of that reality in general and its concrete mediations in particular must necessarily be the guiding thread of the critic's task. Thus, both the fundamental aspects of a literary work, namely, its essence, (containing within itself the essences of the identity and non-identity of the work) and its appearance are the products of a specific historical moment and as such they can be thought of as definite, absolute, final. A synchronic structural analysis* of a literary work, for example, is important and necessary but only so far as its limited character is kept in mind. This finality, however, attributed to both the content and form of a work is relative—to a lesser or greater degree—if the latter are considered outside the historical moment within which they were real and rational. The same kind of reasoning, of course, applies to literary criticism itself: it can be thought of as absolute when it satisfies the necessity of a concrete socio-cultural reality; but in essence it is relative itself because it changes with time.

It should be evident by now that in all the sets of the relationships indicated in the course of our discussion, i.e. the literary work vs. the totality of the reality which gave rise to it, the essence (content) vs. the appearance (form) of a work, literary criticism vs. its socio-historical context, etc., what strictly speaking remains unchangeable over time as already petrified, that is, negated, is the (objective) nature of each relationship itself, never fully known to us for objective reasons, including the variable input of our historical intervention ultimately affecting the presentation of this relationship. The elements of one side of a relationship are in themselves related absolutely to the elements of the other side, forming so to speak a standard toward which human understanding moves but which never completely reaches; because in the final analysis even this standard becomes relative due to the historical input of the investigator. It should also be clear that any attempt on the part of the literary critic to approach merely one side of these relationships can only result in limited conclusions. By the same token, any insistence on the part of literary criticism in just the absolute

---

*See chapter eight.

(synchronic) or just the relative (diachronic) character of any one of these relationships will again produce incomplete results.

From a dialectical standpoint, in order for literary criticism to avoid partiality, incompleteness, one -sidedness, etc. it is necessary that the critic develops his attitude (i.e. his way of viewing reality) in such a way as to be able to move his critical (intellectual) tools simultaneously on a vertical axis* (indicating the path of historical development) and on an horizontal axis,* (suggesting the level which a society has reached in the historical process), while he himself (that is, the resources and needs which define his critical activity) is at the common meeting point of the two axes, namely, *at the center of his own focus.* All this means that the literary critic must possess a dialectical perspective because it alone will enable him to view a totality and its mediations as dialectically related to other totalities and mediations. But as already emphasized, this perspective is both dialectical and materialist, meaning that it aims to approach, understand and explain socio-cultural phenomena not through the shadows of Hegelian or any other idealism, but through their material foundations. This, of course, brings us face-to-face with a central problem of historical materialism as it sets forth to investigate the mode of artistic and literary production: the role played by the material base of society. This problem will be examined further in the chapter on Georg Lukács.

NOTES

[1]Wellek and Warren distinguished three kinds within the general category of the sociology of literature: "the sociology of the writer, the social content of the works themselves, and the influence of literature on society." (Rene Wellek and Austin Warren, *Theory of literature* (3rd ed.; London: Jonathan Cape, 1966), p. 96). For our purposes here however it seems

---

*The terms "vertical" and "horizontal" are only paradigms here; we will return to these terms later on.

preferable just to distinguish two kinds which include all three mentioned by Wellek and Warren.

[2]Joan Rockwell, *Fact in Fiction* (London: Routledge and Kegan Paul, 1974), p. viii.

[3]Robert Escarpit, *Sociology of Literature,* trans. by E. Pick (Painesville, Ohio: Lake Erie College Studies, 1965).

[4]Jean-Paul Sartre, *What is Literature?*, trans. by W. Fowlie (New York: Harper Colophon Books, 1965), pp. 61-154.

[5]Cf. Levin L. Schucking, *The Sociology of Literary Taste* (London: The University of Chicago Press, 1966).

[6]A particular segment of Vico's writings is considered to be the first attempt towards a social approach to literature. It refers to an interpretation of Homer's great works, *The Iliad* and *The Odyssey.* Cf. T. G. Bergin and M. H. Fisch, trans. *The New Science of Giambattista Vico* (Ithaca: Cornell University Press, 1972), pp. 270-271.

[7]Cf. Edmund Wilson, *The Triple Thinkers* (New York: Oxford University Press, 1948), pp. 257-258.

[8]Quoted in Rene Wellek, *A History of Modern Criticism: 1750-1950,* I, (New Haven: Yale University Press, 1955), p. 185.

[9]*Ibid.,* II, p. 220.

[10]*Ibid.,* p. 221.

[11]Hippolyte A. Taine, *Balzac: A Critical Study* (New York: Haskell House Publishers, Ltd., 1973), p. 240.

[12]*Ibid.,* pp. 52-54.

[13]George V. Plekhanov, *Art and Society* (New York: Oriole Editions, 1974), pp. 82-83.

[14]Quoted in Wellek, *A History of Modern Criticism: 1750-1950,* IV, *op. cit.,* p. 29.

[15]Cf. Ruth Benedict, Race: Science and Politics (New York: The Viking Press, 1970), especially p. 127 ff.

[16]Quoted in Wellek, *A History of Modern Criticism: 1750-1950,* IV, *op. cit.,* p. 33.

[17]*Ibid.,* p. 31.

[18]Albert Guerard, *Literature and Society* (Boston: Lothrop, Lee and Shepard Company, 1935), p. 4.

[19]Peter Demetz, *Marx, Engels, and the Poets,* trans. by J. L. Sammons (Chicago: The University of Chicago Press, 1967), p. 228.

[20]Cf. Wellek, *A History of Modern Criticism: 1750-1950,* III, *op. cit.,* pp. 238-239. Also, Demetz, *op. cit.,* pp. 232, 236.

[21]Mikhail Lifshitz, *The Philosophy of Art of Karl Marx,* trans. by R. B. Winn (Bristol: Pluto Press Limited, 1973), p. 7.

[22]Cf. for example, Adolfo Sanchez Vazques, *Art and Society: Essays*

in Marxist Aesthetics, trans. by M. Riofrancos (New York: Monthly Review Press, 1973), pp. 9-11. Also, István Mészáros, *Marx's Theory of Alienation,* (3rd ed.; London: Merlin Press, 1972), p. 190.

[23] Karl Marx, *Theories of Surplus Value,* Part I (Moscow: Progress Publishers, 1969), p. 158.

[24] Georg Lukács, "Appearance and Essence," in G. C. LeRoy and U. Beitz eds. *Preserve and Create* (New York: Humanities Press, 1973), p. 17.

[25] Cf. Bela Kiralyfalvi, *The Aesthetics of Gyorgy Lukács* (Princeton: Princeton University Press, 1975), p. 55.

[26] Georg Lukács, *Studies in European Realism* (New York: Grosset and Dunlap, 1964), p. 1.

[27] Cf. for Example, Lifshitz, Demetz, *op. cit.*

[28] Georg Lukács, *Writer and Critic and Other Essays,* ed. and trans. by A. D. Kahn (New York: Grosset and Dunlap, 1970), p. 61.

[29] Cf. also Stefan Morawski, "The Aesthetic Views of Marx and Engels," *The Journal of Aesthetics and Art Criticism,* XXVIII, no. 3 (Spring, 1970), pp. 301-314. And, Lee Baxandall and Stefen Morawski, eds. *Marx and Engels on Literature and Art* (St. Louis: Telos Press, 1973), which is a collection of the writings of Marx and Engels on literature and art. See especially the Introduction.

[30] *Marx and Engels on Literature and Art, Ibid.,* p. 51.

[31] *Ibid.,* pp. 53, 54.

[32] *Ibid.,* p. 52.

[33] Cf. Mészáros, *op. cit.,* pp. 200-204.

[34] Ernst Fischer, *The Necessity of Art,* trans. by A. Bostock (Middlesex: Penguin Books, 1970), p. 35.

[35] Baxandal and Morawski, eds. *op. cit.,* p. 55.

[36] *Ibid.,* p. 54.

[37] *Ibid.,* p. 61.

[38] *Ibid.,* p. 62.

[39] *Ibid.,* pp. 62-63.

[40] *Ibid.,* p. 63.

[41] *Ibid.,* p. 64.

[42] Karl Marx, *Capital,* I, (Moscow: Progress Publishers, n.d.), pp. 47, 48.

[43] Walter Benjamin, *Illuminations,* ed. Hannah Arendt (New York: Schocken Books, 1969), p. 220.

[44] Mészáros, *op. cit.,* pp. 208-209.

[45] Cf. *Ibid.,* pp. 210-214.

[46] These excerpts are included in Baxandall and Morawski, eds., *op. cit.,* pp. 69-73.

[47]Cf. *Ibid.,* p. 89.

[48]Cf. *Ibid.,* p. 123.

[49]Cf. *Ibid.,* pp. 113-115.

[50]Cf. for example, Diana Laurenson and Alan Swingewood, *The Sociology of Literature* (London: MacGibbon and Kee, 1972), pp. 48-49.

[51]Baxandall and Morawski, eds. *op. cit.,* p. 114.

[52]Peter Brang, "Sociological Methods in Twentieth Century Russian Literary Criticism," in Joseph P. Strelka, ed. *Literary Criticism and Sociology* (University Park: The Pennsylvania State University Press, 1973), pp. 209-251.

[53]Cf. Arnold Hauser, *The Philosophy of Art History* (London: Routledge and Kegan Paul, 1959), pp. 21-40.

[54]Karl Marx, *A Contribution to the Critique of Political Economy* (Moscow: Progress Publishers, 1970), p. 215.

[55]Cf. *Ibid.,* pp. 20-21.

[56]That Lenin's concerns were political rather than theoretical is evident by his consideration of literature as a party weapon. Cf. V. I. Lenin, *On Literature and Art* (Moscow: Progress Publishers, 1970), p. 23.

[57]Paul N. Siegel, ed. *Leon Trotsky On Literature and Art* (2nd ed. New York: Pathfinder Press, Inc., 1972), pp. 56, 45-46.

[58]It should be noted that the Stalinist notion of 'socialist realism' has a romantic core, and it essentially differs from the Marxist concept of realism. Some speeches delivered at the First All-Union Congress of Soviet Writers (1934) demonstrate that the main concern of the party representatives was not artistic and theoretical, but practical and political: the protection and advancement of socialism by all means and at any cost. In this sense 'socialist realism' can be understood as a romantic type of method by which social engineering is aimed at. Cf. for example, John E. Bowlt, ed. and trans. *Russian Art of the Avant-Garde: Theory and Criticism, 1902-1934* (New York: The Viking Press, 1976), pp. 293-294, 297.

[59]Cf. Kiralyfalvi, *op. cit.,* pp. 20-29.

[60]Cf. Mészáros, *op. cit.,* p. 86.

[61]Karl Marx and Frederick Engels, *The German Ideology,* ed. C. J. Arthur (New York: International Publishers, 1973), p. 121.

[62]Quoted in G. V. Plekhanov, *Fundamental Problems of Marxism* (Moscow: Progress Publishers, 1962), p. 31.

[63]Marx and Engels, *op. cit.,* p. 122.

[64]Translated and quoted by Kiralyfalvi, *op. cit.,* p. 30.

[65]Marx and Engels, *op. cit.,* p. 62.

[66]Cf. Kiralyfalvi, *op. cit.,* pp. 30-32.

[67]*Ibid.,* pp. 30-39.

[68]*Ibid.,* p. 34.

[69] Quoted in *Ibid.*, p. 33.

[70] Mészáros, *op. cit.*, p. 192.

[71] Karl Marx, *Grundrisse,* trans. by M. Nicolaus (Middlesex: Penguin Books, 1973), pp. 84, 91-92.

[72] Raymond Williams, "Base and Superstructure," *New Left Review,* no. 82 (November/December, 1973), p. 4.

[73] Cf. for example, the well known passage in Marx's famous Preface to *A Contribution to the Critique of Political Economy.* Also, *The German Ideology* in which it is stated that "The production of ideas, of conceptions, of consciousness, is at first directly interwoven with the material activity and the material intercourse of men, the language of real life" (*op. cit.,* p. 47).

[74] Cf. for example, Gordon Leff, *The Tyranny of Concepts: a Critique of Marxism* (London: The Merlin Press, 1969), pp. 165-184.

[75] Laurenson and Swingewood, *op. cit.,* p. 40.

[76] For a discussion of the basic methodological principles of historical materialism, Cf. J. Witt-Hensen, *Historical Materialism, The Method, The Theories. Book One: The Method* (Copenhagen: Munksgaard, 1960), pp. 46-77.

[77] Cf. Lukács's essay on "The Changing Function of Historical Materialism," in his *History and Class Consciousness,* transl. by R. Livingstone (Cambridge, Massachusettes: The M.I.T. Press, 1973), espec. p. 224.

[78] *Ibid.*, p. 224.

[79] J. Witt-Hansen, *op. cit.,* p. 26.

[80] Lukács, *Writer and Critic and Other Essays, op. cit.,* p. 61.

[81] *Ibid.,* p. 62.

[82] Henri Lefebvre, *Dialectical Materialism,* trans. by J. Sturrock, (London: Jonathan Cape, 1974), pp. 166-167.

[83] Peter Hamilton, *Knowledge and Social Structure* (London: Routledge and Kegan Paul, 1974), p. 23.

[84] For a discussion of Lukács's Marxism, *Ibid.*, pp. 37-54.

[85] The discussion of the dialectical method is primarily based on the following: 1)Plekhanov, *Fundamental Problems of Marxism, op. cit.* 2) Lefebvre, *Dialectical Materialism, op. cit.* 3) István Mészáros, *Lukács Concept of Dialectics* (London: The Merlin Press, 1972) 4) Z. A. Zordan, *The Evolution of Dialectical Materialism* (New York: St. Martin Press, 1967) 5) George Novack, *An Introduction to the Logic of Marxism* (New York: Pathfinder Press, 1973) 6) Guy Planty-Bonjour, *The Categories of Dialectical Materialism* (New York: F. A. Praeger Inc., Publishers, 1967).

[86] For a discussion of the implications involved when this proposition is extended to matter or when dialectics is extended from the realm of

human society and history to nature, Cf. Guy Planty-Bonjour, *Ibid.*, pp.76-77, 166-172.

[87]G. W. F. Hegel, *Encyclopedia of Philosophy,* trans. by Gustav Emil Mueller, (New York: Philosophical Library, 1959), pp. 192, 196, 198.

[88]Cf. Robert Heiss, *Hegel, Kierkegaard, Marx,* trans. by E. Garside (Delacorte Press/Seymour Lawrence, 1975), pp. 96-107.

[89]Bonjour, *op. cit.,* pp. 132-133.

[90]*Ibid.,* pp. 70-77.

[91]Frederick Engels, *Ludwig Feuerbach* (New York: International Publishers, 1941), p. 11.

[92]For a detailed discussion of the relationship between the categories of totality and mediation as it was dealt with by Lukács, Cf. Mészáros, *Lukács' Concept of Dialectic, op. cit.,* pp. 61-91.

[93]*Ibid.,* p. 70.

TWO

PLEKHANOV:
THE CONTENT-ORIENTED SOCIOLOGICAL APPROACH

1. *The Social Determination of Literature*

George Plekhanov, "the first Marxist in Russia,"[1] is credited with being the first Marxist theoretician to undertake systematically the task of laying down a concrete methodology for the materialist study of art and literature. In view of the time, place and conditions under which his endeavor took place, one can understand some of his shortcomings in his diverse works "on philosophy, literature, art, atheism, and the history of social theories and social thought."[2]

Plekhanov's ideas on matters of literary criticism are basically expressed in three of his works: *Historical Materialism and the Arts* (1899-1900), *French Drama and Painting of the 18th Century* (1905), and *Art and Society* (1912). These are rather short studies, yet his name is inseparably linked with the foundation of the sociology of literature.[3] Even though a number of Marxist thinkers dealt also with artistic and literary problems (i.e. Franz Mehring, Rosa Luxemburg, Leon Trotsky, Anatoli Lunacharsky, etc.) his own contribution is considered the most important, remaining unchallenged for a long time given that, after all, Marxist theory was stagnant for decades.[4]

A first acquaintance with Plekhanov's writings will indicate that while considering various factors involved in artistic and literary creation (e.g. biological, psychological, aesthetic), he nevertheless retained an "uncompromisingly sociological approach"[5] which characterizes his overall literary criticism. Artistic and literary phenomena are viewed by Plekhanov as forms of the ideology of the society to which they correspond. The position of these phenomena in terms of the base/superstructure relationship is determined by a formula, the starting point of which refers to the forces of production.[6] Yet, as he states, "all ideologies have one common root—*the psychology of the epoch in question.*"[7]

The fact that Plekhanov appears to advocate at some points the finding of the psychological and at others of the sociological equivalent of a given work should not be taken as a contradiction. On the contrary, this illuminates his conviction of the complementary role of psychology and sociology in the explanation of the ideological (artistic) phenomena which both investigate. That both approaches should be employed is clearly suggested by Plekhanov:

> To understand the Australian native women's dance it is sufficient to know the part played in the life of the Australian tribe by the gathering of wild roots by the womenfolk. But to understand the minuet, for instance, it is absolutely insufficient to have a knowledge of the economy of the 18th century France. Here we have to do with a dance expressive of *the psychology of a non-productive class.* A psychology of *this kind* accounts for the vast majority of the 'customs and conventions' of the so-called good society. Consequently, in this case the *economic* 'factor' is second to the *psychological.*

Does this mean that Plekhanov occasionally rejects the ultimate primacy of the economy in men's socio-cultural life? Evidently this is not the case, because he remains faithful to the fundamental principle of historical materialism. Thus he continues the above argument in the following way: "It should, however, not be forgotten that the appearance of non-productive classes in a society is a product of the latter's economic development. Hence, the economic 'factor' preserves its predominant significance even when it is second to others. Moreover, it is then that this significance makes itself felt, for it is then that it determines *the possibility and the limits of the influence of other 'factors'.*"[8] But let us examine Plekhanov's literary criticism more closely.

In Historical Materialism and the Arts he seems to agree basically with Darwin's idea that the *sense of beauty* is a biological phenomenon, an instinct, that is, an inborn characteristic of human nature. However, neither the origin nor the historical evolution of men's *aesthetic tastes* can be accounted for by the science of biology, and Plekhanov praises Darwin for inviting (indirectly) sociology to take over. But even though Darwin is correct in suggesting the social basis of the "aesthetic sensations" of civilized men, he is mistaken in excluding the primitives. Thus Plekhanov, by pointing out the limitations of Darwin's biological explanations, stresses the indispensability of historical materialism because its "field of investigation begins where Darwin's ended."[9]

There are two terms used by Plekhanov to mark the difference between the inherent and the acquired, the biological and the sociological and their corresponding modes of investigation: a) the *potential,* pertaining to the biological, and b) the *real,* related to the social. "Human nature makes it possible for man to have aesthetic tastes and conceptions. His environment determines the transformation of this potentiality into reality. This environment explains how a given social man (i.e. society, nation or class) has only certain aesthetic tastes and conceptions and no other. . . . Therefore, it is the duty of both the historian and the sociologist to go beyond the limit of discussions about human nature."[10] Even complex psychological phenomena, namely those of "imitation" and "contradiction," which play a fundamental role in men's artistic/literary creations and tastes, can be accounted for sociologically as resulting from the dynamics of social relations.

The tendency opposite to imitation, that of contradiction, is elaborated by Plekhanov through detailed reference to Darwin's "principle of antitheses"[11] which he tries to apply to art and literature.[12] In fact, he concedes that in certain exceptional circumstances human emotions are manifested by gestures and actions opposite to those socially agreed upon as proper, normal, desirable, useful, etc. By referring to a number of examples culminating in the citation of a passage from Taine's *A Tour Through the Pyrenées,*[13] he maintains that Darwin's principle of antitheses can explain men's overall psychological characteristics, the origins of numerous customs, and, to a great extent, the historical development of man's aesthetic response. However, as he repeats time and again, the concrete psychology of a specific society, class, etc. influencing its aesthetic taste is in the course of its evolution and transformation ultimately determined by the prevailing social conditions, due to the action of the principle of antitheses or to that of the psychological law of rhythm and symmetry. Plekhanov states: "the psycho-

logical[14] nature of man enables him to have aesthetic conceptions, and Darwin's principle of antitheses (Hegel's 'contradiction') plays an immensely important role, unappreciated
even to this day, in the mechanism of those conceptions. But
why a given man has certain tastes and not others, why he likes
only certain things and not others—this depends upon his environment."[15]

In this respect, Plekhanov agrees with Madame de Staël's
attempt to explain 17th century French literature "in terms of
the socio-political relationships of the period and the psychology
of the French nobility in its relation to the monarchy."[16] He
also agrees with Hippolyte Taine who suggests that "The literature and art of every society is to be explained precisely by its
psychology."[17] Nevertheless, he does not fail to criticize their
idealist view of history as responsible in the final analysis for a
circular type of reasoning. Plekhanov concludes that despite
the soundness of Taine's aesthetic theory he commits the contradiction of regarding men's psychology as the "final cause" of
the historical conditions surrounding them: "When Taine said
that men's psychology changes with their environment, he was
a *materialist*; but when he declared that the environment of a
people is determined by their psychology he repeated the *idealist*
view of the eighteenth century." Here Plekhanov puts forward
the materialist thesis, but in a mechanical formulation: "The art
of every nation is determined by its psychology; its psychology
by its conditions; and its conditions are determined in the last
analysis by the state of its productive relations."[18] Nevertheless, as occasionally indicated by his own statements, artistic and literary production should be investigated dialectically,[19]
and with this in mind we can now turn to his essay entitled
French Drama and Painting of the 18th Century.

The predominant question here is whether or not there is
a direct causal relationship between the economic foundation
of society and its artistic accomplishments.[20] A case in point
is French drama and painting of the 18th century, and Plekhanov examines the transition from *farce* to *tragedy* and then
to *sentimental comedy,* demonstrating that these three literary genres express the views of the masses of the *people*, the
declining *aristocracy* and the rising *bourgeoisie*, respectively.
The conclusion which his analysis draws is that even though
in primitive society there is a more or less direct correlation
between economic and artistic life, in an advanced society

like that of France in the 18th century, such a relationship is indirect and difficult to reveal because "intermediate stages . . . constitute an obstacle to any true understanding of the situation."[21]

It is by focusing on certain mediations that Plekhanov tries to trace the ultimate influence of the material mode of production on artistic and literary works. He explains: "Social psychology is expressed in the art and aesthetics of a given period. But in the psychology of a society divided into classes, many things are found to seem incomprehensible and paradoxical if we ignore . . . the reciprocal relationships of classes and the meaning of the class struggle."[22] On the one hand, then, the class struggle is suggested as the key mediation which explains the intellectual output of a class society and specifically its art and literature.[23] This general principle refers exclusively to the process of *creation*. On the other hand, Plekhanov endorses Kant's principle of the disinterested nature of aesthetic *taste*. This principle, however, applies only to an individual—in contra-distinction to a social man—because "only that which is useful will seem to him beautiful."[24] In other words, an individual's judgment of the beautiful might be disinterested, while whatever is considered as beautiful by a social man has a utilitarian basis.[25] These assessments are pursued further in Plekhanov's well-known Paris lecture entitled *Art and Society*.

As maintained in this lecture, the question is not whether the *utilitarian* or the *art for art's sake* doctrine is correct, but under what social conditions each one of them is possible. A number of examples from Russian and French literature led Plekhanov to the conclusion that the art for art's sake attitude prevails when artists are in conflict with their social environment, while the utilitarian view predominates when a mutual bond exists between the two, for whatever reason.[26] This is why the utilitarian attitude is favored by conservative and revolutionary regimes alike,[27] even though both attitudes can be either re-actionary or progressive depending on conditions influenced by time and place.[28]

The art for art's sake doctrine, in the form of subjective individualism, disregards the socio-historical reality, while the utilitarian doctrine, in the form of open propaganda, manipu-lates the facts in order to achieve a specific purpose. Plekhanov does not commit himself exclusively to either of these doctrines, indicating that each specific case, (i.e. the romanticists of

France or Pushkin in Russia), should be judged in relation to the relevant socio-historical circumstances and requirements.

One specific proposition put forth in the same lecture marks Plekhanov's approach more than anything else. After stressing that the subordination of art to the state definitely undermines its aesthetic value, he maintains that the *quality* of an artistic or literary work is determined by the *idea* incorporated into it, that is, that *artistic quality and sociological content are causally related* since, after all, "pure art" is but a myth. Plekhanov then focuses on the literary works which result from the art for art's sake doctrine, arguing that they have a positive and a negative aspect. The first is due to the possibility that the artist might free himself from the tight embrace of his social environment and view it anew from a critical perspective. The second is manifested when the detachment of groups of artists from the tastes, manners, etc. of a social establishment (i.e. the dominant social class) does not necessarily aim to change the prevailing social order; this is the case of the romanticists, the Parnassians and the realists in France.[29] Thus, the ideological substance of works produced in the spirit of art for art's sake is often erroneous because of their "inability to rise to an understanding of the great emancipatory ideas of our times."[30]

Plekhanov's name is linked with the so-called "superstructure school" which rejects the direct and open influence of the economic life of a non-primitive society on its literature.[31] He states that "*when a work of art is based upon a fallacious idea,* inherent contradictions inevitably cause a degeneration of its aesthetic quality."[32] Therefore, the main focus of his criticism rests on the principal idea of a literary work, its sociological equivalent, judging literature on the basis of the "falsity" or "rightness" of its ideological content. It seems then that the identification/evaluation of the ideas expressed in literary works is the second task of the literary critic following the principles of historical materialism—after the social determination of artistic and literary production and development.

In this light, it is not surprising that Plekhanov stated that "the modern artist will not find inspiration in a sound idea if he seeks to defend the bourgeoisie in its struggle against the proletariat."[33] As he points out, in painting also "realism fails for want of content and idealist reaction triumphs."[34] He envisages a socialist state of affairs in which the art for art's sake doctrine would be impossible, that is, unnecessary, and the

disinterested aesthetic judgment of the individual would co-
exist with an attitude of collective utilitarianism.[35]   Finally,
he suggests that a literary product cannot but ideologically
correspond to social conditions which surround it, and he insists
that "any artist of proven talent will increase considerably the
forcefulness of his work by steeping himself in the great emancipatory ideas of our time.   For this, it is necessary that these
ideas permeate his spirit and that he express them through his
artist's temperament."[36]

Before completing our account of Plekhanov's literary
criticism, we should emphasize that he viewed the sociological
approach as only one half of criticism. He makes it clear that the
sociological investigation of artistic and literary products ought
to be supplemented by a full-scale analysis of their aesthetic properties.[37]   Unfortunately, by not going beyond the limits of a
sociological quest (*content* and its external relationships),
Plekhanov never expands his field of vision to account adequately for the aesthetic characteristics of works of art and
literature.   Thus, an assessment of his materialist literary criticism has to detect both his actual involvement in matters pertaining to aesthetics proper, and the merits and shortcomings
of his sociological method.

2. Limitations of Plekhanov's Criticism

An evaluation of Plekhanov's literary criticism has to
come to terms with the sharp disagreements among his critics
on certain basic issues.   For example, Lee Baxandall focuses
on Plekhanov's writings in an attempt to clarify the Marxist
standpoint towards three central problems of aesthetics: the
genius of the individual artist, the aesthetic response and aesthetic judgment.   Baxandall seems to credit Plekhanov with overt
awareness of the importance of the artist's individuality and
personal talent, and after presenting some selective quotations
from his works he concludes that "the Marxian finds no difficulty in acknowledging the uniqueness and originality of the
artistic process."[38]   Herri Arvon, however, in his book *Marxist
Esthetics* makes the exact opposite suggestion, indicating that
the striking characteristic of Plekhanov's literary criticism is his
"total rejection of individual creative genius and the absolute

priority of scientific facts."[39]   Arvon makes his inference on the basis of Plekhanov's attack against Gustave Lanson, the defender of individuality in literature.[40]   The question here is which interpretation of Plekhanov's position is more accurate, Baxandall's or Arvon's?

This controversy can be resolved not by merely quoting Plekhanov selectively—his tendency towards contradictory statements is well known—but by focusing on the nature of the sociological approach itself.   The latter, and this is one of its major shortcomings, is practically indifferent to the artist's individuality and to the artwork's uniqueness, viewing both as the outcome of their socio-economic environment.   Of course, individuality might be acknowledged as a factor in the artistic process—this applies to Plekhanov's case—yet it is denied a decisive influence on the latter's end product.   At most, individuality affects some formal elements, such as, style, while, according to Plekhanov, form as well as the content which is dialectically united with it, are objectively given.   His statement in *Ibsen, Petty Bourgeois, Revolutionist,* on the relationship between the individual and the history of literature also expresses the spirit of his literary criticism on the relationship between the individual artist and the artistic creation: "Each individual travels the road of protest in his own way. But where this road leads depends upon his environment. The character of negation is determined by the character of that which is being negated."[41]

Baxandall's treatment of Plekhanov's approach to the aesthetic problem of artistic response seems to be more faithful to the facts.   He rightly credits Plekhanov with explaining the aesthetic response according to the audience's psychological empathy or lack of it, in turn shaped by its class background and other social determinants.   The class explanation of psychological empathy is one of the merits of Marxist sociological approach to literature, and an important improvement over Taine's account of the aesthetic response based on some historical considerations.   A utilitarian attitude toward art and literature is revealed, however, only in the aesthetic response stimulated by the psychological empathy, which is socially conditioned.

To account for the aesthetic response of the individual not directly predisposed by and/or related to social factors, we have already seen that Plekhanov has recourse to Kant.

But it should be noticed that the "disinterested" enjoyment by the individual of artistic and literary works bears the stamp of relativity—in contradistinction to Kant's absolute use of the term—because the same works are necessarily among those which are useful to social man. In relation to this, Baxandall states that "Kant's theory of response as Plekhanov adopted it to this point still does not go to pieces. Plekhanov offers an emendation rather than a contradiction."[42] But another student of Plekhanov's works, Peter Demetz, strongly criticizes his ideas on art and literature, insisting that they are characterized by the contradiction between his Marxist belief in the social conditioning of art, and his Kantian disposition toward art's autonomy.[43]

Even though the notions of "emendation" and "contradiction" in the framework of the particular viewpoints in which they are employed do make sense, the crux of the matter is that the highly problematic nature of Plekhanov's dualism—*individual* vs. *social man*—remains untouched upon. Thus, apart from trying to determine whether or not a fundamental principle of the Kantian idealist aesthetics is compatible with the materialist system of thought, one should also closely analyze Plekhanov's dualism because, after all, as indicated above, the suggested disinterested artistic response of the individual, and consequently the autonomy of art in that instance, is but the appearance, which on another level (social man) becomes null and void.

Kant uses the concept of disinterestedness with epistemological consistency; Plekhanov's epistemological ground, however, makes his Kantian deviation doubtful. Consistency with the Marxist philosophical outlook would imply recognition of the fact that an individual's aesthetic response might *appear* disinterested while in *essence* his aesthetic stand ultimately corresponds in some way, not of course to direct and immediate utilitarian objectives, but to his human, that is *social* needs— otherwise art would by no means represent for him any value whatsoever. On the basis of a dualism and with the help of two different aesthetic theories, Plekhanov attempts to account for the aesthetic response in both its subjective (individual) and its objective (social man) forms. We can suggest that the inherent inconsistencies of his theoretical construction can be removed if the point of departure is not a dualism but a dialectical unity: *the social individual.*

Individuals in no case can be accounted for outside their social environment, and no social man can be considered apart from the particular individual by which he is constituted. Further, if by "a social man's . . . aesthetic view"[44] Plekhanov implies something more specific than the generally uniform aesthetic tastes, habits, etc. which characterize one historical social man as opposed to another, that is, if he implies *the concrete aesthetic feelings as the particular emotional condition arising in the process of the aesthetic perception of a given aesthetic or literary phenomenon, he is in error.* The implied notion of social aesthetic behavior in the sense of a collective aesthetic response is meaningless to the extent that a feeling cannot be shared collectively despite the fact that similar feelings can arise in the process of a collective common experience, i.e. in the theater, in a Beatles concert, in the process of reading a book, etc. Strictly speaking, aesthetic response is of only one kind: individual. It is always a unique personal experience even though every individual aesthetic response always bears the influence of social factors.

The substance of Plekhanov's argument in favor of the compatibility of an objective and at the same time combative literary criticism is weakened by the seeds of a built-in contradiction in his thinking. Thus, on the one hand, a clearly positivistic attitude induces him to speak of a scientific criticism "as objective as physics," and on the other, his Marxist orientation leads him to distinguish the particular dimension of the same criticism: relatively objective, relatively scientific, that is, a socio-historical product itself.[45]

Further, he correctly criticizes a number of "isms" and practices—i.e. naturalism, impressionism, cubism, abstractness, propaganda, etc.[46]—yet he is neither systematic nor dialectical in his comments. He misses, for example, the socio-historical as well as aesthetic necessity to which the various "isms" correspond, and in a dogmatic fashion he rejects them *a priori.* Indicative is his statement that "The beginning of all wisdom . . . must be the distrust of modernism in art."[47] Most significant of all, however, as has already been pointed out, is his failure to develop an effective method for the analysis of the aesthetic structure of artistic and literary works, a failure which definitely marks the Marxist sociological approach influenced by positivism.

Lee Baxandall reaches a similar conclusion after attempting

to relate Plekhanov's work to the key problem of the aesthetic judgment. Plekhanov's essay entitled *The Literary Opinions of W. G. Belinsky* (1897) illustrates the influence of the famous Russian critic on him, especially in relation to the so-called laws of beauty. Plekhanov is quoted by Baxandall as accepting the first law—deriving from Kant's distinction between aesthetic and logical ideas—which states that *showing* not *proving* must be the poet's objective. The second law to which Plekhanov ascribes is a product of the German idealist philosophy and it states that a correspondence prevails between a work's "unity of thought" and its "unity of form." The third law of beauty is of special interest, because formulated by Plekhanov himself it was meant to be the Marxist contribution to aesthetic judgment: "Truth is the subject of poetry. . . . The highest beauty is to be found precisely in truth and simplicity; authenticity and naturalness comprise the necessary condition for truly artistic creation."[48] This law in conjunction with Plekhanov's awareness of the historical nature of truth[49] is the foundation of his proposition (elaborated in *Art and Society*) that a work's central *idea* determines its aesthetic quality. Can he be justified?

Besides the fact that this is a simplistic and very inadequate way for the Marxist principle of realism to be conceived and expressed, it by no means offers a practical solution to the problem of analysis and evaluation of aesthetic structures.[50] Moreover, Plekhanov's distinction between "false" and "right" ideas on the basis of their ideological content not only results in clumsy pronouncements—some of them quoted here—but also demonstrates the truly weak spot of that Marxist sociological approach which shares some common features with Taine's method: its tendency to explain artistic quality by recourse to extraneous factors, e.g. the artist's socio-historical awareness, etc.

The way in which Plekhanov correlates truth and beauty seems to be inappropriate. One can certainly argue that truth is a necessary but not a sufficient condition for beauty, provided—and this Plekhanov fails to notice—that the truth expected by artistic and literary works is not confused with the truth arrived at by scientific analysis. The implication is that while the sociological approach discussed here can identify and communicate the central idea of a literary work, it cannot become a substitute for personal aesthetic experience. In any case, one should refrain from characterizing an idea as false the way Plekhanov sometimes

does, e.g. an idea which supports the bourgeoisie vs. the proletariat, in order to extend this characterization to its artistic
properties. Obviously a logical inconsistency, a contradiction
in the thematic development of a literary work, etc. might be
termed 'false.' But a work's partisanship cannot be used to
judge its aesthetic merits.

To conclude, let us pose the question: is there sufficient
evidence that Plekhanov's emphasis on *the idea* is a useless
proposition: We can unhesitatingly answer in the negative, because his method can successfully determine the sociological
what of a literary work, particularly as it relates to numerous
social factors, and above all, to the class struggle. In other
words—as it is evident in Plekhanov's own writings presented
here—content-oriented Marxist sociology has made a considerable
contribution to the demystification of artistic/literary achievements, the revealing of their ideological roots and overall social
conditioning in the process of artistic creation as well as the
aesthetic response and judgment.

Its merits notwithstanding, Plekhanov's literary criticism
is unable to account for the artistic *how* of a work in either the
creative process or the aesthetic response, while it is necessary
that one goes beyond general sociological considerations—i.e.
aesthetic education, psychological empathy due to class values,
etc.—and into the realm of a work's independent and autonomous existence, and also near to the very deep, personal levels
of the artist's inner desire for creativity as well as to his talent.
The sociological approach in general, influenced by Marxism, is
no less than the primary and prerequisite part of literary criticism, which needs to be supplemented by the psychological
and stylistic. However, when positivistic concerns predominate—
as in Plekhanov's (and Taine's) case—it largely neglects the
literary text itself, moving away from it; it is when inoculated
with structuralism—Lucien Goldmann's case—that it makes the
text the center of its focus.

NOTES

[1] Cf. The "Preface" to the 1962 edition of G. V. Plekhanov's *Fundamental Problems of Marxism, op. cit.,* p. 5.

[2] *Ibid.,* p. 5.

[3] Brang, *op. cit.,* p. 212.

[4] Lee Baxandall, "Marxism and Aesthetics: A Critique of the Contribution of George Plekhanov," *The Journal of Aesthetics and Art Criticism,* XXV, no. 3 (Spring 1967), pp. 267-268.

[5] Henri Arvon, *Marxist Esthetics,* trans. by H. R. Lane, (Ithaca: Cornell University Press, 1973), p. 14.

[6] Cf. Plekhanov, *Fundamental Problems of Marxism, op. cit.,* p. 70.

[7] *Ibid.,* p. 70. Plekhanov is referring to *social psychology.*

[8] Plekhanov, *Fundamental Problems of Marxism, op. cit.,* p. 61.

[9] Plekhanov, *Art and Society, op. cit.,* p. 75.

[10] *Ibid.,* p. 76.

[11] Quoted in *Ibid.,* p. 79.

[12] Cf. Lev Semenovich Vygotsky, *The Psychology of Art* (Cambridge, Massachusetts: The M.I.T. Press, 1971), pp. 212-213, 244.

[13] Plekhanov, *Art and Society, op. cit.,* p. 83.

[14] The terms "psychological nature" of man and "biological nature" as used by Plekhanov have an identical meaning.

[15] *Ibid.,* p. 83.

[16] *Ibid.,* p. 95.

[17] *Ibid.,* p. 95.

[18] *Ibid.,* p. 97.

[19] Cf. for example, Plekhanov's discussion of the relationship between culture and the economic foundation of society as quoted in Baxandall, "Marxism and Aesthetics: A Critique of the Contribution of George Plekhanov," *op. cit.,* p. 269.

[20] Plekhanov, *Art and Society, op. cit.,* p. 162.

[21] *Ibid.,* p. 163.

[22] *Ibid.,* p. 173.

[23] *Ibid.,* p. 185.

[24] *Ibid.,* p. 186.

[25] Cf. *Ibid.,* pp. 186-187.

[26] *Ibid.,* p. 20.

[27] *Ibid.,* p. 24.

[28] *Ibid.,* pp. 37, 43, 44, 59.

[29] *Ibid.,* p. 36.

[30] *Ibid.,* p. 38.

[31] Cf. Strelka, ed. *Literary Criticism and Sociology, op. cit.,* p. 214.

[32] Plekhanov, *Art and Society, op. cit.,* p. 38.

[33] *Ibid.,* p. 46.

[34] *Ibid.,* p. 57.

[35] *Ibid.,* p. 62.

[36] *Ibid.,* p. 65.

[37] Cf. Plekhanov's discussion of the famous Russian literary critic Vissarion Belinsky (1811-1848), quoted in Vygotsky, *op. cit.,* p. 255.

[38] Baxandall, "Marxism and Aesthetics: A Critique of the Contribution of George Plekhanov," *op. cit.,* p. 272.

[39] Arvon, *op. cit.,* p. 13.

[40] Cf. *Ibid.,* pp. 12-13.

[41] Plekhanov, *Art and Society, op. cit.,* p. 121.

[42] Baxandall, "Marxism and Aesthetics: A Critique of the Contribution of George Plekhanov," *op. cit.,* p. 274.

[43] Demetz, *op. cit.,* p. 198.

[44] Plekhanov, *Art and Society, op. cit.,* p. 186.

[45] Cf. some relevant quotations from Plekhanov's statements, in Baxandall, "Marxism and Aesthetics: A Critique of the Contribution of George Plekhanov," *op. cit.,* p. 274.

[46] *Ibid.,* p. 275. Also, Cf. Plekhanov, *Art and Society, op. cit.,* pp. 105, 106, 150.

[47] Quoted in Baxandall, "Marxism and Aesthetics: A Critique of the Contribution of George Plekhanov," *op. cit.,* p. 275.

[48] Quoted in *Ibid.,* p. 276.

[49] *Ibid.,* p. 276.

[50] Cf. *Ibid.,* pp. 277, 278.

THREE

GOLDMANN: THE HOMOLOGY OF STRUCTURES

1. *Genetic Structuralism and Literature*

Lucien Goldmann, whose main ideas were developed in France from the 1950's onwards, became a controversial figure first as a consequence of his new sociological approach to literature, and subsequently as a result of an increasing interest in the wider implications of his theorizing on social and cultural matters. The different accounts of his work in English, however, adopt varied stands towards its validity, ranging from predominantly negative, to moderate and to positive with qualifications.[1]

Goldmann's major studies, *Immanuel Kant* (1945), *The Human Sciences and Philosophy* (1952), *The Hidden God* (1956), *Racine* (1956), *Recherches Dialectiques* (1959), *Towards a Sociology of the Novel* (1964), *Marxisme et Sciences Humaines* (1970), *Structures Mentales et Creation Culturelle* (1970), and *Cultural Creation in Modern Society* (1971), manifest the overall goal of his intellectual life-project: to establish a relationship between cultural products—especially imaginary artistic creations (literature), and conceptual constructions (philosophy)—and the social and ideological structures of the corresponding society. He undertakes this momentous enterprise equipped primarily with the premises of a 'neo-Hegelian' Marxist orientation, the empirical findings of Jean Piaget about the behavior and action of human subjects (individual for Piaget, collective for Goldmann), and a method which he labels 'genetic structuralism.'

Goldmann's merit lies not only in the development of a new methodology, but also in his ability and eagerness to apply and test this promising sociological mode of investigation to specific cultural works, not without impressive results. Despite the more general potential of his theoretical insights, his strength and originality lie with his sociology of literature. Here, a fresh exposition of this will illuminate further Goldmann's accomplishments and shortcomings, providing a comprehensive basis for an equitable evaluation of his actual contribution.

a. *Ahistorical Structuralism and the Content Approach*

French structuralism, the intellectual force of the 1960's which was the outcome of the uncoordinated efforts of such thinkers as Lévi-Strauss, Lacan, Foucault and Althusser, took the form of a system of semiology in the writings of Roland Barthes. This system, faithful to the fundamental guidelines of Ferdinand de Saussure *Course in General Linguistics* (1915) stresses the intrinsic and synchronic study of literary texts.*

This mode of interpretation of linguistic signs (the structuralist *fabrication* of meaning, according to Barthes) succeeds in establishing a consistent relationship between the parts and the whole of a text; yet the text is not considered in terms of its external relations, nor is it treated as also having an historical dimension. Literary works are investigated statically on the basis of their abstract elements, and with complete disregard for those concrete mediations that connect them with the distinct aspects of a given socio-historical reality. Thus, despite structuralism's efficiency in throwing light on the most minute, internal connections of a text, it fails to unveil the latter's unique ties with its author's life-long commitments and stimuli. This exciting "activity"[2] cannot go beyond a dogmatically conceived autonomy of the text, the active presence of which in the socio-cultural world is irrevocably ignored.

From Goldmann's point of view "formalistic" structuralism is unacceptable because, as the theorizing of Lévi-Strauss demonstrates, it is a "system that tends to eliminate in a radical way all interest in history and the problem of meaning."[3] All in all, lacking a coherent philosophy of its own, formalistic structuralism oscillates between a Kantianism minus a transcendental subject[4] (Lévi-Strauss) and a reconstructed materialism (Althusser).

---

*See chapter eight.

In contrast to formalistic structuralism which, for Goldmann, always implies "*the methodological denial of any historical dimension to social facts,*"[5] genetic structuralism is historical: it views philosophical and literary texts in the framework of their historical situation and it ultimately attempts to explain the former in terms of the meanings of the latter. As Goldmann points out, genetic and non-genetic structuralism differ in their perception of human behaviour: for the first, "the whole range of human behavior . . . has a structural character," while the second "sees in structures the essential sector, but only a sector, of overall human behavior," and it leaves "aside what is too closely connected with a given historical situation or a precise stage of a biography, thus leading up to a sort of separation between the formal structures and the particular content of that behavior. . . ."[6]

A noteworthy point of agreement between these two different approaches is their mutual admission of "the incompatibility between structural analysis and concrete history," because at the level of empirical reality—which is dynamic—facts are unstructured and they are better referred to as "processes of structuration and destructuration." Moreover, Goldmann continues, the difference between the appearance and essence of phenomena creates additional problems which, on the plane of scientific analysis, prevent the coincidence of their specific empirical reality with their conceptualization. Therefore, genetic structuralism developed such concepts as those "which are already very close to less comprehensive realities but which continue, of course, to retain a methodological status of the same nature."[7] Shortly, we will see how Goldmann attempts to escape the pitfalls of his initial historicist position by giving it a dialectical turn, at least on the level of theory.

The basic difference between the traditional sociological approach to literature (e.g. Plekhanov) and Goldmann's method derives from the emphasis of the former on establishing the essential similarities between a work's content and the content of its socio-historical environment, that is the content of the corresponding *actual* collective consciousness manifested in the prevailing ideologies. The implication is that a work's content is viewed as a mere reflection of socio-historical dynamics; as the reproduction in the literary realm of men's real involvement in the human community, in all its facets and variations.

Goldmann expresses his misgivings about the drawbacks

of the content approach in a very early article (1947) in which he begins to formulate the main themes of his subsequent studies.[8] Further, in an essay included in his *Towards a Sociology of the Novel* he explains the two principal disadvantages of any exclusive focus on content. The first is due to the writer's justifiable inability to go beyond a limited, selective reconstruction of the empirical social environment. This prevents the sociologist, who is interested in the comparison of contents, from capturing the real "unity" of the work, what Goldmann calls, its "specific literary" nature. The second involves an assumption Goldmann makes which purports that it is the attribute of the mediocre writer—as opposed to the great—to reconstruct only some parts and aspects of men's lives and collective consciousness. Hence, he implies that content oriented sociology "often has an anecdotal character and proves to be especially effective when it studies *works of average importance or literary tendencies*, but gradually loses interest as it approaches the major works of creation."[9]

b. *Foundations of Genetic Structuralism*

Genetic structuralism follows the German neo-idealist distinction between the natural sciences and the cultural or human sciences. Goldmann underlines that the natural sciences study the phenomena of the material world from *without* and, consequently, the use of the scientific method is feasible and adequate. But in the human sciences, any recourse to scientism is completely inadmissible because the investigator perceives his object of study from *within* (a perception which is nevertheless historically and socially preconditioned), being himself a part of it. In other words, in the human sciences the thinking subject is already a part of the analyzed object.

In the course of his intellectual development, Goldmann modifies his attitude towards the subject/object relationship and, viewing history from a dialectical perspective, he attempts to transcend the limitations of his early historicism. Concretely, in his late writings, he abandons his initial uncritical acceptance of the Hegelian notion of *totality* which is based on the *total* subject/object identity, and re-orients himself towards a theory of history that implies the *partial* identity between the subject and the object of thought. At the same time, he criticizes Lukács—the single most important influence on his work—for having approached idealism too closely in his early writings when he adopted the Hegelian position without any modification.[10] There is some reason to suggest that Goldmann's late proclamation of the partial identity of subject and object echoes Lukács' own self-criticism.[11] Be that as it may, Goldmann now maintains that from the dialectical point of view "thought is an important aspect, but only as aspect, of reality: we speak of the partial identity of the subject and the object of research, that identity being valid, not for all knowledge, but only for the human sciences."[12]

Goldmann's mature position on this matter marks his epistemological shift from historicism to dialectics. As a result of his acceptance of the "partial and historical" subject/object identity, the dialectical methodological task of genetic structuralism seems to be twofold: first, to explore the genesis and evolution of the subject/object relationship (diachronic movement), and second, to establish and examine the concrete structure of this relationship at one particular time (synchronic view).[13]

As it will be shown later, despite such *theoretical* pronouncements Goldmann was, ultimately, unable in practice to meet the demands of this double methodological requirement, that is, when he set forth to investigate specific literary and philosophical works. In these studies, including his brief account of the *Nouveau Roman* and Malraux's novels, he remains captive to an historicist stubbornness, and he operates primarily on the level of synchronic structures (within a limited historical period) at the expense of genuine diachronic considerations, such as the effect of literary tradition on works of literature. Unlike its formalist counterpart, genetic structuralism is indeed historical; yet, it is mostly concerned with history as structure and not also as a process.

Goldmann is aware, of course, that the idea of the partial and historical identity of the subject and the object of thought is by no means an epistemological panacea for the human sciences. Nevertheless, by emphasizing the historical dimension (even within the limits of a synchronic perspective) he makes a case for an objective basis of thought, since this is but a part of socio-historical reality. In short, he views the epistemological problem of the human sciences as follows: "L' identité du sujet et de l' objet crée aux sciences de l' homme un statut différent des sciences de la nature. Elle fait de toute affirmation sur la réalité humaine une intervention pratique, une *praxis*, qui rend impossible la séparation des jugements de fait et des jugements de valeur. Il s' ensuit qu' une connaissance positive des faits humains implique toujours une prise de position et une étude à la fois explicative et compréhensive."[14]

Genetic structuralism, takes issue with the central epistemological question of formalistic structuralism: whether social reality could be approached in terms of a conscious subject behaving and acting intentionally, or objectively, that is, in terms of an unconscious linguistic structure, independent of the subject. At the heart of this issue of course is the question of the intelligibility of consciousness.

According to Lévi-Strauss, for example, social reality and consequently its most essential structure, language, cannot possibly be investigated from the standpoint of the subject: language (and its products) is completely autonomous, it is its own truth and its own reality, and it only becomes intelligible by means of an objective structure. In *The Savage Mind* he writes: "Linguistics. . . presents us with a dialectical and totalizing entity but one outside (or beneath) consciousness and will. Language, an unreflecting totalization, is human reason which has its reasons and of which man knows nothing."[15]

Goldmann's structuralism is based on an hypothesis which is found in one form or another in Hegel, Marx, Freud and Lukács, and which might be regarded as the foundation of this approach. The hypothesis about which all these thinkers tend to agree is that there are no absurd human acts (individual or collective) if they aim towards a certain goal, irrespective of whether or not they succeed in achieving it.[16]

In Goldmann's view, the totality of human behavior expresses men's significant response to specific events and situations. Influenced by Jean Piaget, he regards "human realities" as dual processes towards eliminating the old structures (destructuration) which are useless for the new needs of social groups, and towards structuring new "totalities" (structuration) according to the demands of new necessities. These new totalities will ultimately produce equilibria between the subject and the object of action.

The human realities, identified by Goldmann as economic, social, political or cultural facts, are the historical products of a thinking and acting subject. This subject is not the individual but the *collectivity.* A trans-individual subject which is "no more than a complex network of inter-individual relations. . . ."[17] The idea of a collective subject is dominant in genetic structuralism and it requires further elaboration.[18]

c. *The Collective Subject*

In proposing as the true creator of cultural works a collective subject and not their authors, Goldmann does not wish to undermine the latter's singular importance. On the contrary, even though the particularity and uniqueness (i.e. in terms of artistic and intellectual abilities) of exceptional individuals is examined in relation to a social group, it is admitted that the characteristic feature of this group—its distinct collective consciousness—is not simply illuminated but indeed coherently formulated and defined thanks to the special creative skills of those individuals. However, Goldmann maintains that the methodological treatment of a cultural work as the direct, unmediated product of only a single individual can produce little more than limited results: the elucidation of the work's internal unity and the establishment of the links between its parts and the whole. But for Goldmann this is insufficient because neither a relation *"of the same sort"* between a work and its immediate producer can be established, nor can such an approach go beyond an "accidental . . . speculation." Therefore, the psychoanalytical interpretations which regard individuals as the subjects of cultural works are to a great extent inadequate, as will be explained in due course.

Only genetic structuralist sociology is capable of producing a satisfactory account of the works of literature, because it alone can meaningfully connect them and examine them in relation to certain collective units or significant social groups, i.e. the family, professional associations, religious groups, social classes, the nation, etc. Attention should be given to the special importance that some social groups hold over others in the study of cultural works. According to Goldmann, these social groups or "complex networks of interindividual relations" act in certain ways upon the consciousness of their individual members and shape their psychology, which is "an unique, complex and relatively incoherent structure." But an individual's psychology cannot be objectively analyzed and fully comprehended because, among other things, the existing psychoanalytical tools are not adequate for such a task. This difficulty can only be overcome if the investigator moves from the level of the single individual to that of the many, *who belong to a common group.*

On this level, the influence of all other groups—specific to each individual—on his consciousness and consequently on his particular psychological traits acquired by these various influences, "cancel each other out," in the sense that there remains a predominant feature common to all individuals which is suitable for a complete study: *a fairly simple and coherent structure.* In effect, Goldmann continues, "the relations between the truly important work and the social group, which—through the medium of the creator—*is, in the last resort, the true subject of creation,* are of the same order as relations between the elements of the work and the work as a whole. . . . (These relations are) of both a comprehensive and an explanatory kind."[19] It is on the basis of this analysis that the content approach to literary and philosophical works is rejected and replaced by a new approach, the key term of which is *structure.*

d. *The Homology of Structures*

Structures are for Goldmann *functional* totalities bound to change with time[20] and be succeeded by new structures according to the dynamics of the already mentioned process of structuration and destructuration. The basic hypothesis of genetic structuralist sociology can be found in the following excerpt from Goldmann's writings: "the collective character of literary creation derives from the fact that the *structures* of the world of the work are homologous with the mental structures of certain social groups or is in intelligible relation with them, whereas on the level of content . . . the writer has total freedom."[21]

Before we specify which social groups and structures are implied here, we should refer to certain interrelated premises stemming from this hypothesis, which reveal the cardinal importance of these structures for Goldmann's sociology: a) The basic relation between cultural creations and their social environment is between mental structures rather than between

contents; b) These structures are always social phenomena;
c) Even though the content of cultural works and their social
environment might appear unrelated, their mental structures
can be homologous. d) The greater the cultural work, the easier
its study through its mental structure which gives it unity: a
manifestation of high literary quality; and e) The illumination
and analysis of these structures cannot be achieved by literary
or psychological techniques, i.e. by focusing on the writer's
conscious plan or on his unconscious. These mental structures
are *non-conscious processes* and they can usually be inferred
only by genetic structuralist sociology.[22] In this framework,
the question arises which concrete social groups and mental
structures are immediately connected with the production of
artistic and conceptual works.

Given that a collective subject is the real creative force,
the social groups which "encourage cultural creation" are those
"whose consciousness tends to an over all vision of man."[23]
These social groups are none other than social classes, the essential mental structures of which—namely, those that are homologous to the structures of a work's universe—are world visions.
Goldmann argues that social classes have been proven to be
the only social groups capable of generating world visions, at
least for a long period of human history. Further, that philosophical and literary currents can be understood on the basis
of an examination not just of any social group but of social
classes alone. Lastly, he adds that the world visions which can
be expressed in cultural works are the manifestations of "the
maximum of potential consciousness" of these social classes.[24]

Even close to the end of his life, Goldmann still viewed
social classes as the real subject of cultural creation, but only
for those historical periods where they could structure the world
in a coherent way, that is, insofar as they were able to produce
world visions.[25] Thus, he observes, in regard to works of culture, "social classes have a particular importance and a privileged
status inasmuch as they are the only trans-individual subject
whose consciousness and action are directed to the organization
of the sum of interhuman relationships and relationships between
men and nature, with a view to either keeping them as they are
or transforming them in a more or less radical manner. . . ."[26]
But in order to grasp fully the role of social classes as the subject
of cultural creation, we must focus on what might be characterized as the very core of Goldmann's ideas: the interrelated

notions of *potential consciousness* and *world vision.*

e. *Potential Consciousness and World Vision*

Goldmann's key concepts and some of his theoretical standpoints derive from Lukács' early writings: the pre-Marxist works *Soul and Form* and the *Theory of the Novel,* and the Marxist *History and Class Consciousness.* The concepts of potential consciousness and world vision, in particular, are certainly found in Lukács,[27] even though their first systematic consideration can be traced back to Max Weber, who had some influence on the Hungarian philosopher. The notion of potential consciousness holds a central position in the sociology of Max Weber, who does not differentiate it sufficiently from the concepts of *ideal type* and *objective possibility.*

Among these three instruments of scientific analysis used by Weber, the notion of potential consciousness is regarded by Goldmann as the "principal (methodological) instrument" of social science.[28] For this reason, in contrast to the *real or actual consciousness* of social classes, which is the object par excellence of content oriented sociology, their *maximum of potential consciousness* is the focal point of genetic structuralist sociology. Goldmann refers to the difference between the two as follows: "Real consciousness is the result of the limitations and deviations that the actions of other social groups and natural and cosmic factors cause class consciousness to undergo." Yet, despite these obstacles to class consciousness it should be realized that "*Man is defined by his possibilities. . . .* 'Class-for-itself' (as opposed to 'class-in-itself') and the maximum of potential consciousness express possibilities on the level of thought and action *within a given social structure.*"[29]

The concepts of potential consciousness, social class and world vision are closely linked, and we shall now carefully examine the latter, which is no less than the main tool of the genetic structuralist method. World vision is certainly a very problematic concept and thus it is preferable to let Goldmann describe it himself: "a 'world vision' is a convenient term for the whole complex of ideas, aspirations and feelings which links together the members of a social group (a group which, in most cases, assumes the existence of a social class) and which opposes them

to members of other social groups."[30]   In effect, Goldmann
continues, the members of a social class have various degrees of
awareness of this vision, the full grasp of which is the privilege
of only a few: the great writers and philosophers who alone are
able to achieve and express the maximum of potential consciousness of a given class. A world vision, then, is the full expression
of the consciousness of a social class.

Evidently, a new question arises here: is a world vision
an ideology? Goldmann answers negatively and points out that
from a Marxist perspective ideology is false consciousness; that
is, a *partial* distortion of reality. In contrast, a world vision has
a total character, not only in regard to its perception of human
relationships, but also in its capacity to visualize the future
from the standpoint of its experience of the present, preconditioned by its understanding of the past. World visions are, so
to speak, the masterplans of thought and action of the rising
classes; ideologies are but the rusty weaponry of classes in
decline, pertaining also to those social groups which cannot
develop more than a limited and one-sided view of the world.

This distinction is not absolute; in the sense that ideologies depict reality falsely and world visions provide correct
estimations verging on the 'truth.' For example, Jansenism and
Cartesianism are not ideologies but world visions. As for Marxism, it appears to be the only possible world vision of the present.   However, Goldmann suggests that these philosophical
systems "as conceptual works . . . can and must be judged at the
level of *truth.* But since they are at the same time conceptual
expressions of different visions of the world, 'false' philosophies
can for a long time retain a certain value because of their internal
coherence and because they consistently represent a certain way
of thinking and feeling life and the world. . . ."[31] The distinction between world vision and ideology in terms of artistic
production is further clarified within the framework of Goldmann's discussion of the problem of genius, which, as he states,
is *"the most important problem of aesthetics."*[32]

f. *Genius and World Vision*

As we have seen, it is the rare individual alone—the genuine
philosopher or the exceptional writer—who is capable of approxi-

mating the potential consciousness of a social class, that is, its world vision. Even before his major writings, Goldmann was convinced that a writer's *ouevre* constitutes the *objective ground* on which it could be decided whether or not he was a genius, despite the many disagreements and difficulties in determining his special characteristics, such as talent, patience, extraordinary capacity to work, etc., and regardless of any subjective aesthetic judgments and personal preferences.

Goldmann credits genius with the "widest," "richest" and "most universally human sensibility," and observes that certain writers, i.e. Baudelaire, Rimbaud or Rilke, were able to create complete imaginary worlds *for the first time,* that is, they were able to present the universe in a new way. He also views the status of a genius as the *upper limit* of an ambitious process, toward which the great creators advanced—more or less succesfully—in the approximation of this target. And he arrives at the conclusion that "a literary work can be reactionary and retain its aesthetic and human validity. However, genius is by contrast *always progressive,* because in any given epoch, the perspective of the rising class alone can ensure, despite all its ideologies and risks of error, the widest knowledge and the richest sensibility."[33]

World visions are not individual but social facts, and this makes more explicit the notion of the collective subject discussed earlier.[34] The sociology of knowledge, Goldmann asserts, may approach world visions either on the level of real consciousness, or on that of the maximum of potential consciousness, coherently expressed in the great philosophical and literary works. He also suggests that "The two planes *complement* and usually support each other,"[35] therefore the lack of a systematic typology of the world visions is an obstacle to the development of both the sociology of knowledge and intellectual history.

Goldmann believes that the immense difficulties in the construction of such a typology notwithstanding, it alone can tell us "whether (all world visions which are limited anyway) have found expression already in the intellectual and artistic history of the periods known to us."[36] Future world visions, as well as the historical transformations which the old ones undergo, reappearing in different forms from those already known, can be continuously added to that typology at the time of their occurence. This would constitute a 'map' of world visions in the course of human history. Such a typology would greatly contribute to a better understanding of man's most precious accomplishments—his literary and philosophical products—as well as of their collective creators and individual geniuses.

g. *The Study of Tragic Vision*

A literary work, Goldmann claims, has three main characteristics. It constitutes a concrete universe presented from a certain point of view; it is internally coherent; and it achieves unity of content and form.[37] It is primarily coherence and the homology of a work's significant structure with the mental structure of a social class (its world vision) that can make it great as opposed to one that is mediocre.[38] Thus, the question here, becomes, how are these ideas applied in Goldmann's concrete studies? For example, how is he able to demonstrate in his most successful work, *The Hidden God,* that the main structure of Pascal's philosophy and of Racine's theatre is homologous to the tragic vision (another mental structure) of the Jansenists and of the *Noblesse de Robe?*

This question can be answered by referring to the genetic-structuralist method as a process consisting of two distinct phases. First, the phase of *comprehension,* in which a work's internal unity is studied *until its significant structure is revealed.* And second, the phase of *explanation,* the placing of the main structure of a work into the context of another structure external to it, *until the work's genesis appears as a function of the other structure.*

Goldmann stresses that all factors relating to a text but *outside* of it are merely explanatory in nature.[39] In addition, he advocates that the phase of comprehension should be evaluated "solely and exclusively in relation to the proportion of the part of the text which it succeeds in integrating." As for the phase of explanation, it should be evaluated "solely and exclusively in accordance with the possibility of establishing at least a rigorous correlation—and as far as possible a significant and functional relationship—between, on the one hand, the development of a vision of the world and the genesis of a text originating from it, and, on the other hand, certain phenomena external to the latter."[40]

In the specific case of *The Hidden God*, for example, we first comprehend the significant structure of Pascal's *Pensees* in itself, and then we explain it by placing this structure within the structure of Jansenism which we comprehend. We then view Jansenism within the larger structure of the history of Jansenism, and thus we explain the first and comprehend the second. Further, we consider the structure of the latter within the structure of the *Noblesse de Robe,* explaining again the first and comprehending the second. Subsequently, we view the structure of the *Noblesse de Robe* within the structure of the history of French society, which we then comprehend while the former is explained.

Goldmann gives paramount importance to the coherence of a literary work because he considers a work's internal unity as the result of a concrete world vision, the *values* of which are directly expressed in it. This is in contrast to formalistic structuralism which favors, as we have noted, a completely intrinsic approach. In other words, the coherence of a literary text is impossible without a coherent value system and this means that ultimately it is this system which gives an aesthetic structure to a text.

Value analysis is an integral part of Goldmann's studies, and in conjunction with the notion of *crisis* it aims at explaining the genesis of *great* works. In effect, Goldmann perceives their immediate creators—the literary geniuses—as struggling for and against values in a gigantic effort to achieve a synthesis of the old and the new, within the content of their invariably "progressive" works.[41] However, even though periods of social crisis and transformation appear to be linked with "the birth of great works of art and of literature,"[42] there is only one world vision, the *tragic vision,* in its various forms and consequently in the literary genre in which it is expressed, tragedy, that Goldmann specifically associates with the notion of crisis. Thus, given that the real creative subject is collective, the following scheme is suggested for the genesis of great tragedies: crisis⟶ tragic vision⟶mediating geniuses⟶tragedies.

Goldmann distinguishes "three great forms of tragic awareness,"[43] for the entire period of human history, and he points out the three corresponding forms of great tragic creation which express this awareness: the Greek tragedy, the Shakespearian tragedy and the "tragedy of refusal" of Pascal and Racine. To his mind, these three forms of tragic vision have one essential point in common: "they all express a deep crisis in the relationship between man and his social and spiritual world."[44]   Certainly, these three forms of tragic awareness have been transcended by other world visions.[45]   This alternation between tragic vision and world visions going beyond it is not elaborated by Goldmann, who concentrates rather on the relationship between crisis and the great cultural works stemming from it: "it is in periods of social and political crisis that men are most aware of the enigma of their presence in the world. In the past, this awareness has tended to find its expression in tragedy. At the present day it shows itself in existentialism."[46]

h. *Goldmann: Limitations of the Genetic-Structuralist Method*

Goldmann's exclusive focus on a work's coherence, that is, on the ensemble of those elements which contribute to its unity, creates a problem of which he took notice quite late in his productive life, and which is more serious than he had probably thought: his case studies totally neglect those elements which negatively affect the unity and coherence of a work—the "antagonistic" elements. The issue was brought to his attention by Julia Kristeva's study of the work of the Russian Dostoevsky scholar, Michail Bakhtin, who divided literary works into *homophonic or monological* (Tolstoy) and *polyphonic or dialogical* (Dostoevsky), and who was primarily interested in those elements which oppose unity—the critical elements.[47]
Goldmann defends his own position as being the consequence of his background in German classical aesthetics, mostly acquired through the study of the early works of Lukács. Literary value, for example, is defined by Lukács as "a tension overcome between, on the one hand, sensible multiplicity and richness and, on the other hand, the unity which organized this multiplicity into a coherent whole."[48]   Goldmann argues that all those who are influenced by the early works of Lukács tend to examine only one side of this tension: unity. In this sense, he does not assume responsibility for his one-sidedness. Instead, he states that the sociology of literature which follows Lukács' early guidelines is still undeveloped. Despite these justifications, he admits this deficiency of his genetic-structuralist method,[49] and accepts that "almost all literary works have a function that

is partially critical. . . ," because "even if they express a particular vision of the world (they) are led, for literary and aesthetic reasons, to formulate also the limits of this vision. . . ." Therefore, he concedes, literary criticism should "go much further than we have done hitherto, by bringing to light all the antagonistic elements of the work which the structured vision must overcome and organize."[50]

It is mentioned in *The Hidden God* that the contribution of the historico-sociological method (genetic structuralism) is twofold: first, to reveal the diverse world visions existing at the time a work is produced (historical consideration), and second, to investigate and explain the relationship between a work's universe and *one* world vision (sociological aesthetic). This was as far as Goldmann could actually go in regard to those factors that were negatively related to a given work.[51] Despite the dialectical aspects of his thought, it did not occur to him that from the standpoint of the dialectical way of thinking and viewing the world, the existence of antagonistic elements—in one form or another—in a work is not simply due to "literary and aesthetic reasons" but also to a larger necessity, which dialectical logic alone could comprehend. In essence, there always exists an antithesis to what is presented, explicitly or implicitly, as the thesis of any given work.

In his study of Racine's tragedies, Goldmann suggests an additional limitation of genetic-structuralism: that the use of world vision as a methodological tool cannot be a substitute either for textual and aesthetic analysis or for historical studies. This he mainly attributes to the immaturity of his method at its present stage. He has undoubtedly considered the aesthetic analysis of literary works as an indispensable supplement to an approach based on their world vision, having declared that "Aesthetic value proper always remains the fundamental criterion for studying both the objective significance of the work and the validity of the writer's own testimony about it."[52] He refocuses on the same issue in *The Hidden God,* where he views the existence of a coherent world vision in a literary work as only one of the two basic prerequisites for the achievement of an aesthetic result. The second prerequisite is that there should exist a "correspondence" between the literary world created by the writer and the particular "literary devices" that he uses, i.e. style, images, etc.[53]

Moreover, Goldmann makes it absolutely clear that the

genetic-structuralist method is efficient only in the study of *great* works. Average and inferior works are inaccessible to his method because they are created by complicated individuals who do not represent their social class.[54] He finally adds that his method is necessarily restricted to the study of the great works of the *past*. He argues that contemporary works can certainly be approached on the basis of their world vision, but this task would be fruitless given that accidental factors (i.e. advertisement, fashion, etc.) will mislead the research, and the sole fundamental factor for the evaluation of a work—the test of time—will be missing. In the course of time, all parasitic factors involved in a work's position within the cultural life of society disappear and what remains is the only true criterion of enduring literary value: "it is the fact that in certain works of the past, men rediscover what they themselves think and feel in a confused and obscure manner today."[55]

i. *The Writer and his Work*

Goldmann makes a sharp distinction between the *conscious intentions* of a writer, i.e. historical, philosophical, political, etc., and the *objective significance* of his work. The "disjuncture" between the two is sometimes apparent in the case of great creators, i.e. Dante, Goethe and Balzac, and it is of special interest to the researcher who can reveal it by aesthetic analysis. He criticizes such philosophers as Descartes and Sartre, and he claims that the realm of consciousness is much smaller than that of the totality of human behavior; therefore a work's significance must always be separated from its author's intentions.

It is not unusual for the structure of a literary work to express a world vision other than that which its writer consciously endorses. Consequently, the writer's conscious intentions should be treated as only one suggestive element among others. An obvious corollary to this is that a great writer's biography is of little importance in the explanation of his work, first because the latter has a logic of its own, and second because the explanation of his work can be directly based on the world vision of a social class. What then of the input of the actual creator to his own products?

The individual's personal stamp on his work is undeniable:

"the greater the work, the more personal it is;" also, *"the more the work is the expression of a thinker or writer of genius, the more it is comprehensible by itself."* It is the privilege of genius to identify "with the essential forces of social consciousness" to the maximum degree possible, which means that in the case of a genius the individual and the collectivity intermingle.[56] Hence Goldmann insists that the creator's biography and psychology alone—as well as other "influences"—cannot explain his work. The test must always be the basis of literary criticism, but its significance from the point of view of its own author should not be identified with its objective significance.[57]

A point worth noting is that Goldmann's concrete studies led him to the conclusion that it is possible for a writer to pass from one philosophical position to another, and thus, to express in his works two different world visions. His suggestion is that the works of a writer should not be studied in their chronological order; they should be grouped provisionally, and subsequently the common structures of these groupings should be compared with the structures of their surrounding social groups with the purpose of establishing homologies where possible. This procedure proved fruitful in the case of Pascal.[58]

j. *Genetic Structuralism and Psychoanalysis*

We can embark on a discussion of the relationship between genetic-structuralist sociology and psychoanalysis by refocusing on the phases of comprehension and explanation, the status of which, according to Goldmann, is not the same when the viewpoint alters. From the psychoanalytical perspective, where libido and the unconscious are involved, comprehension and explanation are inseparable; from the point of view of sociology, however, such a separation is feasible. As Goldmann maintains, this is so because on the level of libido, that is, "on the plane of the behavior of an individual subject aiming directly at the *possession of an object*" (my italics), consciousness does not function autonomously; in contrast, on the social level the independent function of consciousness becomes evident, and it "tends to constitute a significant structure."

Apart from this difference, genetic-structuralist sociology and psychoanalysis have certain features in common, which also give the latter the appearance of genetic structuralism.[59] What interests us mostly here is their opposing features: psychoanalysis attempts to account for all human behavior by merely investigating one form of the behavior of the individual, that of the desire of an object; genetic-structuralist sociology distinguishes between libidinal behavior—recognized as the exclusive domain of psychoanalysis—and behavior which is *historical in nature,* and which by having a trans-individual subject results in cultural creations.

The whole of human behavior is incorporated in two structures, the libidinal and the historical; but their significance is not the same. Goldmann writes: "depending on whether the libidinal satisfaction predominates to the point of destroying the autonomous coherence almost completely, or whether, inversely, it is incorporated in the latter, whilst leaving it almost intact, we shall have before us either the product of a madman or a masterpiece. . . ."[60]

Within this new framework, Goldmann stresses that comprehension and explanations are neither opposite nor different processes, and freed from subjective influences, such as sympathy, empathy, etc., one can regard them as strictly intellectual practices, constituting "one and the same process, related to different co-ordinates."[61] The point which he wishes to make is that while in the course of research comprehension and explanation are carried on simultaneously as supporting one another, (the previous reference to them as 'phases' was only for convenience), after the end of the research the hypotheses pertaining to comprehension must be presented independently of those pertaining to explanation.

In Goldmann's time, the major explanatory hypotheses were dealing with the creator's individual psychology or the mental structure of a social group. However, he is against a psychological approach because there is usually little information available about a writer's psychology—especially in the case of dead writers—and because such an approach is unable to account for more than just a limited portion of a text; lastly, no psychological approach can deal with the literary, aesthetic and philosophical elements of a work.[62]

From a methodological point of view, Goldmann holds that psychoanalysis is largely inadequate (unlike Marxism) not only because it regards the individual as the only subject "for whom other men can only be *objects* of satisfaction and frustration," but also because the Freudian method, emphasizing the analysis of childhood, totally neglects the temporal dimension of *future*. Nevertheless, it should not be presumed that Goldmann rejects psychoanalysis altogether. He rather looks to the integration of its promising elements with historical materialism, and he credits psychoanalysis for its unique capacity to explain the individual and biographical meaning of a work, which sociology lacks. Lastly he underlines psychoanalysis' inherent inability to provide information about the nature and overall meaning of a literary work.[63]

k. *Capitalism and the Novel*

The genetic-structuralist method would require modification if its object of investigation were changed. Thus, we have seen that the notion of social class is useful for the analysis of literary works within certain limits, that is, when social classes demonstrate an ability to destructure and restructure the world coherently. We have also mentioned Goldmann's realization that as great literary works are searching for true values—even though they express a specific world view—they are partially critical. This notion extended to the novel creates a tension in his argument.

As Goldmann moves from an examination of Pascal's tragic philosophy and Racine's tragic theater—that is, from conceptual and imaginary works created before the industrial revolution—to an account of the literary phenomenon of the capitalist era, namely, the novel, he considers it imperative to base himself on a new analysis of the relationship between culture and society, and to adjust his method to meet the demands of a different situation. Specifically, instead of the utilization of a theory accounting for the relationship between social classes, world visions and the great literary and philosophical achievements of the pre-capitalist past, the starting point of his analysis of the novel is that it differs from the masterpieces of traditional literary genres, not merely in form but mainly in the sense of not expressing the world vision of social classes. Moreover, ever since its appearance, the novel has been taking an increasingly critical stand against bourgeois society.

Here, Goldmann follows Lukács' analysis and accepts that

the novel has developed as a consequence of the sharp class divisions of capitalist society, dealing essentially with man's estrangement from the world. Unlike epic literature, the novel is not primarily concerned with the destiny of the human community but with that of the individual, its central figure being the "problematic hero." The novel is individualistic by nature, and its outward form is biographical. Its distinct aim is the desperate search for true human values in a world governed by the impersonal rules of the market, and it is one of the few possible channels of critical opposition to the evils of capitalism. Hence the tension in Goldmann's argument is that given that the novel is not expressing the world vision of a social class—not even the world vision of the class which gave rise to it, i.e. the bourgeoisie—the source of its coherence and greatness is uncertain. But he does provide us with an answer.

To begin with, due to the exploitative nature of capitalism, the values of the social class which identifies with it cannot possibly be expressed (i.e. approved and defended) in the great literary creations. It is impossible for capitalism to exist without the suppression of true human values, and this suppression enacted by the bourgeoisie results in its inability to reconstruct an already degraded world. Therefore, the notion of social class is inadequate for the approach to great novels, because they reflect the reality not only of one social class (including a class's perception of it) but of society as a whole. The coherence, then, of the novel derives from the homology of its main structure with the predominant (economic) structure of capitalism. For Goldmann, the novel is *"the transposition on the literary plane of everyday life in the individualistic society created by market production."*[64] Consequently, as capitalism has taken different forms in the course of its evolution, so has the novel, which responds to the changes of the former and develops alongside it.

Goldmann postulates three distinct periods of capitalism to which he attributes three corresponding forms of the novel, on the assumption that there exists between the two a direct structural homology. First, there is the period of economic liberalism, and the novel is characterized by its exclusive focus on the individual, the problematic hero. Second, there is the period of monopoly capitalism, and the novel's major concern here is the dissolution of personality, psychologism, and the suppression of the individual hero by an all-expanding bureau-cratization—Joyce and Kafka are the most noticeable examples. Third follows the period of advanced capitalism, with the bureau-cratic state assuming the role of a giant capitalist; the literary equivalent of this period is the *nouveau roman.* The French novelist, Robbe-Grillet, is an example of this last kind of novel, the underlying thesis of which is, according to Goldmann, the relative autonomy of objects.[65]

As previously indicated, all forms of the novel demonstrate man's estrangement, the predominance of market relations in the daily interaction of people, as well as the novel's own increasing distance from class values and class consciousness, that is, from a particular world vision. For these reasons, the basis of Gold-mann's analysis of the third form of the novel, *the nouveau roman,* which he regards as the culmination of a process, is not, as already stressed, a theory of class but a phenomenon which for the first time in human history permeates the lives and relationships of human beings irrespective of the social class to which they belong: the phenomenon of *reification.*

1. *Reification and the Nouveau Roman*

According to Goldmann, the *nouveau roman* is the literary expression of reification, and it emerged decades after the sys-tematic exposition of the latter because of the mystifying effects of reification on men's consciousness. Lukács deals with rei-fication extensively in his well-known essay in *History and Class Consciousness,* and it became, one might say, Goldmann's fixation when he embarked on an investigation of the relation-ship between culture and capitalism in his writings in the 1960's.

Reification is a very complex and problematic concept. Its full elaboration—particularly a critique of Lukács' valuable contribution on the subject, as well as of the excesses, errors and inadequacies of his analysis—would require a study of its own, and even then significant questions would probably remain unanswered. Its brief consideration here can begin with its meaning, which derives from a combination of the meanings of three concepts found in the early and late works of Marx and in the sociology of Max Weber, respectively: *alienation, com-modity fetishism* and *rationalization.*

Reification is a characteristic phenomenon of a social formation in which commodity production is generalized and universalized, and according to which: a) the productive activity of men is alienated from themselves; b) the relationship between human beings takes the form of a relationship between things; and c) rationalization—that is, calculation, specialization and mechanization—turns men's productive activity into a routine-like operation, devoid of initiative, creativeness or innovative challenges.

In his essay "Reification and the Consciousness of the Proletariat," Lukács maintains that reification has infiltrated the totality of human consciousness in an all-embracing process, and consequently, all bourgeois thought—especially philosophy and political economy—is itself reified as manifested in its inability to unveil the essence of reality. On the other hand, this consciousness, (the proletariat's included) is forced to adopt a passive, *contemplative stance* toward life. In sum, every single aspect of consciousness, including economic, political, philosophical, artistic, and even everyday thinking, is not simple invaded but indeed strangulated by the devastating influence of reification, and the outcome for capitalist society is frightening, (as this process continues alongside the ongoing socialization of labor—meaning that the vast majority of people are in *essence* workers.)[66]

To paint the picture of capitalist reality more bleakly, Lukács states that the effects of reification—on a society in which commodity has become "the universal structuring principle" at both the *objective* level (historical evolution of society) and the *subjective* level (man's stance towards society)—are also manifested in the "fragmentation" and "atomization" of the worker, as his "own existence is reduced to an isolated particle." The same effects are further visible in the elimination of the worker's human attributes because quality surrenders itself to quantity due to "the dehumanized and dehumanizing function of the commodity relation."[67] Let it be emphasized that speaking of the worker, Lukács believes that he speaks of the entire capitalist society.[68]

Obviously, a number of questions could be posed about the nature and workings of reification. For example, what are the factors determining the extent of its domination of life in capitalist society? How is its alleged omnipotence reconciled with the appearance and function of critical consciousness? Or, how in the midst of reification's reign can Lukács say that for the proletariat and for him alone, "the process by which a man's achievement is split off from his total personality and becomes a commodity leads to a revolutionary consciousness?"[69] In other words, to ask by what means an objectively negative situation (negative for "as long as [the worker] does not consciously rebel against it)"[70] can be turned, by force of the everyday experience of the proletariat while it sells its labor-power to capitalists, into a subjectively positive one, namely, the worker's capability for rebellion against his own reified existence, to which he eventually becomes fully conscious, putting mysteriously behind him his initial contemplative stance?

To make things worse, this contemplative stance, this passive participation in the world, apart from being a direct product of the capitalist mode of material production, is skillfully cultivated further and reinforced during the continual process of reproduction of capitalist society, realized through the various institutions of the state and other weaponry available in the system's arsenal: the mass media; all means and resources at the disposal of all levels of the administration, which is entirely controlled by a bureaucracy carefully selected along ideological criteria and initiated in the ideals of the established social formation; and, above all, by the general mobilization of the formal and informal mechanisms of the capitalist educational system which reproduces the bourgeois values resulting in the reified social relations of production, as well as the individuals who will preserve, defend and continue the reproduction of these values. Here we are not only referring to what Gramsci defines as "organic" intellectuals, who, in his words, "are the 'officers' of the ruling class for the exercise of the subordinate functions of social hegemony and political government....,"[71] but to all members of society to the extent that each one of them is an 'intellectual.'[72] In view of these observations, the question reoccurs: how are critical consciousness, rebellion and ultimately revolution possible?

It can certainly be argued that essential links are missing in the complex chain of Lukácsean analysis. However, the following suggestions might be useful before an uncritical rejection of the Hungarian philosopher's ideas. First, reification is presented by Lukács as a characteristic phenomenon, as a main trend in a process, and not as a total one in the absolute meaning of the word. In this sense, one should view reification as the upper limit toward which capitalist society is moving, with innumerable gradations, rather than as a gigantic contaminated and contaminating pool in which the totality of the society has already sunk. Second, while a passive and contemplative stance predominated as a thesis of capitalism, critical consciousness is not only possible but also inevitable because of the unavoidable antithesis which this consolidated and consolidating thesis is bound to generate (that is, the novel) first of all in the most sensitive parts of the system, those which for one reason or another are immediately affected by reification: the workers, both mental and manual. And third, more than half a century after Lukács' pioneer study on the subject, the presence of reification is becoming more and more felt by an ever-increasing number of people. The outcries from various quarters—mostly from the intellectual and artistic community—about the quality of life largely because of the deteriorating living conditions and social relationships in the populous metropolitan centers, indicates among other things that reification is becoming an unbearable reality. Reification should not be mystified. Yet, it is not just an abstraction: it is a phenomenon manifesting itself in frustrating experiences.

Goldmann accepts the fundamental points of Lukács' analysis of reification. But he overemphasizes its consequences for contemporary society, as shown in his own discussion of the same phenomenon in *Rechearches Dialectiques.* He is struck by the suppression of true human values, and he is particularly concerned about the degenerating relationships among human beings within capitalism.[73] As he focuses on the effects of reification on consciousness, he is very much alarmed by the contemplative stance contributing to men's apathy.

The situation, of course, is not desperate for Goldmann and he still looks upon the proletariat as humanity's hope. This confirms his belief in Marxism as the unique world vision of our time, expressed in literature as the critical viewpoint which gives it coherence and greatness, given that aesthetic requirements are met. For example, in *Towards a Sociology of the Novel,* he maintains that Andre Malraux's famous novel, *Man's Estate,* highly critical of both the values of capitalist society and Stalinism, is indeed an excellent literary work asserting dignity and fraternity. In contrast, the same author's *Days of Hope,* an unproblematic novel which accepts uncritically the party's disciplinarian line and dogmatic policies, is far from a real specimen of what might be considered great literature. Once more, the interrelationship between literary structure and the value system of society is affirmed, while the critical stand toward the workings of human community is always one of the indispensable elements of exceptional literary works.[74]

Malraux's *Man's Estate* is rather an exception, since, as pointed out earlier, the literary expression of advanced capitalism is the *nouveau roman*, characteristically represented by Robbe-Grillet. In Goldmann's view, the basic theme of Robbe-Grillet's novels is men's contemplative stance, whereas the demonstration of the autonomy of objects—in contrast to the classical novel where objects are always related to human beings—underlines man's passivity which results from his reified existence, that is, his dehumanization.

Because of their success in faithfully depicting the essence of the reified reality of advanced capitalism, Goldmann regards the novels of Robbe-Grillet as great realistic works which portray society in a very critical manner.[75] Indeed, Robbe-Grillet presents human beings as meaningless entities, wandering around an object-dominated world. Thus he supports Goldmann's theory according to which the structures of the three stages of capitalism are homologous to the structures of the three forms of the novel. But eventually Goldmann modifies his initial stand and criticizes Robbe-Grillet for the exclusion of the dimension of future, and consequently, of hope, from the imaginary universe he is creating.[76] His final conclusion is that the lack of diversity which characterizes the *nouveau roman* ultimately results in the limitation of men's choices in both the literary and social planes.[77]

m. *The Essential and the Accidental; the Whole and the Parts*

In *The Hidden God*, Goldmann speaks of three basic approaches to literary and philosophical works: the positivistic, the intuitive (which he does not consider as scientific) and the dialectical. He further underlines two fundamental difficulties which, in his view, usually hinder the historian of literature and philosophy. The first is that "not everything which an author writes is equally important for an understanding of his work." The second arises because "Words, sentences and phrases which are apparently similar, and in some cases even identical, can nevertheless have a different meaning when used in a different context."[78]

According to Goldmann, in order to overcome the first difficulty, the investigator should be able to distinguish between what is *essential* from what is merely *accidental*. The second difficulty can be resolved on condition that the relationship between the *whole*—be it a literary work, a man's behavior and personality, the structure of society, etc.—and its *parts* can be established. The establishment of this relationship marks for Goldmann the difference between the traditional methods of approaching cultural works and the dialectical approach.[79]

These two serious obstacles, however, are interrelated, and so they can be dealt with simultaneously. Goldmann writes: "in the study of man, we can separate the essential from the accidental only by integrating the individual elements into the overall pattern, by fitting the parts into the whole."[80] Thus, a primary methodological requirement is the classification of the facts at the investigator's disposal into relatively autonomous wholes, which will subsequently constitute the frame of reference of the entire investigation.

If no relatively autonomous whole exists on the level of a given work, or on that of its author's personality, the investigator can seek it in larger entities, for instance that of society and particularly on the level of its class divisions. Finally, Goldmann answers a self-imposed question: "How can we define the meaning either of a particular text or of a fragment? The reply is . . . by fitting it into the coherent pattern of the work as a whole. The word to be stressed here is 'coherent'."[81]

2. Goldmann's Achievements and Failures

Now that we have mentioned the special difficulties which the historian of literature and philosophy is likely to meet, as well as Goldmann's suggestions as to how they may be overcome, it seems necessary to ask two questions, each related to a different period of his creative life. First, to what extent can his admittedly limited method (to recapitulate: adequate for the study of the great works of the past, but inadequate for the study of mediocre and/or contemporary ones; unable to substitute not only for historical studies but also for textual and aesthetic analyses; and one-sidedly restricted to the examination of a work's uniting elements, neglecting the antagonistic ones) be considered as satisfactory, that is, *qualified for the task it set itself forth to fulfil?* And second, what is the validity of its avowedly unsystematic theorizing on the characteristic literary product of the capitlist era, the novel, and particularly on the *nouveau roman?*

Before proceeding with any answers, a decision should be made as to how we are going to judge Goldmann's genetic structuralism: as a method of *sociological analysis* of imaginary and conceptual works, or as a *self-sufficient literary criticism?* Obviously, such a decision cannot be made arbitrarily, disregarding factors such as Goldmann's own realization that a sociological approach is *no more* than an indispensable element for the overall analysis of literary works.

There should not be any doubt that Goldmann's approach is merely sociological and in no case can be judged as an autonomous literary criticism. Therefore it is erroneous to blame him for indifference to the individual creator's project or the formal attributes of a work, in the way, for example, Glucksmann does.[82] By the same token, one should be very skeptical of criticisms that Goldmann is greatly underestimating traditional aesthetics— e.g. the painstaking examination of style, syntax, imagery, etc.— when he claims that his method alone can succeed in accounting for ninety-five per cent of the text:[83] this percentage refers exclusively to a work's *sociological* understanding and explanation.

As a strictly sociological approach, then, Goldmann's genetic structuralist method can be viewed as a promising development in the study of the literary achievements of the past, going beyond the limits of the content-oriented sociological investigations. On the one hand, it shows that the coherence of great works is based on social values expressed through world visions, and on the other, it meaningfully links the latter with social classes from a historical perspective. Relating social classes to literature in concrete studies, that is, demonstrating the social-ideological rather than merely the individual character of imaginary products is a significant contribution to the sociology of literature, while the general linking of class consciousness to culture is one of Goldmann's praiseworthy merits.

It should be noted that by exploiting the possibilities of the notion of potential consciousness he ultimately escapes the traps of reflectionism, at least in his main studies. Raymond

Williams points out that the notion of potential consciousness offers a real way out of the deadlock which the conception of consciousness creates as it is controlled by a determining base. In this sense he is right in reminding us that "art . . . can succeed in articulating not just the imposed or constitutive social or intellectual system, but at once this and an experience of it, its lived consequence. . . ."[84]

To answer the second question, let it be stated with emphasis that Goldmann's limited writings on contemporary literary works are devoid of the virtues manifested in his early analyses. His study of Malraux's novels offers no more than a value analysis on the basis of the main themes of these works which reflect the cultural, social and political themes and values of Western European history from World War I onwards.

Goldmann's internal analysis of Malraux's *oeuvre* and of the *nouveau roman* justifies some of his critics, who accuse him of reflectionism as well as of being dominated by the idea of reification. It might be said in his defense that by postulating three stages of capitalism to which he attributes three corresponding forms of the novel, he is just trying to illuminate the main effects of the capitalist process on the novel, and is not intending to be as rigid and absolute as he appears or to suggest that he is depicting reality in its entirety. Such arguments would perhaps create some positive reactions, but only if he had left some room for doubt, if his late theorizing were not so mechanical and shallow,[85] and if he were not so guilty of being selective, exclusively concerned with a few carefully chosen writers.

In effect, his view of Robbe-Grillet's *nouveau roman* as the literary form corresponding to advanced capitalism is far from persuasive (disregarding at this point his possible misunderstanding and misinterpretation of Robbe-Grillet's novels),[86] because he bypasses a whole range of great authors and novels which are neither 'infected' not particularly interested in what Goldmann perhaps regards as the 'epidemic' of reification. In other words, he fails to see that reification is a part, albeit influential, of contemporary social reality, but not the whole of it. The consequences of reification are evidently felt by more and more people; nevertheless a great part of humanity, both inside and outside the capitalist world has also other problems to occupy it. In the final analysis, capitalism is not an air-tight system where all life and activity are maintained under laboratory conditions.

Preoccupied with separating the essential from the accidental, as well as with fitting the parts into comprehensive wholes, Goldmann attempts to put modern literature into a pre-fabricated mold, with poor results. Also, unable to continue the meaningful linking of cultural products to social classes,[87] since reification and other factors, such as a satisfactory theory of class are in the way, Goldmann rejects the notion of social class in his analyses. For him, a social class is no longer an autonomous totality, which he seeks to find in the capitalist structure perceived as a unity.

Goldmann's eagerness for classifications and generalizations leads him to be victimized by his own methodological perspective. Thus, the closer he comes to his object of investigation, in both time and detail, the less he is capable of a sound account, evidently being more at home with big schemata and large categories. The novel is certainly a phenomenon of the capitalist era, but in saying this one is not saying everything. Not only are there plentiful variations of the novel in essential respects, but also it co-exists with other literary forms flourishing within the dominion of advanced capitalism; these variations and forms Goldmann ignores. Even the random mentioning of just a few names, such as Hemingway, Solzhenitsyn, T.S. Eliot, Sartre and Borges, points to the erroneous path of Goldmann's thinking, partially explained by his critics as the outcome of his strong attachment to certain early ideas of Lukács.

Goldmann's historicist treatment of society and culture seems to be largely responsible for his inability to give due consideration to art's autonomy and the paramount importance of formal and cultural traditions. Despite his declaration that aesthetic considerations are outside his interests, his failure to deal with the evolution of the formal elements of literature partially explains his methodological and theoretical weaknesses. Form and content—to use these two outmoded notions—are dialectically related and, Goldmann's understanding of this notwithstanding, he does not take into account that meaning, for example, is inseparably related to style when formulating his methodological statements. More than that, his neglect of significant elements contributing to the formation of the artist's consciousness —which is revealed through the world vision and values he expresses—points right to the crux of Goldmann's limitations.

It can be argued that Goldmann is only partially successful in illuminating the complex foundations of consciousness, especially when by taking a critical stand this consciousness is immediately connected to great literature, as he himself believes. He relates consciousness to the economic structure of society, but he does not pay enough attention to other influential factors: intellectual traditions, the educational system, and above all, the contradictions generated by and within the established social formation. Could Goldmann be unaware of the existence of these factors? It has already been said that he was not. Nonetheless, his attitude in this respect was shaped by his conviction that i) a writer's conscious intentions should be distinguished from the objective significance of his work, and ii) that among the various influences on a writer's consciousness "only a single one has really had any effect"[88]: as far as the great works of the past are concerned it is the world vision of a social class; in the case of the novel, it is a theme with a structure homologous to the most significant structure of capitalism.

Goldmann's contribution to the advancement of our knowledge of the relationship between culture and society is weakened because he does not exhaust all the possibilities available within the framework of the sociology of literature. As Glucksmann rightly observes, monism is the main characteristic of his method. In this sense, and in addition to his emphasis on the homology of structures, there is a methodological continuity in all his writings. Ultimately he is unable to fulfil the varying methodological requirements of individual works by adequately utilizing the entire body of the general principles orienting his investigations. He is only equipped to meet anticipated demands, to deal with the past's great achievements—defining greatness with partiality—and only with those novels built upon certain themes, while content-oriented sociology is kept in reserve for the study of mediocre works. In all, Goldmann lacks flexibility and adaptability, that is, the capacity not simply to confront expected situations but also to allow his methodological tools, and consequently his ideas, to be shaped in turn by the unexpected, in order for his inquiry to go beyond the boundaries of a prescribed account into the complicated depths of a work's manifold properties and unpredictable singularity. To use the proper term, Goldmann's method is in essence undialectical.

NOTES

[1] The following is a partial list of commentaries in English on the work of Goldmann: Miriam Glucksmann, "Lucien Goldmann: Humanist or Marxist?," *New Left Review*, no. 56 (July-August, 1969); Diana Laurenson and Alan Swingewood, *op. cit.*; Raymond Williams, "Introduction" in Lucien Goldmann's *Racine* (Cambridge: Rivers Press, 1972); Miriam Glucksmann, *Structuralist Analysis in Contemporary Social Thought* (London: Routledge and Kegan Paul, 1974); Francis Mulhern, "Introduction to Goldmann," *New Left Review*, no. 92 (July-August, 1975); Terry Eagleton, *Marxism and Literary Criticism* (London: Methuen and Co. Ltd., 1976); Ilena Rodriguez and Marc Zimmerman, "Lucien Goldmann: Cultural Creation in Modern Society," *Telos*, no. 28 (Summer, 1976); William Mayrl, "Introduction," in Lucien Goldmann's *Cultural Creation in Modern Society* (St. Louis: Telos Press, 1976); William Mayrl, "Genetic Structuralism and the Analysis of Social Consciousness," *Theory and Society*, Vol. 5, no. 1 (January, 1978); and, Marc Zimmerman, "Lucien Goldmann: From Dialectical Theory to Genetic Structuralism," *Berkeley Journal of Sociology*, Vol. XXIII (1978-1979).

[2] Cf. Roland Barthes, "The Structuralist Activity," in Hazard Adams, ed. *Critical Theory Since Plato* (New York: Harcourt Brace Jovanovich, Inc., 1971), pp. 1196-1199.

[3] Lucien Goldmann, *The Human Sciences and Philosophy* (London: Cape Editions, 1969), p. 12.

[4] Cf. "A Confrontation," *New Left Review*, no. 62 (July-August, 1970), p. 59.

[5] Goldmann, *The Human Sciences and Philosophy, op. cit.*, p. 15.

[6] Lucien Goldmann, "The Sociology of Literature: Status and Problems of Method," *International Social Sciences Journal*, XIX, no. 4 (1967), p. 510.

[7] *Ibid.*, p. 511.

[8] Lucien Goldmann, "Dialectical Materialism and Literary History," *New Left Review*, no. 92 (July-August, 1975), pp. 50-51.

[9] Lucien Goldmann, *Towards a Sociology of the Novel* (London: Tavistock Publications, 1975), p. 159.

[10] Lucien Goldmann, "The Early Writings of Georg Lukács," *Triquarterly*, no. 9 (Spring, 1967), p. 179.

[11] Cf. Goldmann, *The Human Sciences and Philosophy, op. cit.*, pp. 35, 44; and, Lukács, *History and Class Consciousness, op. cit.*, pp. XXII-XXIII.

[12] Goldmann, "The Sociology of Literature: Status and Problems of Method," *op. cit.*, p. 494.

[13]Cf. Lucien Goldmann, *Marxisme et Sciences Humaines* (Paris: Gallimard, 1970), pp. 211-212.

[14]*Ibid.*, p. 254.

[15]Claude Lévi-Strauss, *The Savage Mind* (Chicago: The University of Chicago Press, 1966), p. 252.

[16]Lucien Goldmann, "Reflections on History and Class Consciousness," in István Mészáros, ed. *Aspects of History and Class Consciousness* (New York: Herder and Herder, 1972), pp. 75, 76.

[17]Goldmann, *Towards a Sociology of the Novel, op. cit.*, p. 157.

[18]Goldmann criticizes the positivist and individualist modes of thinking (i.e. rationalism, empiricism, Enlightment thought, positivism, neo-Kantianism and Sartrian existentialism) which presume the individual status of the subject and thus see dualities everywhere. Cf. "Reflections on History and Class Consciousness," *op. cit.*, pp. 71-75.

[19]Goldmann, *Towards a Sociology of the Novel, op. cit.*, p. 158.

[20]Cf. Goldmann, *The Human Sciences and Philosophy, op. cit.*, pp. 14-15; and, *Marxisme et Sciences Humaines, op. cit.*, p. 220.

[21]Goldmann, *Towards a Sociology of the Novel, op. cit.*, p. 159.

[22]Cf. Goldmann, "The Sociology of Literature: Status and Problems of Method," *op. cit.*, pp. 495-496.

[23]Goldmann, *Towards a Sociology of the Novel, op. cit.*, p. 160.

[24]Goldmann, *The Human Sciences and Philosophy, op. cit.*, pp. 102-103.

[25]As we shall see later on, under conditions of reification social classes are unable to construct world visions, hence, they become relatively unimportant to cultural creation.

[26]Goldmann, "Reflections on History and Class Consciousness," *op. cit.*, p. 72.

[27]Cf. *Ibid.*, pp. 76-77. Also, Lucien Goldmann, *The Hidden God*, transl. by P. Thody, (London: Routledge and Kegan Paul, 1970), pp. 14-15.

[28]Goldmann, *The Human Sciences and Philosophy, op. cit.*, pp. 112-117.

[29]*Ibid.*, pp. 118-119.

[30]Goldmann, *The Hidden God, op. cit.*, p. 17.

[31]Goldmann, "Dialectical Materialism and Literary History," *op. cit.*, p. 47.

[32]*Ibid.*, p. 48.

[33]*Ibid.*, p. 50.

[34]For a discussion see, *Ibid.*, pp. 40-41. As for the contribution of both individual and social subjects to the creation of cultural works, see, *The Human Sciences and Philosophy, op. cit.*, p. 129.

[35]*Ibid.*, p. 130.

[36]*Ibid.*, pp. 131-132.

[37]Goldmann, "Dialectical Materialism and Literary History," *op. cit.*, p. 48.

[38]Goldmann, *Towards a Sociology of the Novel, op. cit.*, p. 160.

[39]Goldmann, "The Sociology of Literature: Status and Problems of Method," *op. cit.*, pp. 500-501.

[40]*Ibid.*, p. 501, no. 1.

[41]Goldmann, "Dialectical Materialsm and Literary History," *op. cit.*, p. 49.

[42]*Ibid*, p. 50.

[43]Goldmann, *The Hidden God, op. cit.*, p. 47, no. 1.

[44]*Ibid.*, p. 41.

[45]*Ibid.*, p. 46.

[46]*Ibid.*, p. 48.

[47]Cf. Julia Kristeva, "The Ruin of a Poetics," in Stephen Bann and John E. Bowlt, eds. *Russian Formalism* (Edinburgh: Scottish Academic Press, 1973).

[48]Goldmann, "The Sociology of Literature: Status and Problems of Method," *op. cit.*, p. 514.

[49]*Ibid.*, p. 515.

[50]*Ibid.*, p. 515.

[51]Goldmann, *The Hidden God, op. cit.*, p. 316.

[52]Goldmann, "Dialectical Materialism and Literary History," *op. cit.*, p. 43.

[53]Goldmann, T*he Hidden God, op. cit.*, p. 315.

[54]*Ibid.*, p. 315.

[55]*Ibid.*, p. 316.

[56]Goldmann, "Dialectical Materialism and Literary History," *op. cit.*, p. 43.

[57]Goldmann, "The Sociology of Literature: Status and Problems of Method," *op. cit.*, pp. 497, 498.

[58]*Ibid.*, p. 504, especially n. 1.

[59]*Ibid.*, pp. 498, 499.

[60]*Ibid.*, p. 499.

[61]*Ibid.*, p. 500.

[62]*Ibid.*, pp. 506, 507.

[63]Goldmann, *Towards a Sociology of the Novel, op. cit.*, p. 164.

[64]*Ibid.*, p. 7.

[65]For Goldmann's analysis of the *nouveau roman* see, *Ibid.*, pp. 132-151.

[66]Lukács, *History and Class Consciousness, op. cit.*, p. 89.

[67]*Ibid.*, pp. 83-92.

[68] *Ibid.*, pp. 90-91.

[69] *Ibid.*, p. 171.

[70] *Ibid.*, p. 172.

[71] Antonio Gramsci, *The Modern Prince and Other Writings* (New York: International Publishers, 1967), p. 124.

[72] Cf. *Ibid.*, p. 121.

[73] Lucien Goldmann, *La Creation Culturelle Dans la Societe Moderne* (Paris: Denoel/Gonthier, 1971), pp. 99-100.

[74] Goldmann, *Towards a Sociology of the Novel, op. cit.*, pp. 18-131.

[75] Lucien Goldmann, "Criticism and Dogmatism in Literature," in D. Cooper, ed. *The Dialectics of Liberation* (London: Penguin Books, 1968), p. 147.

[76] Cf. Goldmann, *Marxisme et Sciences Humaines, op. cit.*

[77] Goldmann, "Criticism and Dogmatism in Literature," *op. cit.*, p. 143 f.

[78] Goldmann, *The Hidden God, op. cit.*, pp. 9, 10.

[79] *Ibid.*, p. 8.

[80] *Ibid.*, p. 12.

[81] *Ibid.*, p. 12.

[82] Cf. Miriam Glucksmann, *op. cit.* For Goldmann's own stand see, "Dialectical Materialism and Literary History," *op. cit.*, pp. 45, 51.

[83] Cf., for example, Laurenson and Swingewood, *op. cit.*, p. 67, n. (+).

[84] Williams, *op. cit.*, p. XVIII.

[85] Cf., for example, how he relates the difference between two distinct conceptual works with the difference between two corresponding stages of capitalism, in *Towards a Sociology of the Novel, op. cit.*, p. 123.

[86] Glucksmann, "Lucien Goldmann: Humanist or Marxist? ", *op. cit.*, p. 59.

[87] Cf. Goldmann, *Towards a Sociology of the Novel, op. cit.*, p. 124. The use of the marxist notion of social class in pre-industrial societies is very problematical, and one should expect Goldmann to give full qualifications of its unrestricted use in relation to world visions.

[88] Goldmann, "The Sociology of Literature: Status and Problems of Method," *op. cit.*, p. 498.

FOUR

LUKACS: DIALECTICAL CRITICISM

1. *Foundations of Marxist Aesthetics*

We already had the opportunity to present aspects of Georg Lukács' ideas, especially in the previous chapter. Here, we will concentrate on those elements which characterize his contribution to Marxist literary criticism. For our purposes, then, we will focus on certain aesthetic problems and discuss Lukács' final stand on them, rather than to follow his views as they were developed and modified essay after essay and book after book. In addition, we will refer to his perception of some fundamental dialectical relationships with special emphasis on that between the material and the artistic/literary production of society.

Lukács' first major publication, *Soul and Form* (1910) reveals the influence on his thinking of some of the ideas of Kant, Dilthey and Husserl. In this book the notions of "form" (Kant), "signification" (Dilthey) and "atemporal essence" (Husserl) are prevalent, as is indicated by Lukács' view of "significant atemporal structure of 'forms', as expression of different and privileged modalities in the relationship between the human soul and the absolute."[1]

In his second major work, *The Theory of the Novel* (1920), Lukács is still attached to his idea of forms, while Hegel's influence on him is more than obvious. The main concern of the book is with the development of a typology of various kinds of cultural—primarily literary— products, and exclusive attention is given to the novel because, as he states, it is not only "the representative art form of our age" but also "because the structural categories of the novel constitutively coincide with the world as it is today."[2]

The Theory of the Novel—idealist in nature and for this reason subsequently criticized by Lukács himself[3]—is an ambitious work, yet its major contribution rests in the problems which it reveals rather than in the solutions which it offers. This failure was probably the first Lukácsean victory because as a result of it Lukács began systematically to explore the Marxian heritage in order to find some answers to his questions. Also, from then on, he abandoned the grandiose idea of the development of a general typological theory, and for a long period of time he engaged himself with "concrete historical monographs."[4]

His famous *History and Class Consciousness* was published in 1922, and despite its failures and shortcomings, as well as Lukács' later denunciation of it, this work opened the road towards a real dialectical Marxism and provided the epistemo-logical and theoretical foundation for his subsequent studies on literature in the framework of a new perspective. However, the theoretical explorations within the context of this new world vision were not easy and thus Lukács' significant fresh writings in literary criticism appear after the passing of a good number of years, most of which he spent in Moscow engaged in many activities.

Some of his well-known studies were published in the following order: *Goethe and his Age* (1947), *Essays on Realism* (1948), *The Turning-Point of Destiny* (1948), *Russian Realism in World Literature* (1949), *German Realism of the Nineteenth Century* (1951), *The Historical Novel* (1955), and *Balzac and French Realism* (1957). Finally, his most important works in aesthetics were written even later, when he was an aged man. The first is the *Specialty, as a Category of Aesthetics*, and the second, *The Peculiarity of Aesthetics*. These works include a discussion of four issues which cover the following: the notion of totality; the problem of realism and the meaning of typicality; the theory of aesthetic reflection; and specialty as an aesthetic category.

a. *Totality*

The category of *totality* is central in the Lukácsean problematic. The conception of totality is a historical one and it can be first understood as the potentiality of a certain point of view to encompass the total, to see the whole in its completeness. For Lukács, this potentiality can only be attributed to historical materialism which, in contradistinction to bourgeois social science, it alone can distinguish "the all round, determining *domination of the whole over the parts.*"[5] In this sense, totality is seen as a standpoint, while the same category can also be understood as the property of an event, phenomenon, etc. According to Lukács, totality in this respect can be found in art because the latter is always striving to achieve it. It should be made clear, though, that art cannot grasp *whichever* totality one can think of. Concretely, it cannot portray the totality of the "universal human condition;" the parts of a literary work, for example, cannot be seen as expressing totalities of the "particulars of reality . . . " or "a copy of a segment of life."[6]

To understand the kind of totality art is trying to achieve, one should be familiar with what Lukács calls *extensive* and *intensive* totalities. The first includes everything which is outside of man; it is the totality of the whole spectrum of objective reality. This totality is, for example, the main object of investigation of science, which of course can only hope for an approximate idea of it; but even this approximation by no means can be reached by art. The latter's main object is the domain of intensive totality, that is, the totality of "man in the full context of interaction with the relevant elements of his socio-historical environment."[7]

The grasping of intensive totality is, for Lukács, the ultimate aim of art. But how can such an ambitious project be realized? "*The totality of the object* can be posited only when *the positing subject* is itself a totality,"[8] answers Lukács. This phrase appears as a simple statement yet it is probably one of the most far-reaching insights which, focused on the area of literature, may illuminate first of all the limitations of all one-sided approaches to literary creation. Second, it may throw light on the mystery—for some literary critics—of the greatness of a literary work. Third, it can show above all that the truth of notions like individual standpoint, individual creation, individual (personal) explanations is only relative in character.

b. *Realism*

To grasp the nature of the totality which art strives to

master, we must refer to the concept of realism[9] which is central
to Marxist aesthetics and the axis of Lukács' literary criticism.
Nevertheless, it is often misunderstood, misinterpreted and
misused.

Realism is often taken to mean simply the *technique* by
which an artist mirrors the objects of his sensuous experience,
a meaning which, among other things, presents realism as a
stylistic device only. This understanding is far from correct
and it has often been employed to ridicule the abuses of socialist
realism as practiced by Stalinism. In the Lukácsean sense, however, realism should be understood as possessing two distinct
characteristics: one, historical, according to which it undergoes
a constant change; and the other, permanent, which gives it its
central meaning. The first, represents the formal and stylistic
devices which an artist employs in his work. These devices
or techniques change and develop from artist to artist and
from time to time. The second characteristic—on the basis of
which the artistic and literary production of any society and
period can be approached—has to do with the relationship
between an art-work and the *essential* features of the society
within which it was created.

Realism is not a mere technique, but a standpoint, a way
of understanding and approaching reality. A writer, for example,
may employ the artistic techniques used by the great naturalists,
e.g. Zola, yet even the most faithful photographing and most
accurate enumeration of the objects of sensory reality can
never make him a realist artist.[10]   Realism, like classicism
and romanticism, is a genuine *artistic method* which must be
distinguished from mere *artistic style* even though the two
are inseparable being dialectically united.[11]

Does this mean that a writer should be exclusively concerned with the essence of objective reality and thus neglect
(and suppress) the expression of his own emotions and feelings?
And if so, does this imply than an artist can only achieve greatness if he is completely preoccupied with the common affairs?
Lukács' answer is clear as it articulates in an unambiguous way
the non-individual character of an individual's subjectivity:

> everything in a writer's life, every individual experience,
> thought and emotion he undergoes, however subjective,
> partakes of an historical character. Every element in his
> life as a human being and as a writer is part of, and

determined by, the movement from and towards some goal. Any authentic reflection of reality in literature must point to this movement. The method adopted will vary, of course, with the period and personality. But the selection and substruction he undertakes in response to the teleological pattern of his own life constitutes the most intimate link between a writer's subjectivity and the outside world.[12]

It is due to the necessarily realistic character of great art and its primary concern with man's place within society and nature that Lukács feels free to state: "science is mankind's *awareness* while art is mankind's *self-awareness.*"[13] Now, let us see how his doctrine of realism is related to his notion of *typicality,* another misunderstood and misused concept.

c. *Typicality*

By a *typical* situation or a typical hero, Lukács does not have in mind the average, that is, the situation or hero with characteristics and properties which represent the statistical mean derived from similar personalities in similar circumstances. The literary *type* is a rather complex category, which is defined as such on the basis of its *breadth, essentiality, enhancement,* and *self-awareness.*

A hero has breadth if he demonstrates the characteristics of a specific individual, who nonetheless is well fitted within his socio-historical situation. Essentiality refers to the hero's capability to concentrate in his person the fundamental traits of those social forces which through their struggle make history themselves. The notion of literary enhancement underlines the importance of the projection of the various sides of an individual's complexity in such a manner that man's full potentiality will be revealed, yet without the latter giving the impression that he is capable of achieving what is humanly and historically impossible. Finally, Lukács' typical hero should demonstrate self-awareness; that is, his ability to see himself in perspective, and to also be able to distinguish the links which bridge the events and conditions of his individual life with the events and conditions which constitute the collective history of his society.

In the light of these four proconditions, the Lukácsean notion of typicality is a concept unique and rich in meaning, inseparable from his overall theory of literary realism. Thus, making the concrete distinction between the *type* and the *average*, Lukács leaves no doubt about the particular meaning of his category of typicality. He writes:

> according to Marx and Engels, the type is not the abstract type of the classical tragedy . . . and even less what the Zola and post-Zola school writers and critics said it was: the average. The type is characterized by the fact that all the prominent features of that dynamic unity in which true literature reflects life run together in their contradictory unity and that in these contradictions the most important social, ethical and spiritual contradictions of an epoch are woven into a living unity. The representation of the average, on the contrary, has as a necessary consequence that these contradictions, always reflecting the great problems of the epoch, appear toned down, weakened in the soul and fate of an average man and thus lose their essential traits.[14]

d. *Reflection*

Realism, according to Lukács, is but another name for the Marxist theory of aesthetic reflection, that is, the theory on the basis of which his own literary criticism is founded. However, it should be made clear that by *reflection* is not meant any of the well-known ideas of copying or imitating reality in a mechanistic, passive and static way. We should be reminded that the Marxist theory of reflection is rooted in Aristotle's theory of *Mimesis,* yet it is a revolutionary improvement upon it, built around the axis of the dialectical relationship of *essence* and *appearance.*

These two categories cannot be considered independently from each other. Essence, of course, is more significant than appearance which is included in the former, however, the essences or laws of socio-historical phenomena are not as rich as the objective reality. The latter is, in Lukács' words, "always richer in content than the most perfect laws," because, no matter how well-founded are the various laws or essences of the different phenomena constituting reality, they are no more than *"approximations* of the constantly changing, transforming, infinite totality of objective reality."[15]

The Marxist concept of *law* does not have an absolute meaning. As Lukács stresses, this is not *relativism* either because such a possible relativistic position can be transcended on the basis of dialectics. Thus, as a dialectical thinker, he sees not a dualism between *absolute* and *relative* truth but a dialectical relationship between the two. He states that on the one hand, the relative aspects of an absolute truth "tie it to place, time and circumstance," and on the other, "relative truth, inasmuch as it is indeed truth, by faithfully reflecting reality, has absolute validity."[16]

The fundamental hypothesis of the theory of reflection is expressed by Lukács as follows: "all we do, all we know and all we are, in the final analysis, is the product of our reaction to reality."[17] As we have already indicated, this does not mean that the objective character of literature—in the Lukácsean sense—precludes man's subjectivity from its concerns. On the contrary, as it was pointed out in our discussion of the notion of typicality, the individual, the personal, is considered and the totality of its meaning is transcended by the larger meaning of the totality of a whole epoch and society.

But does literature, in order to reflect reality objectively, have to be scholastic and accurate in its depiction of reality, the way for example entomologists describe and classify ants? Lukács' answer is negative simply because, according to the Marxian system, every particular aspect of the objective reality is but an instance of a long historical process, a temporary phenomenon in the chain of an infinite number of ever changing phenomena. In this sense, what is important for us to know is how and why these changes become possible and what are the underlying forces of this process, keeping constantly in mind that man himself is at the center of this history-in-the making, notwithstanding that his freedom to act is not unlimited.

This is why, from Lukács' point of view, an objective evaluation of a literary work is perfectly possible if this work is considered on the basis of its capability to reflect the essential features of objective reality (the permanent aspect of realism) by the use of certain artistic means (the temporary aspect of realistic art: the historically conditioned styles, techniques, etc.) And it is also for this reason that artistic talent, for which we do not have an adequate theory, cannot be viewed as a mystical property but as a special capability of the artist to properly understand and express the patterns of the objective movement of the overall cosmos with which his subjective being is in a permanent dialectical relationship and of which he is but a tiny part himself.

This artistic capability, however, this talent, is not manifested only after the work is completed but it can be detected even before the work begins as it is demonstrated by the writer's perspective. Lukács writes: "In any work of art, perspective is of over-riding importance. It determines the course and content; it draws together the threads of the narration; it enables the artist to choose between the important and the artificial, the crucial and the episodic. The direction in which characters develop is determined by perspective, only those features being described which are material to their development."[18]   It is for lack of an adequate perspective that Lukács blames the modernist artist; similarly, he blames the bourgeois social science for their failure to see the world from the standpoint of totality. Finally, it is the writer's adequate perspective or lack of it which determines the meaningfulness of literary products because as he writes, "Every human action is based on a presupposition of its inherent meaningfulness at least to the subject. Absence of meaning makes a mockery of action and reduces art to a naturalistic description."[19]

e. *Specialty*

A basic category in Lukács' theory of artistic reflection is that of *specialty*, an understanding of which is indispensable for a complete idea about the main features of his literary criticism. To begin with, Lukács makes clear that all modes of reflection deal with the same objective reality and that from the point of view of historical materialism the question of the hierarchy between them is non-existent. All modes of reflection, however, are *relatively autonomous* and they also have some special characteristics distinct to each one of them. Within this framework, for example, Lukács underlines the *anthropomorphic* character of art (centered about man's relationship between his subjective being and objective reality) and the *disanthropormorphic* (i.e. the impersonal search for the purely objective) character of science.[20]

The main similarities and differences between the various modes of reflection can be understood on the basis of three categories—elements of objective reality: the *individual*, the *universal* and the *special*. All three categories are present in every mode of reflection, yet a single category is more dominant in one mode of reflection and less in another.

The category of individuality is concerned with the specifics of individual phenomena and it is the dominant category, for example, in the mode of reflection of history. The category of universality seeks to find out what is common to all phenomena and attempts to establish general laws. It is obviously the dominant category of the scientific mode of reflection, as well as the mode of reflection of philosophy.

Neither the category of individuality nor that of universality can satisfy the demands of the artistic mode of reflection. This task lies in the third category, namely the category of *specialty* which can be thought of as occupying a place anywhere between the two extreme points of individuality and universality. This is so because only the artistic/literary mode of reflection aims at achieving the unity of the *particular* with the *total*, that is, toward the artistic/literary construction of a world which, while retaining its individual characteritics, it also preserves elements of its universal character.

For the fulfillment of the demands of the category of specialty, then, the artist/writer should tirelessly seek the golden mean between the two extreme categories of individuality and universality, because a divergence toward any one of them will affect negatively the presence of the other. In other words, it is the category of specialty (or category of *uniqueness*) which unites in a work of art the subjective (individual) with the objective (universal) elements on any level, in any phenomenon or circumstance. Lukács writes: "Only uniqueness as the midpoint of the aesthetic reflection of reality, is in a position to illuminate the specific dialectical unity of subjective and objective factors as a principle of opposition animating the whole sphere."[21]

It should be emphasized that for Lukács, and from the point of view of men's life and activity, subjectivity and objectivity do not constitute a duality but a genuine *dialectical relationship*. This implies that neither category can be thought of in its pure form, that is, independent from the other. Bela Kiralyfalvi, who presents Lukás' position on this important matter, reports: "On the one hand, even the most objective discovery (law, fact, etc.) is the result of a subjective effort. On the other hand man's subjectivity, his inner world, cannot be known in its complexity and depth without a thorough understanding of its context, the objective world."[22]

2. Socio-Economic Structure and Literature

The above statement brings us again to what we have already referred to as a central problem of historical materialism: the relationship between the economic base of society on one hand, and its artistic/literary achievements on the other.

To begin with, the position of vulgar ('scientific') objectivity propounded by orthodox Marxism, according to which art and literature are but the direct reflection of the material conditions of society (i.e. the economic relations of production) in a straightforward cause and effect manner, is already overdiscussed and overdebated, an elaboration of which is rather needless here. For our specific objective, we can mention Lukács' early attack in his *History and Class Consciousness* on crude economic determinism, his suggestion that the artistic mode of production has properties distinct from the other modes of production, and his belief that art and literature are relatively autonomous from the material processes of society.

This initial Lukácsean position was somehow based on the self-contradictory assumption that within the framework of capitalist societies (characterized by complexity), the principles and hypotheses of historical materialism apply to some modes of production (i.e. economic, scientific, etc.) but they do not apply to some others (i.e. artistic, religious, etc.), while within the framework of pre-capitalist (relatively simple) societies the same principles and hypotheses seem to apply to all modes of production. Before we rush to criticize Lukács for this contradictory and indeed relativistic kind of thinking, we must add that such a rather easy and convenient solution to an extremely difficult problem did not allow his mind to rest. Thus, decades after the writing of *History and Class Consciousness*, in the preface to which Lukács wrote for the 1967 edition of the book, he speaks about "the great uncertainty prevailing with regard to its essential content and its methodological validity," admitting that "this volume encompass my years of apprenticeship in Marxism."[23]   But in order to see how he tried to overcome some of his early shortcomings, it will be more fruitful to focus on the famous interview given by him near the end of his life.

In this important document Lukács expresses his mature position about social reality in the following way: "society is an extraordinarily complicated complex of complexes, in which there are two opposing poles. On the one hand there is the social totality, which in the final analysis determines the interaction of the individual complexes, and on the other, the complex of the individual person which forms an indissoluble minimal unity within this process. The process is determined by the interaction of both poles. This is the process of man's coming to be."[24]

The extent of these complexities becomes apparent when for example one wishes to determine the kind of social totality which surrounds the individual, or when one wishes to understand the uniqueness of the latter. Is one going to determine just an individual's national social totality? The international social totality? Their interrelated and interacting context? What aspects of it? Or how specifically can one determine the totality of the interaction between an individual's objective condition and his subjective properties in an ever changing process?

In the face of such difficulties, Lukács takes such a position as to maintain the golden mean between *necessity* and *freedom.* This is another essential dialectical relationship which demonstrates that man is a decision maker. Bela Kiralyfalvi gives the following account of Lukács' position: "Freedom and necessity form a contradictory inseparable unity, meaning that in man's most characteristic activity, work, teleological decisions (based on knowledge of essences), on the one hand, and their casual-compulsory preconditions (the infinite richness of reality), on the other, also form a contradictory inseparable unity."[25]

Referring to the specific phenomenon of literary creation, Lukács points out that the two-thousand year old division of literature into three basic kinds, namely, *lyric, epic* and *drama* was never altered or transcended in essence. This fact led him to the conclusion that "the unprecedented flux of social determinations and hence of alternatives is not a river without course or banks, but rather produces very definite determinations and then sticks to them."[26]

This way Lukács definitely by-passes the narrow cause-and-effect approach which views the immediate economic relations of production as the determining factor of the socio-cultural phenomena and indicates that the latter while obliged to follow a certain general direction are neither restricted to pre-appointed positions nor predetermined in their exact characteristics, but can rather move and develop following a path of their own within of course the huge river of human history. This amounts to a full realization by Lukács of the significant input which men can have into the course of their own history since they have the capability by exercising their freedom to the fullest to strengthen their activity until this freedom reaches its upper limit, i.e. until it stumbles on the banks of the great river. He states: "No matter how much it is the economy that makes all these things possible, they can only be realized through the alternative choices of men."[27]

The immense complexity which human society and history —as well as the actions, creations, etc. of individuals—have already reached, led Lukács to another conclusion, namely that socio-cultural phenomena, literary products, etc. can only be understood genetically, that is, traced back to their origins and development. In other words, he suggests that only an "ontological" approach can answer our very many questions about human phenomena, maintaining that both the categories of *individuality* (the totality of the specific characteristics of each individual phenomenon, human being, etc.) and *objective reality* (independent of the individual's subjectivity) must be dialectically employed.

The "ontology" proposed by Lukács is not some abstract procedure, but rather a definite method aiming at discovering "the forms of being that new movements of the complex produce."[28] As for the main category of objective reality, it originates in human labor because the latter necessitates human conceptualization, (in contradistinction to other higher animals which develop only "mental images"), and, ultimately, human consciousness, on the basis of the absolute necessity of human labor, for the survival, preservation and development of the species. Let us quote Lukács again:

> The concept of things only becomes necessary in la-
> bor. . . . In the labor process, a whole sphere of life,
> i.e. science, grew up out of what was originally one
> particular aspects of labor. . . . I would just like to
> say summarily that we men gradually attained in this
> way a consciousness of the objective character of the
> world, a consciousness which provides a picture of reality,
> naturally with the necessary ontological control. Of
> course the ontological control is itself something his-
> toric. . . .[29]

In view of the ontological approach which Lukács proposes as an adequate method of analysis of socio-cultural phenomena, a question might be asked as to whether or not and to
what extent such a method is always useful. If we consider the
genesis and development of the phenomenon of literature,
for example, Lukács' ontology seems not only adequate for
its explanation, on the basis of some concrete (material) foundation—verifying thus the basic premise of the materialist outlook—
but also able to account for what he calls, "the typical moments,
those necessary for the process itself."[30]   In short, ontology is
able to account for the characteristics of those turning points
of history which result in the emergence of new phenomena,
and for phenomena within phenomena (i.e. the historical novel
which developed under certain conditions within literature in
general).

When, however, we are not concerned with the genesis
and development of whole phenomena, e.g. literature, but rather
with the particular case of the collective or individual manifestations of phenomena, e.g. some literary works, or just one
specific work, how useful is the ontological approach proposed
by Lukács? To answer this question, a discussion of the limits
of historical materialism for the study of individual literary
creations is prerequisite but this will be postponed for the
chapter dealing with the literary criticism of Jean-Paul Sartre.
We can just say for the moment that according to Lukács the
study of specific literary works should begin with the establishment of the concrete (socio-historical) mediations between the
complex totality of objective reality (in its process) and the
complex totality of the individual creator (in its development).
This, of course, on condition that the balance between the
relative autonomy (freedom) of the creator's mental activities

which is manifested in the artistic/literary works produced and the concrete objective basis of these activities (the necessity with which the creator's freedom was exercized) is maintained.

The importance of the category of *individuality* as it interacts with that of *objective reality* comes into focus once more. Therefore, it should be re-emphasized that individuality is for Lukács a uniquely decisive category for the realization of artistic and literary creations. This is what he states about individuality: "Even in the most heterogeneous complexes of social life, a man must act in a unified way, for he must also reproduce his own life. Thus, something arose which we call the individual personality of the man. Here also you can see an ontological gradation. . . . The development of this individuality into a personality belongs to the realm of social ontology."[31]

In general, we can say that a close reading of Lukács' first conversation on "Being and Consciousness" discloses some aspects of his intellectual evolution from the days of *History and Class Consciousness*. Among other things, his final stand admits the incorrectness of his early assumption that historical materialism is applicable in some cases (i.e. some societies, modes of production, etc.) and inapplicable in some others. The universal methodological validity of historical materialism for the study of both general and specific socio-cultural phenomena, i.e. literature and a given literary work correspondingly, is reaffirmed.

Yet, notwithstanding the soundness of the materialist principle that being determines consciousness, this principle alone cannot account for all the unique characteristics of specific phenomena, e.g. a given novel: certain *mediations* pertaining to this particular novel should be closely scrutinized with the additional use of *auxiliary tools*. But, as already indicated, this will occupy us in the chapter on Sartre. We can just mention here that from Lukács' perspective, *aiming primarily towards generalizations*, the task of the application and verification of historical materialism as one moves from simpler to more complex phenomena becomes increasingly difficult.

In the case of general phenomena, this is partially due to the fact that the movement from the lower to the higher (in complexity) implies a constantly increasing distancing of the various phenomena from their concrete material basis which can be detected with considerable difficulty. Nevertheless, any socio-cultural phenomenon seems to be unavoidably linked to a concrete basis which includes not only the socio-economic relations of men but also those natural forces and phenomena which affect directly or indirectly, positively or negatively, the existence and life of men.

The co-existence of the two, however, namely the material basis and the specific phenomenon which it has preconditioned, either in their initial or mutually corresponding forms is not indispensable. This means that while the necessity of a socio-cultural phenomenon is initially created in order to satisfy directly or indirectly the needs of a particular material situation, in the course of their development both phenomena follow a dynamic of their own, meaning that the transformations which the latter undergoes does not necessarily cause a corresponding transformation in the former. This increasing removal of a socio-cultural phenomenon from its material foundation does not mean that the two are not still linked with each other on the basis of the rationality of the initial necessity which created them. If this link is severed at some point in time, due to the non-necessity (subsequently evolved) of that aspect of a material basis which gave rise to a particular phenomenon, then the latter, as we have seen, is already irrational, unreal, an appearance without an essence, bound to perish.

To focus again on the real, rational phenomena which mainly interest us here, we can say that both their own transformation (toward complexity) from some of their initial conditions, as well as their progressive removal (distance) from each other, makes it extremely difficult to establish the connecting threads between them and their material foundations. With these considerations in mind, it is no wonder that an investigator becomes more and more perplexed as he tries to distinguish within the complexity of phenomena the mediations which link the one with the other, and the totalities of which they themselves are primary, secondary, etc. aspects.

In conclusion we can say that the attempt of the approach, understanding, evaluation or interpretation of a literary phenomenon (either general or specific) on the basis of those concrete mediations (separating thus the immediate from the distant, the significant from the insignificant, etc.) which link it with a concrete material basis (either obvious or hidden), as it is indicated above, is a very much different enterprise—based on a different (i.e. larger, richer) objectivity—from the enterprise suggested by 'scientific,' vulgar materialism. Finally, it should be evident by now that the old argument of subjectivity vs. objectivity is indeed transcended on the basis of the category of the dialectical totality of the interactive complexes of objective reality and individuality.

3. *The Unresolved Problem of Individuality*

Lukács, the architect of Marxist aesthetics, became both the object of admiration and of criticism. Here we cannot deal with criticism concerning his overall work because the latter covers many disciplines and areas of intellectual endeavor. To concentrate just on his literary criticism, we can mention that he is often criticized for matters of secondary importance. Also, he is often misunderstood and misinterpreted, mainly because a good number of his critics fail to treat his ideas as dynamically evolving totalities, in a dialectical movement of self-correction.

Some of the most serious accusations against Lukács, the literary critic, stress (correctly) that he ignores numerous modern novels solely praising those characterized by him as *critical realist* and that he rejects offhand expressionism and subjectivism.[32]   Further, he is criticized by Galvano della Volpe, for example, as being "materialist" (in quotation marks) in contradistinction to Engels who is presented as a true materialist.[33].   Moreover, he is criticized by della Volpe as having committed certain mistakes in his practical critical studies on Flaubert, Proust, Joyce, Kafka, etc., while his concept of *critical realism* associated with the work of Thomas Mann is viewed as inadequate which needs to be replaced by the concept of "artistic realism."[34]

Certainly, della Volpe is right as far as some aspects of Lukács' concrete studies are concerned, nevertheless, his judgment merely scratches the surface of the entire Lukácsean contribution to the development of a Marxist criticism, because, among other things, Lukács' major works, i.e. *Specialty, as a Category of Aesthetics,* and *The Peculiarity of Aesthetics*, published after della Volpe's study, are not considered.

These latter works, of course, are examined by some others, e.g. G. H. R. Parkinson, who in a long article argues that specialty is not a general category of aesthetics because it does not apply to all art (i.e. music), not even to all literature (i.e. the lyric). Parkinson does not reject Lukács' position on aesthetics altogether. After his attack on specialty, he states: "This, however, does not mean that Lukács' aesthetics is valueless. His work contains a number of discussions—i.e. his account of the distinction between art and science, and of the relations between works of art and aesthetic 'laws'. . . ."[35] We can say that as his article demonstrates, Parkinson's understanding of Lukács' thinking is limited, and his assessment of the work of the Hungarian critic short-sighted.

Admittedly, Lukács' theoretical and practical literary criticism is not infallible; errors, contradictions and limitations are present in it. Yet, we can overlook his various shortcomings at this point, *mostly due to Marxism's inability to account alone for literary creation*, since our primary concern is to elucidate how much and to what extent one might profit from Lukacs' literary criticism for any subsequent step toward a theoretical and practical move in this area. From this point of view, we can say that Lukács offers more than anyone else among his Marxist contemporaries.

In reference to his major limitations, we can only emphasize here that although he pays the proper attention to the (philosophical and ontological) category of individuality, he does so only from the side of the latter's socio-historical and ideological determinants. This is perhaps the result of his firm opposition to all varieties of irrationalism as a "discernible trend in philosophy in all countries from about 1800 until the present time,"[36] as well as to psychological and psychoanalytical methods.

The positive and negative aspects of the Lukácsean literary criticism will be evident in the light of this approach to literature which is based not only on historical materialism but also on disciplines which succeed where the latter does not have the means to adequately perform. We are, of course, referring to Sartre's methodological synthesis on the theoretical and especially the practical level, where his great merit lies.

Indeed, we should not fail to notice that there is usually a gap separating the various methodological statements from their application, which is often as wide as that between theory and practice. For example, Sartre himself points out that "everyone knows and everyone admits . . . that psychoanalysis and Marxism should be able to find the mediations necessary to allow a combination of the two. . . . Likewise, everyone says that there are American sociological notions which have a certain validity. . . . Everyone agrees on all this. Everyone, in fact *says* it—but who has tried to *do* it?"[37] It is none other that Sartre himself who actually *did* it, as it will be shown in the last chapter of this study.

NOTES

[1]Cf. for example, Lucien Goldmann, "The Early Writings of Georg Lukács," *Triquarterly, op. cit.*, p. 169.

[2]Georg Lukács, *The Theory of the Novel* (Cambridge, Massachusetts: The M.I.T. Press, 1971, p. 93.

[3]Cf. Glucksmann, "Lucien Goldmann: Humanist or Marxist?" *op. cit.*, p. 56.

[4]Cf. Fredric Jameson, *Marxism and Form* (Princeton: Princeton University Press, 1971), p. 180.

[5]Quoted in Mészáros, *Lukács' Concept of Dialectic, op. cit.*, p. 62.

[6]Kiralyfalvi, *op. cit.*, p. 84.

[7]*Ibid.*, p. 85.

[8]Quoted in Mészáros, *Lukács' Concept of Dialectic, op. cit.*, p. 62.

[9]For an account of the historical development of this concept Cf. Rene Wellek, *Concepts of Criticism*, ed. by Stephen G. Nichols, Jr., (New Haven and London: Yale University Press, 1964), pp. 222-255.

[10]For a discussion of this matter Cf. Mészáros, *Marx's Theory of Alienation, op. cit.*, pp. 195-200.

[11]Avner Zis writes: "*Artistic method . . . constitutes a specific type of approach to the subject of art, to the reflected reality, for which it provides the artistic analogy; style on the other hand constitutes a system or principle for the organization of artistic expression,*" (*Foundations of Marxist Aesthetics* (Moscow: Progress Publishers, 1977), p. 242.)

[12]Georg Lukács, *Realism in Our Time* (New York: Harper and Row, Publishers, 1971), pp. 54-55.

[13]Kiralyfalvi, *op. cit.*, p. 37.

[14]Lukács, "Appearance and Essence," in Le Roy and Beitz, eds.

op. cit., p. 19.

[15]Quoted in Kiralyfalvi, *op. cit.*, p. 27.

[16]Quoted in *Ibid.*, p. 27.

[17]Quoted in *Ibid.*, p. 55.

[18]Lukács, *Realism in Our Time, op. cit.*, p. 33.

[19]*Ibid.*, p. 36.

[20]Kiralyfalvi, *op. cit.*, pp. 35, 36.

[21]Lukács, "Art as Self-Consciousness in Man's Development," in Berrel Lang and Forest Williams, eds. *Marxism and Art* (New York: David Mckay Company, Inc., 1972), p. 229.

[22]Kiralyfalvi, *op. cit.*, p. 38.

[23]Lukács, *History and Class Consciousness, op. cit.*, p. ix.

[24]Theo Pinkus, ed. *Conversations with Lukács* (Cambridge, Massachusetts: The M.I.T. Press, 1975), p. 135.

[25]Kiralyfalvi, *op. cit.*, p. 27.

[26]Pinkus, *op. cit.*, p. 135.

[27]*Ibid.*, p. 137.

[28]*Ibid.*, p. 21.

[29]*Ibid.*, p. 28.

[30]*Ibid.*, p. 16.

[31]*Ibid.*, pp. 30-31.

[32]Glucksmann, "Lucien Goldmann: Humanist or Marxist?," *op. cit.*, pp. 57, 58.

[33]Galvano della Volpe, "Theoretical Issues of a Marxist Poetics," in Lang and Williams, eds. *op. cit.*, p. 185.

[34]*Ibid.*, pp. 191-197.

[35]G. H. R. Parkinson, "Lukács on the Central Category of Aesthetics," in G. H. R. Parkinson, ed. *Georg Lukács: The Man, his Work and his Ideas* (London: Weidenfeld and Nicolson, 1970), p. 145.

[36]Cf. H. A. Hodges, "Lukács on Irrationalism," in *Ibid.*, p. 86.

[37]Jean-Paul Sartre, "The Itinerary of a Thought," in *Between Existentialism and Marxism*, transl. by John Matthews (London: NLB, 1974), p. 43.

FIVE

FREUD AND JUNG: PSYCHOANALYTIC CRITICISM

1. *Psychology and Literature*

a. *The Extrinsic Approach*

Extrinsic literary criticism is characterized by the study of
setting, environment and other external relations of literature,
and it can be classified as follows: First, the criticism which
approaches literary works via the biography of their authors.
Second, that which examines literature in relation to the socio-
historical circumstances within which it arose. Third, the kind
of literary criticism which views literature simply as the artistic
expression of the philosophical ideas of a specific society at
a given time. And, fourth, that which maintains that a literary
work can be investigated in the light of the general intellectual
climate which surrounds it, and particularly in relation to the
other arts.[1]
This is a rather tentative classification, as one category
usually overlaps with another, but it gives a good indication of
how an approach to literature can be pursued on the basis of
some extraliterary element. It is within this spirit, that the
relationship between literature and history, myth, biography,
psychology, sociology, religion, etc. can be established.[2] One,
however, does not have to follow such compartmentalization
because two dominant categories of extrinsic criticism, the
sociological and the *psychological,* seem to include an examination of all these relationships. For example, one might discuss
historical, religious, etc. factors within the sociological approach,
and biographical as well as other elements (e.g. the motives of
individual artists) within the psychological. These two modes
of investigation of literary works comprise the cornerstone of
the extrinsic approach. We can agree then with Arnold Hauser
who points out that a work of art—and this applies to literary

creations as well—is "the outcome of at least three different types of conditions: psychological, sociological and stylistic."[3]

The sociological and the psychological approaches to literature are completely distinct from one another, as suggested more than four decades ago by the Russian psychologist Lev Semenovich Vygotsky, who in his study *The Psychology of Art* refers to the "psychological" and "non-psychological" aesthetics. Vygotsky, separates the "sociology of art" from the "psychology of art,"[4] leaving no doubt about their different albeit complementary tasks.[5] In this chapter, we will briefly examine the psychological perspective of literature with special emphasis on psychoanalysis.*

b. *Psychological Theories of Literature*

The impact of Freudian theories on the one hand and the many inadequacies of the speculative method of post-Kantian idealism on the other, at a time when the aftermath of the First World War made the "imaginative writers of psychological bent . . . suddenly famous. . .",[6] gave a great impetus to an aesthetic based on psychology. Additional reasons were a) the fact that the generation of intellectuals of 1905 were more conservative in comparison to the generation of their fathers,[7] and b) the fact that individualistic, esoteric problems captured the minds of the European intelligentsia.[8]

The expressions 'psychology of literature' and 'psychoanalysis of literature' are often used indistinguishably. Frederic C. Crews, for example, defends such a usage maintaining that "psychoanalysis is the only psychology to have seriously altered our way of reading literature."[9] One might argue, however, that the two terms should be differentiated first, because psychoanalysis is one kind of psychology among many,[10] regardless of its comparative weight, and second, because the psycho-

---

*Psychoanalysis is also discussed in chapter three from the point of view of Goldmann's genetic structuralism and in chapter eleven in contrast to Sartre's existential psychoanalysis.

logical approaches to literature employ different methods.
It is a fact that psychoanalysis has paid incomparably
more attention to literature than any other kind of psychology.[11]   Its predominance in the study of literature has been
prevalent not only because general (objective) psychology tends
to favor the examination of empirically verifiable phenomena—
as it is manifested by its alleged predisposition against the subjective point of view which the study of literature implies in
the case of non-psychoanalytic psychologies—, but also because
general psychology avoids entering a field where psychoanalysis
is viewed as having failed to deal with successfully, and thus
to associate itself with the latter.[12]

By pointing out the reluctance of general psychology
to engage in the study of literature, it is not our intention to
suggest that the attempt to explain the creative process is a
phenomenon originating in psychoanalysis.   It goes as far back
as Plato's *Ion* and it had certainly preoccupied the romantic
critics, i.e. Wordsworth.[13]   By the same token, elements of
an attempt toward a psychological study of writers can also
be found in the literary criticism of various times, but it was
Freud's and Jung's investigations which gave it the appearance
of a scientific venture.

The fact to be stressed here is that—psychoanalysis excluded—"At best, objective psychology is indifferent to literature.   To the psychologists, literature offers a loose set of post
hoc generalities or charming illustrations."[14]   As already mentioned, however, psychoanalysis is not the only psychology
which became interested in artistic creation and especially
literature.   Before we enter into a discussion of Freud's and
Jung's ideas on the nature of literary production, then, let us
take a look at the various psychological theories of literature.[15]

According to Vygotsky, the numerous psychological theories of art are characterized in the greatest part by incompleteness.   They can be classified though on the basis of three psychological systems.   The first, which identifies art with *perception,*
goes as far back as antiquity when representation was considered
the fundamental element of artistic experience; it is also related
to the work of the German philologist, philosopher and historian
Wilhelm von Humboldt (1767-1835).   In the framework of
this system, art differs from science in nothing but method,
since "art is the perception of wisdom, and teaching and instruc-
tion are its main tasks."[16]

This system resulted in the development of a psychological theory of art and despite a number of corrections brought to it by "the second generation of researchers" it reached such an extreme position (supported by Valerii Brisnov) as to profess "that any work of art, by some special method, leads to the same perception as does the course of a scientific proof".[17] This exclusively intellectual theory of art was justified by D. N. Ousianiko-Kulikovskii, by the addition of another theory which sees a psychological distinction between the 'lyric' and the 'epic,' the former being but a special element in the total artistic process. If this differentiation is accepted "the essence of lyrical art can be reduced to processes of perception or to pure brainwork."[18] In respect to this, Vygotsky quotes Ousianiko-Kulikovskii as follows:

> Emotions play a dominant role in artistic creativity. They are generated by the content itself. . . . These emotions per se are not lyrical, but they may incidentally include a lyrical 'streak' if the work of art has a lyrical form. . . . Let us take the scene of Hector's farewell to Andromache. In reading it we may experience a strong emotion and may even by moved to tears. But this emotion has nothing lyrical in it, since it is caused only by the emotional scene. However, accompanied by the rhythmic effect of the flowing hexameters, it causes lyrical emotion. . . . The lyrical element is strengthened and occasionally may even have replaced the emotion caused by the subject matter. To get this emotion in its pure form, without the admixture of its lyrical component, all we have to do is transpose the scene into prose devoid of any rhythmic cadence.[19]

Obviously, while a psychological theory is developed to explain artistic creation (i.e. art as perception), the same theory is insufficient to account for some art forms, e.g. poetry. Therefore, some operation is needed which by destroying the form of a work of art will try to reveal the purified emotion generated by the latter's content by simply getting rid of its lyrical components. This insensitivity for the artistic and aesthetic properties of a work of art demonstrates the ultimate inadequacy of the psychological theory which regards art exclusively as perception "to explain the special and quite specific effect generated by artistic form."[20]

An immediate reaction to this crude intellectualism was another psychological theory of art emphasizing the primary importance of the artistic *form*. This theory, based on the second psychological system which views art as technique, is nothing else but the formalism developed in Russia. Since, however, the latter is discussed in a separate chapter we can just mention here that for Russian formalism artistic emotions are generated solely by the form of an artistic or literary work. For the formalists, "A literary work is pure form; it is neither a thing nor a material, but a relationship between materials. And like any relationship, it is one of zero dimension."[21]

The main difference between these two psychological systems and the third one, namely psychoanalysis, is that while the former deal with the *conscious* life of individuals, the latter undertakes the task of exploring the *subconscious* (or unconscious), considered as the avenue towards the unlocking of the secrets of human behavior, artistic creativity included.

Psychoanalysis, in contrast to all previous pre-analytical psychological systems, paid close attention to the *irrational* side of human conduct, regarding it not only as the outcome of accidental circumstances but also as the result of meaningful motivation. The inaccessibility of the subconscious to a direct observation was overcome by psychoanalysis through the careful study of its two principal manifestations: *dreams* and *neuroses*. The knowledge acquired from the scrutiny of these two phenomena was utilized for a fresh examination of art and literature perceived as phenomena strongly resembling both dreams and neuroses, albeit identical with none. To do justice, however, to the psychoanalytic approach to literature, we must first of all situate it historically.

2. *Freud: Between Play and Daydreaming*

a. *The Psychoanalytic Outlook*

It seems certain that the father of the psychoanalytic movement, Freud himself, was influenced by one kind of literary criticism: the romantic. As Arnold Hauser rightly observes[22] the similarity between the romantic world view and the tenets of psychoanalysis as a way of viewing human existence is striking. The idea of "a loss of reality" or the "discomfort with civilization" as the exclusive characteristic of both the artist and the neurotic was unknown prior to romanticism. Up to the time of the romantics art was thought of as socially based and the artist as a well-integrated member of his society.

Freud, influenced by the romantic way of thinking, saw in the artist a frustrated being uncomfortable in his social setting. Art therefore, became an escape mechanism, a bridge connecting the artist with the reality which he could not reach otherwise. To defend the artist's precarious social standing the romantics veiled him in such a way as to create a new image of him according to which he was endowed with mysterious powers originating in the depths of his disturbed mind. Hence, psychoanalysis' claim that the source of artistic creativity is located in unsatisfied desires, in a neurotic frame of mind, that is, in illness.

As Hauser correctly notices, the romantic view of the artist can be sociologically explained if one considers the insecurity of the individual artists and writers after the loss of their patrons—that is, after the French Revolution and the decline of the aristocracy in Western Europe—and their "anxiety in a never-ending struggle for material existence, success, influence, and power. . . ."[23] In fact, while real life was denying the romantic creators a leading role in society, they themselves created around them the protective (illusory) walls of an attitude which brought them in opposition to the new social order.

The romantics, present themselves as sacred persons whose artistic abilities are based on unique inspiration and special talent emanating from the unseen layers of their minds. This is why "Psychoanalysis regards, as did romanticism, the unconscious as the origin, if not of a higher, at least of a more genuine, more perennial form of truth." In this sense, a point well made is that "psychoanalysis came into being as an answer to the problem of a civilization in which as a result of the romantic crisis, an individual's life and his work have become two separate provinces."[24]

b. *Towards a Psychoanalytic Theory of Literary Creation*

Freud's impact on literary criticism, as well as on literature itself, was immense.[25] On the one hand, this was due to his revolutionary views on human behavior: the psyche is divided in the *id* (consisting of instictual needs and drives), the *ego* (consciously mediating between oneself and reality) and the *superego* (functioning unconsciously to check the id); behavior is guided by such unconscious processes as projections, displacement, rationalization, etc.; aspects of the unconscious are primarily manifested in dreams and neuroses; and *libido*, that is, the sexual drive of individuals, is at the root of many of their actions.

On the other hand, Freud's influence is due to his concrete ideas on art and the artists. In his *Introductory Lectures*, for example, he refers to art as a bridge connecting fantasy and reality. Thus, the (male) artist, who is often a person with unsatisfied instinctual desires, takes refuge in fantasy by means of his artistic creativity. If he finally becomes successful and popular he gains in reality what he could previously entertain only in his imagination: fame, power and an exciting love life. These ideas were systematized and expanded in Freud's essay entitled "Creative Writers and Daydreaming." In this essay he sets forth the argument that art is close to children's *play* and the *daydreaming* of adults:

> The child's best-loved and most intense occupation is with his play or games. Might we not say that every child at play behaves like a creative writer, in that he creates a world of his own, or, rather rearranges the things of his world in a new way which pleases him? It would be wrong to think he does not take that world seriously; on the contrary, he takes his play very seriously and he expends large amounts of emotion on it. The opposite of play is not what is serious but what is real. In spite of all the emotion with which he cathects his world of play, the child distinguishes it quite well from reality; and he likes to link his imagined objects and situations to the tangible and visible things of the real world. . . .
> The creative writer does the same as the child at play. He creates a world of fantasy which he takes very seriously—that is, which he invests with large amounts of

emotion, while separating it sharply from reality. . . . [26]

Inevitably, the child grows up: on the one hand, he cannot continue his familiar play, and on the other, he strongly misses the pleasure derived from it. According to Freud, the solution to this problem by the adult is the replacement of play by daydreaming: "we can never give anything up; we only exchange one thing for another. . . . In the same way, the growing child, when he stops playing, gives up nothing but the link with real objects; instead of *playing*, he now *fantasies.* He builds castles in the air and creates what are called *daydreams.*"[27]

Freud makes a distinction between children's play and the daydreaming of adults: children do not conceal their play from others; adults tend to keep their daydreams secret as being ashamed of their own fantasies. He also points out that while all children participate in play, only unsatisfied adults have fantasies and engage in daydreaming where the stimulus of artistic creation lies.

Daydreams, according to Freud, are directly connected to *purely creative* writing, that is, writing based not on available material, i.e. myths, legends, etc., but on the imaginative powers of its own author. Evidently, Freud realizes that creative writing is not just equivalent to "naive daydream." It is, however, regarded by him as wish-fulfillment related to the three periods of time: past, present and future. A literary work, for example, is inseparable from the writer's biography in its present and past manifestations as well as its future anticipations. Hence, the singular importance of childhood, both as a formative period of an individual's life and as a rich ground for the application of the psychoanalytic method is emphasized:

> A strong experience in the present awakens in the creative writer a memory of an earlier experience (usually belonging to his childhood) from which there now proceeds a wish which finds its fulfillment in the creative work. The work itself exhibits elements of the recent provoking occasion as well as of the old memory . . . I am inclined to think that this way of looking at creative writing may turn out not unfruitful. You will not forget that the stress it lays on childhood memories in a writer's life—a stress which may perhaps seem puzzling—is ultimately derived from the assumption that a piece of creative

> writing, like daydream is a continuation of, and a sub-
> stitute for what was once the play of childhood.[28]

In "Creative Writers and Daydreaming" Freud deals with the question of how writers—these "strange beings"—manage to stimulate our emotions and make us experience great pleasure, elevating themselves above the general daydreamer who is a-shamed of and secretive about his fantasies. This achievement, Freud answers, is the ultimate secret of the artist, the very essence of *ars poetica*, and it is the result of a special technique based on two methods. First, the writer masks and camouflages his fantasies (egotistical and shameful daydreams) and he presents them in a pleasant, artistic manner.[29] Second, it is within the writer's ability to modify his personal daydreams to such an extent as to give them general significance.[30]

The technical term Freud uses to name the initial pleasure emanating from the artistic form of literary works is *fore—pleasure*. This operates as a kind of emotional fuel, so to speak, and it "makes possible the release of still greater pleasure arising from deeper physical sources." Therefore, the writer's contribution to the creation of a pleasant emotional state in the reader's mind consists in the triggering off of a mechanism residing in the reader himself. Freud states: "all the aesthetic pleasure which a creative writer affords us has the character of a fore-pleasure of this kind, and our actual enjoyment of an imaginative work proceeds from a liberation of tension in our minds."[31] In the final analysis we—as readers—can enjoy a literary work (which is but the artistic form that a writer's daydream takes) because it ultimately enables us "to enjoy our own daydreams without self-reproach or shame."[32]

Freud's theoretical construction then regards art and literature as substitute gratification, an illusion, operating on the reader as a narcotic and stimulant. By the same token, the writer is perceived as a neurotic, and his creative work, the fulfillment of his wishes. On the basis of these assumptions both the meaning of literary works and the motives of the individual writer's creating them—the creative process—can be explained. Freud himself, however, seems to have been aware of the problems which the psychoanalytic approach to artistic creation leaves unsolved, and resorting to the inadequacy of "the present state of our knowledge"—as he writes—he characterizes the body of ideas that have often been taken as his theory of art as mere "encouragements and suggestions."[33]

Be it as it may, the artist redeems his sufferings in the world by exercizing his "power of sublimation"[34] and his capacity of "symbolization."[35]   As for the reader's, spectator's, etc. pleasure emanating from the 'consumption' of an artistic work it is fundamentally the result of released internal tensions. Thus, to use the central concept of Aristotle's aesthetics, *catharsis* is the main effect of art.   Now, the question arises of how the enjoyment of an artistic work communicating something disagreeable, even terrifying, is possible.

From a Freudian standpoint, the possibilities of enjoyment in such cases can only be explained if we search "beyond the pleasure principle."   Our attention should be concentrated on the inner necessity of human beings to overcome, to transcend a situation which generates in them displeasure, (i.e. the fear of death) by confronting it face-to-face.   Evidently, the 'consumption' of artistic and literary works producing such a desirable result resembles ordinary psychoanalytic therapy, and again, catharsis is achieved.

The core of Freud's theory of artistic creation as well as one of its most debatable elements is the proposition that the ultimate foundation of creativity is the libidinal energy of men, originating in infantile sexuality: *the Oedipus complex*. The latter is considered to be at the root of the artistic masterpieces of all people and times.[36]   In this sense, the sexualism underlying works of art—based on the Oedipus complex as a universal[37] characteristic of childhood—determines not only artistic creation itself but also its effect.   The study then of the Oedipus complex takes on an enormous significance because it is presented as greatly influencing human culture in general, art and literature in particular.

A usually misunderstood aspect of the Oedipus complex is the nature of its universality.   This complex should not be conceived as a phenomenon with standard and inevitable characteristics.   The degree and form of its manifestation varies from society to society, from time to time, and even from one family to another.   On the one hand, each concrete complex of this kind does not exhaust the entire spectrum of the possible relations that may develop between children and their parents. And on the other, every Oedipus complex is unique to the extent that it is conditioned by its specific social and family environment.   This qualification of the universal nature of the

Oedipus complex, however, should be considered in the framework of Freud's suggestion that it is far more preferable to
overestimate its importance than to underestimate it.[38]

c. *Freud Under Attack*

The most well-known examples of a psychoanalytic approach to works of art and literature are Freud's own study
of Leonardo da Vinci, and Ernest Jones' study of Shakespeare's
Hamlet. Both analyses, however, have been attacked as simplistic, deterministic and arbitrary. In addition, Freud's ideas
were subject to severe criticism, because among other things
he often expressed hostility towards art and the artists.[39]
One argument against Freud's approach is that psychoanalysis lacks scientific validity and that it does not have a
unified view on art. Therefore, it can neither prove that the
writer is a neurotic nor can it account for the creative process.
But the outright rejection of psychoanalysis on these grounds
disregards those psychoanalytic insights which seem to be indispensable for the study of human behavior, i.e. the importance
given to the formative years of childhood.
Another argument is that the problem of the psychoanalysis
of dead writers cannot really be resolved. This criticism too,
fails to draw the line between those creators about whom we
have very limited information—if any—and so many others
about whom there exists a wealth of biographical details in
respect to their mode of life, relationships, innermost thoughts,
ambitions, actions, etc. through private letters or some other
trustworthy testimony. The possibility of at least one kind of
psychoanalysis of dead writers, namely existential psychoanalysis, is confirmed by Sartre's monumental study of Flaubert.
Certainly, the establishment of indisputable facts in such cases
is very difficult, and the element of doubt cannot be eliminated
considering that the investigator is after unconscious motives
and drives unknown to the subject himself. Nevertheless, useful
hypotheses might be formulated which in turn can be tested
on the basis of the artist's work.
One of the loudest criticisms is that directed against the
psychoanalysis of literary characters. Concretely, it is argued
that fictional characters do not have an unconscious; that their

childhood is seldom properly presented in a story; and that the psychoanalytic critic considers it to be his duty to attribute to their behavior as many irrational elements as possible. The counterargument from defenders of psychoanalytic criticism is that fictional characters should be treated as real persons—otherwise they would be incomprehensible—and their psychoanalysis should not be excluded.[40]   Some psychiatrists, however, express their doubts considering such a practice unrealistic. In a televised interview, for example, a psychiatrist, director of a mental penitentiary, replied to a question about the psychology of the vicious criminal character—portrayed by Richard Widmark—in the 1947 movie 'Kiss of Death', by asking rhetorically "How can you psychoanalize someone you haven't examined?"

This brings us back to the writer himself. If the creator has provided the necessary material for a psychoanalytic examination of his characters, that is, if he has made them real, then, they can be psychoanalyzed—as can be Raskonlikov in *Crime and Punishment*.   The objection that psychoanalytic criticism is improper for those literary works whose authors were not familiar with Freud's ideas is shallow. Writers were always able to observe and describe the same reality as Freud, only their objectives were different to the extent that the artistic mode of reflection differs from the scientific.   It should also be taken into account that there are cases in which leading fictional characters are meaningfully related to the writer's own personality and as such they can by psychoanalyzed if, again, the adequate information exists.   One should not forget Flaubert's statement: "I am madame Bovary."   This does not suggest the generalization that the main literary characters should be identified with their creators.   Rather, that they are positively or negatively interrelated in terms of their preferences and dislikes, prejudices and appreciations, hopes and fears, longings and world outlook.

Lionel Trilling, in his two essays "Freud and Literature" and "Art and Neurosis," opposes some of the Freudian ideas by arguing that they are more concerned with the emotional expression of writers than with anything else; that Freud's distinction between reality and illusion is both "didactic" and "crude"—a very good point, indeed; above all, that in contradistinction to a neurotic, an artist is aware and "in command" of his fantasies, his creation being a conscious act; finally, that the neurotic or the sick artist is but a myth favored by the artist himself and those closely related to him.[41]   Despite all that, Trilling praises Freud first for his regard of the mind as a "poetry-making organ,"[42] and second for the general contribution of psychoanalysis to the understanding of art and literature.

An overall assessment of Freudian psychoanalytic criticism cannot fail to concentrate on its basic pitfalls, emphasized over and over again by its critics.   First, is the inability of psychoanalysis to deal with the artistic form because it is exclusively preoccupied with the development of a theory of content. This failure of the psychoanalytic approach has often become the principal target of its critics.[43]   Freud himself was not unaware of this lack of the necessary theoretical and methodological tools for an account of the artistic form, and defending in a sense this weakness he states that "where the artist gets his ability to create is not concern of psychology," and that "before the problem of the poet, psychoanalysis must lay down its arms."[44]   This admission, of course, does not solve the problem, and psychoanalysis is rightly accused of "psychologism," that is, the tendency to pay too much attention to the relationship between the work of art and the biography of its creator at the expense of any artistic consideration.[45]

This brings us to the second major pitfall of psychoanalysis, namely, the "genetic" one,[46] which not only consists of the attempt to examine artistic and literary works through the biography of their creators, but also to reduce all manifestations of the latter's behavior to sexual impulses.[47]   Thus, as Hauser observes, psychoanalysis' primary shortcoming is that "it treats all art as symbolic and all symbolism as sexual," maintaining that "poetry is nothing but an oral outlet" and "every artist is unconsciously a voyeur."[48]

Another serious shortcoming of psychoanalysis is its totally unhistorical character.[49]   It has further been noticed that since "every person is inexorably chained to his Oedipus complex," psychoanalysis seems to indicate that every man is "the slave of his early childhood."[50]   Some critics also make a strong case against psychoanalysis' complete disregard of the conscious —committing a similar error as the previous psychological theories which totally neglected the unconscious—and they are even tempted to reject the psychoanalytic approach in spite of its positive aspects.[51]   Others, consider psychoanalysis highly useful, but they limit its possible field of operation to those artistic works or their aspects which indeed originate in the unconscious.[52]

What then can be our assessment of Freudian psycho-analytic criticism? Is it justifiable to view it as an unsuccessful attempt to account for phenomena beyond its reach or as a revolutionary body of ideas full of possibilities for a better understanding of complex mental processes and their artistic/literary manifestations? A simple answer should unhesitatingly suggest the latter, provided that it is adequately qualified.

Freud should be credited for his dynamic conception of the human mind (conscious vs. unconscious), and psychoanalysis as a comprehensive model and a theory of mental processes potentially able and necessary to supplement the task of historical materialism.[53] Yet, despite the unquestionable validity of the psychoanalytic method, the use of this approach as a self-sufficient literary criticism would resemble the erection of high walls around the distinct area of literary creation, which would artificially separate it from the other spheres of human production and activity, material, mental or otherwise.

In fact, a strict psychoanalytic approach could mark art and literature as alien and unrelated objects to society as a whole. Such a situation can be avoided, however, if the psycho-analytic critic is willing and able to liberate psychoanalysis from its deterministic and reductionistic elements, and if along with the study of the unconscious as well as the irrational aspects of human behavior, he would take into consideration the decisive part played by the conscious. Likewise, artistic form must be treated as that special property of art and literature without which it would be devoid not just of its independent status, but, more significantly, of its essence.

Psychoanalysis could be proven perhaps invaluable on condition that it constantly refines and updates its concepts and techniques, and it is enriched with the explanatory power of the socio-historical method. Thus, as far as the reader is concerned, the psychoanalytic critic should always keep in mind that the enjoyment of a literary work is historically bound depending on a whole range of cultural factors. As for the creator himself, his psychological traits cannot be examined independently of his society and the latter's historical determinants. The complete disregard of the socio-historical dimension by the psychoanalytic model can only result in the undermining and distortion of its own search for valid explanations. It is this apparent weakness of the Freudian theory of art and literature which a number of its adherents tried to correct by having recourse to Marx as well as to Anthropology.[54]

3. *Jung: The Archetypes*

Carl Gustav Jung, sums up the difference between what he calls 'analytic psychology' and psychoanalysis by characterizing the latter as psychotherapy with a narrow purpose: the readjustment of the individual to his social environment. On the contrary, the target of his analytic psychology is psychotherapy on a grand scale, aiming at the full development of the personality until the complete realization of the self is achieved.

Analytic psychology was ignored for decades, largely characterized as inefficient, and the Jungian writings as confused.[55] At the same time, Freudian psychoanalysis was established as the dominant psychological movement, and it came to be regarded as a major breakthrough in man's self-awareness.

It was only lately that Jung began to attract some attention for a number of reasons. Concretely, in England a distrust for psychoanalysis was noticed from the end of the 50's onwards and, as a consequence, an interest was shown for less deterministic psychological approaches to personality as well as for the great Eastern philosophical systems. Jung himself was credited for his visit to Benares, India, in 1938 and for his early admiration for the spiritual achievements of the East to the extent that he considered them as superior to the "barbarism" of the West: "Our Western air of superiority in the presence of Indian understanding is a part of our essential barbarism, for which any true perception of the quite extraordinary depth of those ideas and their amazing psychological accuracy is still but a remote possibility."[56]

In France, Freudianism had a monopoly for a long period of time. Thus, psychoanalysis remained firmly rooted even after the eminent Freudian structuralist Jacques Lacan introduced linguistics in the study of the ego, and attacked those Freudians who were attached to an ego-psychology which had given more autonomy to the ego than Freud ever advocated. Following the events of May 1968, however, the rejection of the Western way of life and ideology, and a desire for liberation from the restrains of intellectualism lead to an orientation toward ideas developed in the East. Here too, Jung began to attract some attention. As a result, the French association of analytic psychology (S.F.P.A.) was established in 1969. At the same time, another group appeared with less interest in analytic psychology and more concern for the Eastern philosophies. Both groups began to publish, among other things, the works of Jung, an indication that an interest in his writings is reviving. This, makes an examination of the relationship between analytic psychology and literary criticism more timely.

a. *Psychological and Visionary Art*

Jung himself, in a lecture delivered to the Society for German Language and Literature in Zurich in 1922, presents his views on the relation between poetry and analytic psychology. First of all, he limits the role of psychology to the study of the creative process, and he indicates that the examination of the artistic nature of literary works, for example, is unaccessible to it.[57] Hence, he condemns Freud's reductionism of the explanation of all behavior to the sexual drives of childhood, as well as his dogmatism, the premises of which Jung views as arbitrary.[58]

For Jung, the "great" literary works are the proper subjects of analytic psychology due to their special psychic significance (for the reader)—in contradistinction to Freud for whom the qualitatively lower literature is more useful to psychoanalysis—and to their capability to transcend the personal situation of their creators.[59] Thus, the artist as such cannot be analyzed by biologically oriented psychology, and Jung regards art as an autonomous, "living" organism resembling a plant. In this sense, art is above its creator because it simply "uses man only as a nutrient medium, employing his capacities according to its own laws and shaping itself to the fulfillment of its own creative purpose."[60]

In effect, not all art is able to manipulate its own creator, therefore, Jung distinguishes two separate modes of artistic and literary creation. First, the *psychological* mode, totally planned and controlled by the artist's conscious. This mode, as Jung maintains, results from the *introverted* attitude of the artist—an orientation towards himself—and is in line with Schiller's category of 'sentimental' poetry. Here, the involvement of a psychologist would be useless because the meaning intended by the artist is communicated in a straightforward manner. The second mode of artistic creation, the *visionary*, is that which Jung had in mind when he defined art as a living, autonomous entity. This category of art—corresponding to Schiller's 'naive' poetry—is the result of the artist's *extroverted* attitude—an orientation towards the world. For the understanding of this type of art and literature the help of psychology is indispensable, and even the artist himself "is aware that he is subordinate to his work or stands outside it. . . ."[61]

According to Jung, then, in the psychological (introverted) mode of artistic creation the artist's consciousness is identical with the creative process, but in the visionary (extroverted) mode it is not. Therefore, in the case of the latter, the creative process far from being an exercise of the artist's freedom is in reality subordinated to the unconscious. This is why Jung views the creative process, "as a living thing implanted in the human psyche," or as an "autonomous complex," that is, "a split-off portion of the psyche, which leads a life of its own outside the hierarchy of consciousness."[62]

Jung, foresees the problem deriving from the possibility that one and the same poet may manifest both introverted and extraverted attitudes alternately. Yet, the most serious difficulty emerges when an apparently "psychological" work is in reality "visionary" i.e. full of symbolic meanings often beyond our (present) power of comprehension.[63] Literary works of this type (i.e. with latent meanings) are contrasted to those which are conscious products "shaped and designed to have the effect intended," and Jung maintains that the more the symbolic meaning of a work is hidden from us, the more it attracts our interest, although the aesthetic enjoyment derived from it might not be completely satisfying. He further suggests that art "in itself" has no meaning at all; it merely "is". But if, by disregarding the creative process, we perceive art from the outside, that is, in relation to other phenomena, then we can establish its various meanings. This is precisely the scientific task of analytic psychology.[64]

b. *Collective Unconscious and Primordial Images*

It is Jung's belief that any "autonomous complex" results from the activation of a part of the unconscious caused in turn by energy originating in consciousness. However, as consciousness transmits energy to the unconscious it itself becomes apathetic (this happens to many artists) or it regresses to an "infantile and archaic level." When Jung focuses specifically on the autonomous *creative* complex—about which he admits we know nothing—he tries to relate the visionary mode of creation with primordial words and images. By emphasizing that he as a psychologist is only interested in the symbolic artistic and literary works, he puts forward the idea that they originate in the *collective unconscious*, while the non-symbolic ones, of no interest to him, are just "symptoms" emanating from the *personal unconscious*.65 An elaboration on Jung's distinction of the unconscious in collective and personal is necessary for an understanding of its effects on literary criticism.

By *personal* unconscious Jung means a "superficial layer" of the unconscious which rests on a deeper layer, inherent in every individual: the *collective* unconscious. This collective part of the unconscious is universal, with more or less common features for all individuals, that is, it is of a "suprapersonal nature." Jung explains: "The contents of the personal unconscious are chiefly the *feeling-toned complexes*, as they are called; they constitute the personal and private side of psychic life. The contents of the collective unconscious, on the other hand, are known as archetypes."66 In a more explicit statement he adds: "We mean by collective unconscious a certain psychic disposition shaped by the forces of heredity; from it consciousness has developed."67 Put it differently, the collective unconscious which normally remains hidden "is no more than a potentiality handed down to us from primordial times in the specific form of mnemonic images or inherited in the anatomical structure of the brain."68 At exactly this point Jung's own contribution to literary criticism begins, consisting of his theory of *archetypes* which derives from his theory of the collective unconscious. In Jung's own formulation:

> the primordial image or archetype is a figure—be it a demon, a human being, or a process—that constantly

recurs in the course of history and appears wherever creative fantasy is freely expressed. Essentially, therefore, it is a mythological figure. When we examine these images more closely, we find that they give form to countless typical experiences of our ancestors. They are, so to speak, the psychic residue of innumerable experiences of the same type.[69]

Analytic psychology places tremendous emphasis on the archetypes because they can affect human life in many respects including the causation of neuroses and psychoses. Their importance lies in the fact that deriving from our "collective psychology . . . which changes our whole life, which changes the surface of our known world, which makes history . . . and . . . moves according to laws entirely different from those of our consciousness," they are themselves "the great decisive forces" which "decide the fate of man."[70]

Archetypes in no case should be confused with predetermined contents. In Jung's view, they should better be regarded as predetermined, to some extent, forms. By the same token, they are not ideas but just the possibilities of ideas, the disposition towards a particular kind of possible behavior.[71] But despite their form-like nature, Jung insists that,

> In each of these images there is a little piece of human psychology and human fate, a remnant of the joys and sorrows that have been repeated countless times in our ancestral history, and on the average follow ever the same course. It is like a deeply graven river-bed in the psyche, in which waters of life, instead of flowing along as before in a broad but shallow stream, suddenly swell into a mighty river. *This happens whenever that particular set of circumstances is encountered which over long periods of time has helped to lay down the primordial image.*[72] (My italics).

When this takes place (i.e. either as a direct experience as for example in the case of the artist, or through some medium like language, as in the case of the audience), and these forms are filled-up with concrete contents resulting from the influence of innumerable factors, then the original mythological situation is reconstructed in the psyche of the individual and an emotional tension overflows him. It is the moment that he undergoes an experience typical to his race and therefore familiar to him. And, as Jung argues, while the everyday struggle for "adaptation" is greatly "laborious" because each one of us is confronted with strange and "atypical situations . . . it is not surprising that when an archetypal situation occurs we suddenly feel an extraordinary sense of release, as though transported, or caught up by an overwhelming power. At such moments we are no longer individuals, but the race; the voice of all mankind resounds in us."[73] Hence, Jung comes to the conclusion that "The individual man cannot use his powers to the full unless he is aided by one of those collective representations we call ideals, which releases all the hidden forces of instinct that are inaccessible to the conscious will."[74]

The most "effective ideals" derive from one and the same archetype. For example, the archetype of mother produces the ideal of the "mother country," and the archetype of father the ideal of "fatherland." The moment an archetype acquires a content, that is, when it becomes conscious through some kind of experience, e.g. through language, it moves up so deeply that we are at its mercy. Therefore, we can appreciate the uniqueness of the artist whose "relative lack of adaptation turns out to his advantage; it enables him to follow his own yearnings far from the beaten path, and to discover what it is that would meet the unconscious needs of his age . . . so art represents a process of self-regulation in the life of nations and epochs."[75] Thus, along with the archetypes the artist emerges as a powerful being, because "whoever speaks in primordial images speaks with a thousand voices; he enthralls and overpowers, while at the same time *he lifts the idea he is seeking to express out of the occasional and the transitory into the realm of the ever-enduring. He transmutes our personal destiny into the destiny of mankind. . . .*"[76] (My italics).

Finally, Jung feels confident enough to attempt an explanation of both "the secret of great art, and of its effect upon us":

> The creative process, so far as we are able to follow it
> at all, consists in the conscious activation of an archetypal
> image, and in elaborating and shaping this image into the
> finished work. By giving it shape the artist translates it
> into the language of the present, and so makes it possi-

ble for us to find our way back to the deepest springs of
life. Therein lies the social significance of art: it is constantly at work educating the spirit of the age, conjuring
up the forms in which the age is most lacking. . . . The
artist seizes on the primordial image and in raising it
from deepest unconsciousness he brings it into relation
with conscious values, *thereby transforming it until it
can be accepted by the minds of his contemporaries
according to their powers.*[77] (My italics).

c. *Analytic Psychology and Literature*

An evaluation of analytic psychology as the basis for the
development of a distinct approach to literature cannot fail
to consider the numerous critical studies which have been produced over the years, ranging from Edward Glover's forceful
attack on Jung, to Stanley Hyman's acceptance of him as in
some respects more important for literary criticism than Freud
himself, and to Morris Philipson's moderate standpoint, evidently
coming to Jung's defense.[78]   In effect, this interest in Jung's
work is mostly due to his varying influence—along with the
works of some anthropologists, particularily J. G. Frazer's
The Golden Bough—on such eminent literary critics as Maud
Bodkin, G. Wilson Knight, Robert Graves, Herbert Read and
especially Northrop Frye, that is, to Jung's co-influence on
the development of a mythological or archetypal kind of criticism.[79]   In addition, it should be reminded that some great
poets have themselves expressed, one way or another, ideas
essentially similar to Jung's as, for example, T. S. Eliot and
W. B. Yeats.[80]
In confronting the question of the validity of Jung's theories for literary criticism we should not loose focus on the
limited, albeit unique, role Jung assigns to psychology. This
role is restricted to the investigation of the creative process
of the purely symbolic works with the aim of establishing their
meaning (or psychic significance, or psychological essence)
which are inaccessible not only to non-psychological literary
criticism but even to their own authors.[81]   We shall return to
this matter shortly, but for the moment we will proceed by
pointing out that Jung's comparison of an art-work to a natural

thing, e.g. a plant, is at best a distortion of the distinguishing characteristic of an artistic creation, namely, its being the product of man, a fact which the Jungian aesthetic theory seems to ignore.

By the same token, the classification of art and literature according to the creator's introverted or extroverted attitude is a simplification, because the two can hardly be separated as influencing one another. One might detect here Jung's intention to establish the indispensability of analytic psychology without falling into Freud's reductionism to the sexual.

In regard to one of the most provocative Jungian concepts, the collective unconscious, it should be stated at the outset that its existence is not confirmed by the findings of anthropology and biology.[82] This concept is even unacceptable to literary critics attracted to Jung's ideas like, for example, Northrop Frye who in his *Anatomy of Criticism* limits the field of operation of archetypal criticism only to the relationship between form and content, excluding that between source and derivation.[83] Thus, one might agree with Hauser that the concept of collective unconscious "originates in an unscrupulous direct application of the principles of the psychology of the individual to the psychology of groups."[84]

Jung's theory of archetypes is severely attacked by some of his critics.[85] Yet, instead of arguing that he simply "confuses theory with tradition"[86]—since the existence of archetypes cannot be scientifically verified—one can view archetypes not as universal forms engraved in the human brain, able to "rearise spontaneously, at any time, at any place, and without any outside influence,"[87] but as socially necessitated and maintained common experiences, occasionally useful to literary criticism as auxiliary tools.

Northrop Frye, again, noticing that classical mythology is a "grammar of literary archetypes"[88] asserts that the application of archetypal criticism to myth results in *comedy* (myth of spring), *romance* (myth of summer), *tragedy* (myth of autumn) and *irony* (myth of winter). However, for Frye, this is just one possible approach among others. Maud Botkin's *Archetypal Patterns in Poetry* is another case in point: Jung's ideas were the precondition for this study, but they are not accepted blindly.[89] In effect, Jungian archetypal criticism is, like Freud's, reductionist since all female figures become Magna Mater, all male figures the Wise Old Man, all evil persons the

Shadow, etc. This is a very simplistic view indeed of man's sophisticated and complex literary achievements.

In relation to literature, the Jungian construction has an extremely limited field of possible operation, due to its neglect of stylistic, socio-cultural, historical, etc. considerations. It is also retrogressive and utterly conservative in nature. On the one hand, Jung limits great literature solely to symbolic works—which unconsciously reveal primordial images—, and he saves for the group of psychologist-critics the privilege of establishing their meaning, that is, of mediating between the archetypes of great literary works and the audience plus the authors themselves, the latter being unable to understand them directly. On the other hand, he entrusts the education of the "spirit of the age" to the lessons derived from the message passed on by the archetypes as these are decoded by the Jugian critic who should presumably always strive for the primordial images to "be accepted by the minds" of the audience "according to their powers."[90]

By what kind of education can symbolic works enlighten the present and, consequently, prepare the way for the future of mankind? In other words, what is the kind of knowledge which the unconsciously activated archetypal forms can offer through the mediation of the Jungian critic? Morris Philipson, Jung's supporter, after clarifying that the message of great works should not be taken as a scientific proposition, explains: "The new knowledge (the wisdom) of such criticism lies in its appreciation of the intuitive or prospective values of the artworks; and its effectiveness lies in its ability to make connections between the symbol and the re-organization of psychic life. . . . The valuable critic, like the effective analyst, is the one who helps the audience (like the cooperating patient) to intepret those manifestations that are symbolic in purport. By so doing, he exemplifies the expression of wisdom, relating what is known to proposals for how to live better."[91] The likening of the critic to analyst and of the audience to patient is, at best, silly. Even this, however, is surpassed by the last statement which implies a perception of the Jungian literary critic as a social philosopher.

Our trip into Jung's thinking taught us that the moral treasure of the present and future is well preserved into primordial images, released to us drop by drop through literature (poetry) which is pregnant with archetypes, and that the analytical psychologist-critic acts as society's intellectual midwife. If one is not already consumed by the muddy Jungian sea, one wonders whether there was a short-cut to the same conservative destination.

NOTES

[1] Cf. Wellek and Warren, *Theory of Literature, op. cit.*, p. 73.

[2] Cf. James Thorpe, ed., *Relations of Literary Study* (New York: Modern Language Association of America, 1967).

[3] Hauser, *op. cit.*, p. 13.

[4] Vygotsky, *op. cit.*, pp. 9-11.

[5] Cf. *Ibid.*, p. 13.

[6] H. Stuart Hughes, *Consciousness and Society* (New York: Vintage Books, 1961), p. 393.

[7] *Ibid.*, p. 341.

[8] *Ibid.*, p. 393.

[9] Frederic C. Crews, "Literature and Psychology," in Thorpe, ed. *op. cit.*, p. 73.

[10] Cf. H. B. English and A. C. English, *A Comprehensive Dictionary of Psychological and Psychoanalytical Terms: A Guide to Usage (New York: David McKay Company, Inc. 1968), pp. 420-426.*

[11] Cf. Martin S. Lindauer, *The Psychological Study of Literature* (Chicago: Nelson Hall, 1974), p. 9.

[12] *Ibid.*, p. 26.

[13] David Daiches, *Critical Approaches to Literature* (Englewood Cliffs, New Jersey: Prentice-Hall, Inc. 1956), pp. 340-341.

[14] Lindauer, *op. cit.*, p. 41.

[15] It should be noted that Lindauer emphasizes the neglect of objective psychology to study literature basing himself mostly on an examination of recent American scholarship. Vygotsky, however, bases his study mainly on the works of European and particularly Russian scholars produced at the beginning of this century.

[16] Vygotsky, *op. cit.*, p. 31.

[17] *Ibid.*, p. 38.

[18] *Ibid.*, p. 33.

[19] *Ibid.*, p. 33.

[20] *Ibid.*, p. 35.

[21] Quoted in *Ibid.*, p. 53.

[22] Hauser, *op. cit.*, pp. 54-63.

[23] *Ibid.*, p. 62.

[24] *Ibid.*, pp. 62, 63.

[25] Cf. Jack J. Spector, *The Aesthetics of Freud* (New York: McGraw Hill Book Company, 1974), especially chap. 4.

[26] Sigmund Freud, "Creative Writers and Daydreaming," in Adams, ed., *op. cit.*, p. 749.

[27] *Ibid.*, p. 750.

[28] *Ibid.*, pp. 752-753.

[29] *Ibid.*, p. 753.

[30] Cf. Harry Slochower, "The Psychoanalytic Approach to Literature: Some Pitfalls and Promises," *Literature and Psychology*, XXI, no. 2 (1971), p. 110.

[31] Freud, *op. cit.*, p. 753.

[32] *Ibid.*, p. 753.

[33] *Ibid.*, p. 753.

[34] *Sublimation* as it is used by Freud refers to "a process of deflecting libido on sexual-motive activity from human objects to new objects of a non-sexual, socially valuable nature." (*The Basic Writings of Sigmund Freud*, transl. and ed. by A. A. Brill (New York: The Modern Library, 1965), pp. 18-19) For Freud's conviction that sublimation originates in the domain of the sexual, cf. *Ibid.*, p. 568, especially n. 1.

[35] Hauser, distinguishes *sublimation* from *symbolization* and points out the the latter endows the artistic works with multiple meanings. However, he rejects the idea that symbols are produced by the unconscious. Cf. Hauser, *op. cit.*, p. 49.

[36] Quoted in Vygotsky, *op. cit.*, p. 78.

[37] Freud is categorical about the universality of the Oedipus Complex. Cf. Brill, transl. and ed., *op. cit.*, p. 308.

[38] Sigmund Freud, *A General Introduction to Psychoanalysis*, transl. by Joan Riviere (New York: Pocket Books, 1969), p. 217.

[39] Cf. Phillip Rieff, *Freud: The Mind of the Moralist* (New York: The Viking Press, 1950), pp. 120-121.

[40] Cf. Morton Kaplan and Robert Kloss, *The Unspoken Motive* (New York: The Free Press, 1973), pp. 4-7. Also, Leonard Tennenhouse, ed. *The Practice of Psychoanalytic Criticism* (Detroit: Wayne State University Press, 1976), p. 12.

[41] In Adams, ed., *op. cit.*, pp. 948-967.

[42] *Ibid.*, pp. 956.

[43]Cf. Vygotsky, *op. cit.*, pp. 68, 84. Also, Hauser, *op. cit.*, p. 76.

[44]Quoted in Spector, *op. cit.*, p. 79.

[45]Hauser, *op. cit.*, p. 73.

[46]Slochower, *op. cit.*, p. 107.

[47]Vygotsky, *op. cit.*, p. 76.

[48]Hauser, *op. cit.*, pp. 50, 51.

[49]*Ibid.*, pp. 78, 80.

[50]Vygotsky, *op. cit.*, p. 81.

[51]*Ibid.*, pp. 81, 83, 84-85.

[52]Hauser, *op. cit.*, pp. 88, 89. 90.

[53]*Ibid.*, pp. 66, 67, 69.

[54]Wellek and Warren, *op. cit.*, p. 83.

[55]Cf, for example, Edward Glover, *Freud or Jung?* (Cleveland: World, 1967), p. 19. Also, Aldous Huxley, *Tomorrow and Tomorrow and Other Essays* (New York: Harper, 1956), p. 178.

[56]Carl Jung, "The Problem of Types in Poetry" in *Psychological Types; or The Psychology of Individuation*, transl. by H. Godwin Barnes (New York: Harcourt, Brace and Company, Inc., 1923), p. 245.

[57]Carl Jung, "On the Relation of Analytical Psychology to Poetry," in Adams, ed., *op. cit.*, p. 810.

[58]*Ibid.*, p. 812.

[59]*Ibid.*, p. 813.

[60]*Ibid.*, p. 813.

[61]*Ibid.*, pp. 813, 814.

[62]*Ibid.*, pp. 814, 815.

[63]Jung defines a symbol as "the intimation of a meaning beyond the level of our present powers of comprehension." *Ibid.*, p. 815.

[64]*Ibid.*, p. 816.

[65]*Ibid.*, p. 817.

[66]Violet S. deLaszlo, ed., *The Basic Writings of C. G. Jung* (New York: Modern Library, 1959), p. 287.

[67]C. G. Jung, *Modern Man in Search of a Soul*, transl. by W. S. Dell and Cary F. Baynes (New York: Harcourt, Brace & Co., 1933), p. 165.

[68]Jung, "On the Relation of Analytical Psychology to Poetry," *op. cit.*, p. 817.

[69]*Ibid.*, p. 817.

[70]Jolande Jacobi, ed., *C. G. Jung: Psychological Reflections* (Princeton: Princeton University Press, 1970), p. 39.

[71]C. G. Jung, *Four Archetypes*, transl. by R. F. C. Hull (Princeton: Princeton University Press, 1973), p. 13.

[72]Jung, "On the Relation of Analytical Psychology to Poetry," *op. cit.*, p. 818.

[73]*Ibid.*, p. 818.

[74]*Ibid.*, p. 818.

[75]*Ibid.*, p. 818.

[76]*Ibid.*, p. 818.

[77]*Ibid.*, p. 818.

[78]Cf. Glover, *op. cit.*, p. 173. Also, Stanley Edgar Hyman, *The Armed Vision* (New York: Vintage Books, 1955), pp. 134, 160. And, Morris Philipson, *Outline of a Jungian Aesthetics* (Northwestern University Press, 1963), p. 178.

[79]Cf. M. H. Abrams, *A Glossary of Literary Terms* (3rd ed., New York: Holt, Rinehart and Winston, Inc., 1971), pp. 11-12.

[80]Cf. Daiches, *op. cit.*, pp. 356-357.

[81]Jung, "On the Relation of Analytical Psychology to Poetry," *op. cit.*, p. 816.

[82]Philipson, *op. cit.*, pp. 140-160.

[83]Northrop Frye, *Anatomy of Criticism* (Princeton: Princeton University Press, 1957), p. 109.

[84]Hauser, *op. cit.*, p. 78.

[85]Cf. Kaplan and Kloss, *op. cit.*, pp. 294-299.

[86]Glover, *op. cit.*, p. 151.

[87]Jung, *Four Archetypes, op. cit.*, p. 13.

[88]Frye, *op. cit.*, p. 135.

[89]Cf. Maud Bodkin, *Archetypal Patterns in Poetry* (New York: Vintage Books, 1958)

[90]Cf. Philipson, *op. cit.*, pp. 119-131, 180-181.

[91]*Ibid.*, pp. 184-185.

SIX

THE PATH OF RUSSIAN FORMALISM

1. *The Influence of Symbolism and Futurism*

Just before the October Revolution, a group of students of language and literature at the University of Moscow, formed an organization called the Moscow Linguistic Circle (1915). At about the same time in St. Petersburg, a group of philologists and literary historians created the Society for the Study of Poetic Language, the *Opojaz* (1916). Thus, the Russian 'formalist' school came into existence and it contributed not only to the elaboration of a new and rewarding approach to literature but also to the growth of the science of linguistics, as well as to structuralism which was subsequently developed.[1]

From a historical point of view, Russian formalism was a reaction in the realm of literary studies against the positivist sociological, biographical and psychological determinism, following up the epistemological revolt against positivism initiated in Germany by the neo-Kantians W. Dilthey, W. Windelband, and H. Rickert. The contempt of the Russian formalists for an extrinsic approach to literature was first manifested in their attack against the three existent orientations in Russian literary criticism: the *historical*, which neglected the literary work itself; the *sociological*, which viewed a work of literature as a means to be employed for the social and moral betterment of society; and the *philological*, which was also interested in the historical relations of a literary text.

A major adversary of the Russian formalists—and their initial immediate target—were the *symbolists* who were very influential in Russian literary criticism. The symbolists upheld the positivist view of language as a mere medium with a purely referential function. Every word used by the poet is but a sign pointing to an extraliterary symbol, i.e. religious, philosophical, magical, etc. As victor Erlich explains, "To the Symbolist theoretician, poetry is a revelation of ultimate Truth, a higher form of cognition, a 'theurgy', capable of bridging the gap between empirical reality and the 'Unknown'. The poetic word is seen as a mystical Logos, reverberating with occult meanings. The metaphor, one of the poet's basic devices, is elevated from a mere figure of speech to a Symbol." Erlich quotes one of the leading Russian symbolists, the poet and scholar Vjaceslav Ivanov, who wrote that the "macrocosm is reflected in each microcosm, in the same way in which the sun is reflected in each drop of rain."[2]

According to the Russian symbolists then the sign and the object, the signifier and the signified are not related conventionally but organically. Poetic language corresponds to hidden meanings of a higher order and it conveys messages that need to be deciphered. For this reason the symbolists felt obliged to concentrate on "the poet's 'words, rhythms, images'—to the metrical pattern, the euphonic devices and the mechanism of the metaphor. In short, it became imperative to concentrate on the problems of poetic form."[3]

The mysticism of symbolism and its absolute separation of poetic from communicative language created a strong reaction within its own camp and a new group, the Acmeists, began to seek "clarity and . . . graphic sharpness of outline."[4] However, the most severe criticism of symbolism came from another literary movement, the *futurists.*

The objective of the futurists was to break away from tradition, and to secure the right of the poet to follow his own syntactical, grammatical and thematic rules. Moreover, whereas the symbolists attributed importance to the word for what it represented, the futurists valued the word as an autonomous and self-sufficient entity. Erlich translated the title of the futurist manifesto as the *Word as Such,* and he provides us with the following excerpt: "We, the Futurist poets, thought more about the Word than about the Psyche, mercilessly abused by our predecessors. Let us rather live by the word as such than by our own experiences."[5]

The subjectivistic and impressionistic practices of literary criticism also were rejected, and a shifting of emphasis took place from content to form, the former being regarded as of minor importance. Erlich has translated the following excerpt from the writings of a leading futurist, Krucenyx: "Genuine novelty in literature does not depend upon content. . . . A new light thrown on the old world may produce a very interesting interplay. If there is a new form, there must also exist a new content. . . . It is form that determines content."[6]

Whereas the symbolists were interested in the 'essence' of a poem, the futurists were absolute relativists, and they also underlined the need for a scientific poetics. For the futurists, the poem was the product of a craftsman, the poet, and not of an individual endowed with extraordinary magical qualities as the symbolists tended to believe. Nevertheless, the futurists, unlike the symbolists, did not produce any major theoreticians, and the construction of the new scientific poetics that they envisaged fell entirely on the shoulders of the formalists.

It should be emphasized at this point that the formalists were greatly influenced by both the symbolists and the futurists. The primary concern of these two movements for poetic form undoubtedly played a constructive role in the shaping of the formalists' ideas. By the same token, the futurists' critique of the symbolists' overall way of thinking, their focus on the word as an independent entity, and their stress on the necessity for a scientific approach to poetry, showed the way to the formalist theoreticians. In addition, the futurists' extremism and their lack of a systematic theory, together with the symbolists' aspiration to go beyond art by developing a distinct philosophy, created the precondition for the initiation of the formalist movement. It was in sharp opposition to the mystifying symbolist metaphysics that the first formalist group was formed. In his informative essay, "The Theory of the Formal Method" (1927), Boris Ejxenbaum—a literary theoretician who became one of the most important members of the *Opojaz*—writes:

> We engaged in battle with the symbolists in order to wrest poetics from their hands and, once having divested poetics of any ties with subjective, aesthetic, or philosophical theories, to redirect it to the route of a scientific investigation of facts. . . . The basic motto uniting the original group of formalists was the emancipation of the poetic word from philosophical and religious biases to which the Symbolists had increasingly fallen prey. . . . That is the source of the new spirit of scientific positivism that characterizes the Formalists: the rejection of philosophical premises, psychological or aesthetic interpretations, and so forth. . . . Art had to be approached at

close range, and science had to be made concrete.[7]

The central question which preoccupied formalism was a work's *how*, at the expense of its *what* or *why*. This common problem became the axis around which the formalist theory and method were constructed step-by-step, as each individual theoretician was advancing his ideas and often revising them according to the criticism they attracted and to his own intellectual maturity. Boris Ejxenbaum warns that one should regard the early formalist writings (1916-1921) as a polemic against rival literary movements rather than as carefully developed theses of an academic standing.[8] He also makes special reference to the collective nature of the formalist achievements.[9]

It is a fact that not a single theoretician can be credited to the entire formalist methodology. As far as its status is concerned, however, it can hardly be accepted that the writings of 1916-1921 were no more than polemical statements, because they were also the programmatic theoretical and methodological principles of the movement, some of which were eventually reformulated and improved in respect to their extremism, one-sidedness and dogmatism. In this brief account of Russian formalism, then, we should consider its fundamental premises and discuss its principal concepts, taking into account their evolution during the life-span of this movement on Russian soil, as well as during the days of its successor movement: the Prague structuralism.

2. *The Study of Literariness*

In the words of Roman Jakobson, the object of study of formalism "is not literature but 'literariness', that is, what makes a given work a *literary* work."[10] In this initial formulation, literariness is that which distinguishes literature from non-literature: a quality pertaining to the mode of being of literature.

The concept of literariness was primarily meant to facilitate the exclusion from the area of concern of literary science of such factors as the author's biography, socio-historical elements, intellectual trends, etc. In this sense, literariness could be studied, (hence the differentiating characteristic of literature from non-literature could be established), if literary research was exclusively focusing not on the literary text in its entirety but on the artistic *devices* employed in it.

The emphasis on the distinctive feature of literature, its *differentia*, was so strong that literariness became indistinguishable from literature which was ultimately reduced to its main quality. Victor Shklovsky—one of the most influential theoreticians of the movement—went as far as to define a literary work as the "sum-total of all stylistic devices employed in it."[11] Notwithstanding its usefulness, this purely formalist position created more problems than it could solve, and this became evident to the formalists themselves when they realized that there were some other factors, e.g. ideological, social, etc., which a critic could not afford to dismiss.

As a result of this re-evaluation, the concept of literariness was redefined, and instead of being the sum-total of its devices, a literary work came to be regarded as "a structured system, a regularly ordered hierarchical set of artistic devices,"[12] according to a statement made by Roman Jakobson in one of his lectures delivered at Masaryk University in Brno in 1935. Thus, it was realized that literariness co-existed with other elements which were also essential to a literary text, despite the fact that literariness was always its key feature, the one that differentiated it from non-literary works. The co-existence of the element of literariness with other factors that were always subordinated to it was understood on the basis of a fundamental formalist concept: the concept of the *dominant*.

Roman Jakobson defines (1935) the concept of the dominant as "the focusing component of a work of art." This component "rules, determines and transforms the remaining components."[13] To make this clear, Jakobson focuses on poetry, regarding verse as a system of values that are in a hierarchical position to one another. One of these values is the most essential because it alone makes verse what it is.

Jakobson mentions, for example, that in the Czech poetry of the fourteenth century, the main value of verse was not the "syllabic scheme but rhyme," while in the Czech realist poetry of the late nineteenth century "rhyme was a dispensable device, whereas the syllabic scheme was a mandatory, inalienable component," and for the modern Czech free verse "intonation becomes the dominant."[14] He then views the dominant as historically conditioned and he observes that even though in the three periods of Czech poetry the same elements are present, i.e. rhyme, a syllabic scheme and intonational integrity, the element which becomes the dominant and regulates the function of the others depends on factors external to the poem.

This standpoint was a great improvement over the monistic position of pure formalism that tended to limit a poetic work to its aesthetic function (literariness). By the same token, Jakobson also rejected the mechanistic position, according to which a poetic work was regarded as a "mechanical agglomeration of functions," i.e. philosophical, didactic, social, aesthetic, etc. all having an equal standing within the work. He goes beyond both the monistic and mechanistic perspectives and defines a poetic work as "a verbal message whose aesthetic function is the dominant."[15] This new definition together with an historical approach to the concept of the dominant enabled linguistic analysis to move towards the overcoming of the separation between synchrony and diachrony. Jakobson took pride in this advanced form of formalist thinking and he concluded:

> The reader of a poem or the viewer of a painting has a vivid awareness of two orders: the traditional canon and the artistic novelty as a deviation from the canon. It is precisely against the background of that tradition that innovation is conceived. The Formalist studies brought to light that this simultaneous preservation of tradition and breaking away from tradition form the essence of every new work of art.[16]

The concept of the dominant was useful and adequate for the consideration of artistic/literary works from a more general to a more specific level: for the distinction between literature from non-literature in general; for the contrast between the artistic works of different historical periods, e.g. Renaissance (emphasis on the visual arts) vs. the Romantic era (emphasis on music); for the differentiation between varied literary genres within the same historical period, e.g. poetry vs. prose, with rhyme being the differentiating element; finally, for the distinction of a particular artist's work from that of another within the same historical period and literary genre.

Richard Sherwood examines the contribution of Shklovsky in the development of early formalist theory on prose literature, and he points out "The Formalists' concern with the prominent, differentiating devices of separate writers, i.e. *neologisms* (Khlebnikov), *making strange* (Tolstoi), *digressions* (Sterne), *oxymorons* (Rozanov, Mayakovsky), *imagery* (Bely)."[17] (My italics). This differentiation and consequently the determination of the dominant element of a literary work was ultimately based on the formalist perception of literature as a predominantly linguistic phenomenon—which either is equated with the sumtotal of certain artistic devices (early formalism), or it is a structured *system* of signs (the Prague structuralism)—by which the poet always manipulates language for his own purposes.

The formalists' perception of the language exclusively used by the poet, derived from their rejection of the idea that literature in general and poetry in particular is a creation bearing a communicative message. To support this argument, the formalists maintained that language, the medium by which both poetry and everyday speech are expressed, should be characterized in accordance with its function. The formalist Lev Jakubinskij, writes (1916): "If the speaker uses (language) for the purely practical purpose of communication, then we are dealing with the system of *practical language* (discursive thought), in which language resources (sounds, morphological segments, and so forth) have no autonomous value and are merely a *means* of communication."[18] Jakubinskij adds that when language does not serve an explicit practical purpose but takes on an autonomous value then we have *poetic language*.

The sharp distinction of language in 'practical' and 'autonomous' served as the basis for the construction of a new scientific poetics, i.e. a poetics concerned with the scientific study of literary facts. It also offered a satisfactory explanation to the notion of "trans-sense language" put forth by the futurists, that is, language which seems to be unintelligible and meaningless. In relation to this, Shklovsky suggested that in certain instances, i.e. prose fiction, folklore, nursery rhymes, religious rituals, etc.[19] we do have trans-sense language in which case the sound is more important than meaning. Shklovsky's inference was that in poetry where the language has indeed a value of its own, sound is more significant than meaning.

This new theory of the supremacy of sound over meaning dealt a blow to the theory of poetry as expressing images and to that which viewed a poem's sounds as indicating secret meaning (symbolism). In this framework, the examination of the rhythm of a poem became of special interest to the formalists since as Osip Brik writes, "Sounds and sound harmonies are not merely a euphonic extra but are the result of an autonomous poetic endeavor."[20]

The formalist theory of versification was based on the autonomous value of poetic language and on the dynamic function of a dominant element. This dominant element and organizing principle of poetry, or, in the words of Jurij Tynjanov, "the constructive factor of verse"[21] is *rhythm*, vaguely defined by Boris Tomasevskij as "a regular alternation in time of comparable phenomena."[22]

Erlich points out that what makes rhythm the dominant factor of poetry is not its mere presence in poems but its "status": in poetry rhythm is the supreme characteristic while in prose or verbal communication rhythm cannot be more than a secondary feature.   Further, Erlich translates the following significant statement made by Jurij Tynjanov: "In poetry the meaning of words is modified by the sound, in prose sound is modified by the meaning."[23]   Before we elaborate on this statement, we should notice that the formalists did not confuse rhythm with meter.   Moreover, they maintained that prosody "must be 'oriented' not toward phonetics, that is, the physical and physiological description of speech-sounds, but toward phonemics, which examines the speech-sounds *sub-specie* of their linguistic function, that is, their capacity for differentiating word-meanings."[24]

The formalist correlation between prosody and semantics served as the ground for their rejection of those theories which related a poem's sound and its meaning *in terms of the music of its verse and aspects of external reality*, i.e. physical, psychological, intellectual, etc.   The formalists did correlate sound and meaning in poetry but from another perspective, namely, *in reference to a correspondence between different forms of poetic expression*.   Erlich explains: "What was emphasized here was the similarity between two sets of devices, two levels of literary craft—poetic euphony and poetic imagery. . . .   The terms of reference were 'intrinsic', and verse was approached as a self-contained entity."[25]

In this framework, the formalists' insistence on the supremacy of sound over meaning and on the former's ability to modify the latter is illuminated.   Rhythm, the dominant element of poetry, "deforms" the meaning of the poem because, in Erlich's formulation, the inflation of rhymes with specific sound-patterns "brings words closer to each other, makes them interact, overlap, crisscross, and in so doing, reveal the wealth of this 'lateral', potential meanings." At this point Erlich quotes Ejxenbaum who states that "The play of these lateral meanings running afoul as it does of habitual verbal associations, is the principal feature of poetic semantics."[26]

In an essay written in 1927, Osip Brik expresses his disagreement with both the theory of trans-sense language which separates poetic from practical language, and the theory which, at the other extreme, fails to distinguish the language of poetry from that of everyday communication. Brik argues that poetic language is similar and at the same time different from communicative language and suggests that the former's "specifically verbal nature has to be underlined."[27]

The nature of poetic language is a highly complicated problem and its study continued under the influence of Saussurean linguistics and Russian formalism. For example, Jan Mukarovsky, a member of the Prague school of structural linguistics, wrote an essay in 1948 in which he examines the relationship between poetic language and standard. In his view, the function of poetic language is "foregrounding," that is, the autonomous use of words which "achieves maximum intensity to the extent of pushing communication into the background as the objective of expression and of being used for its own sake."[28] Foregrounding, however, cannot be complete. Therefore, Mukarovsky goes on, standard language plays a vital role as background to a poem. A poem is a dynamic unity of foregrounded elements, constituting a structure that is manifested as an artistic whole and in relation to which the value of the parts is determined.[29]

The formalists preferred to call their method *morphological*, in order to differentiate it from other approaches to literature, i.e. sociological, historical, etc.,[30] and such a differentiation was carried on at the theoretical and philosophical levels as well. One of the main points of difference between the formalists and the adherents of the sociological, historical, etc. approaches, was the attitude towards the issue of form vs. content.

The formalists rejected completely the notion of the primacy of content over form—in which case form was regarded as merely the guise of the essential thing. Furthermore, they aspired to go beyond the extreme futurist position according

to which content is determined by form, even though this was
initially adopted by the formalist theoreticians, e.g. Shklovsky.
Victor Zirmunskij, for example, views content as an aspect
of form, maintaining that the elements of the content do not
have an existence of their own, that is, outside a work's aesthetic
structure.[31]

Shklovsky himself came to regard form as an independent
and dynamic entity, meaningful in itself. In his pamphlet "The
Resurrection of the Word" (1914), he writes: "We do not sense
the familiar, we do not see it, but recognize it. . . . . . . 'artistic
perception is perception in which form is sensed (perhaps not
only form, but form as an essential part)."[32] And five years
later, he states: "*A new form appears not in order to express
a new content, but in order to replace an old form, which has
already lost its artistic value.* . . ."[33]

What these varied formulations indicate is that the formalists could in no case emancipate themselves from the mechanistic
notion of the primacy of form over content, and this fact was
eventually realized even by Shklovsky.[34] This mechanistic
attitude can be partially explained by the complete opposition
of the formalist thinking to realism, and by the formalist's
initial firm separation of art from life and its various aspects,
ideology included. In relation to this we can quote two excerpts
translated by Erlich. The first is from the writings of Shklovsky:
"Art was always free of life, and its color never reflected the
color of the flag which waved over the fortress of the city."
The second is from Roman Jakobson's writings, stating that
"to incriminate the poet with ideas and feelings is just as absurd
as the behavior of the medieval public which beat up the actor
who played Judas."[35]

The property of artistic form to be sensed is attributed
to the employment of special artistic devices by the poet and
which ultimately make the experiencing of form possible. The
use then of these devices becomes the *raison d'etre* of art. In
this sense, a story is introduced in a novel not because it is of
any particular interest to the author or to his readers, but because he wants to use it as an experimental material in order
to apply to it some artistic techniques. In his essay "Art as
Technique" (1917), which is regarded as the manifesto of Russian formalism, Victor Shklovsky writes:

> art . . . exists to make one feel things, to make the stone

stony. The purpose of art is to impart the sensation of things as they are perceived and not as they are known. The technique of art is to make objects 'unfamiliar', to make form difficult, to increase the difficulty and length of perception because the process of perception is an aesthetic end in itself and must be prolonged. *Art is a way of experiencing the artfulness of an object; the object is not important.*[36]

The concepts of *defamiliarization* and *retardation* which emerge from this excerpt reveal the core of the formalist problematic. Defamiliarization, or the 'making strange', is a device counterposed to the principle of artistic economy and consequently to the traditional idea that the poetic image explains the unfamiliar in terms of the familiar. What actually happens, the formalists argue, is exactly the opposite: poetry presents everything, even the most common things, as seen for the first time. The central objective of art, according to Shklovsky, is not the presentation of life and nature by means of realistic images, but their creative distortion through the employment of adequate artistic devices. This theory of defamiliarization, the main idea of which originates in Aristotle,[37] results in the shifting of emphasis from the poetic use of images to the role of poetry itself, and poetry is now defined in terms of its function.

In his perceptive discussion of Russian formalism, Frederic Jameson stresses that the emphasis on defamiliarization has three consequences: First, that it makes the mode of literary expression distinct from other modes of verbal expression. Second, that in a literary work primacy should be given to a renewed, fresh perception, through which the world is seen. And third, that it allows for the perception of literary history not in terms of a unilinear progression but in terms of abrupt discontinuities and ruptures.[38] In this light, the making strange becomes the supreme challenge of the artist, and *innovation* the ultimate artistic end.

Retardation, the slowing down of action, is the other device that counterposes the principle of artistic economy. The duration of aesthetic perception must be prolonged, since, according to Shklovsky, the process of perception is an aesthetic end in itself. This way, those who can 'read' behind the walls of strangeness built by the artist will enjoy more the artfulness of an object and the literariness of a literary text. It is understandable, then, why *device* was the watchword of the formalist vocabulary.

The central role played by the device of retardation is underlined in an essay written by Shklovsky in 1919, which shows the connection between the special devices of plot construction and general stylistic devices.[39]   Shklovsky utilizes numerous examples from the literary tradition of various cultures and maintains that some devices of plot formation, i.e. staircase construction and framing (that is, the practice of introducing a series of narratives each one placed within another), are closely connected to the device of retardation. What Shklovsky wishes to demonstrate above all is that whereas the basic factor in poetry is the poet's ability to manipulate language, literary prose owes its creation to *syuzhet* (plot) which is its main element of construction.   Whereas poetic language is distinguished from practical language, in literary prose the *syuzhet*, that is, the manner by which a story is constructed, is differentiated from the story itself, or subject matter, or the 'materials'.

Erlich observes that the formalists could not agree on the nature of these 'materials'. He points out, however, that some of them i.e. Shklovsky, Zimunskij and Jakobson, accepted that the 'materials' of literature correspond to its verbal structure, its words: the raw stuff by which ideas, emotions, etc. are expressed.   In this sense, for the formalists, the artist is not the mediator between form and content, but between 'materials' and devices.[40]   On the basis of their distinction between poetic and practical language, on the one hand, and literature and non-literature, on the other, *in terms of the structure of language*, the formalists rejected the genetic study of literary phenomena and developed a descriptive-functional approach.[41]

3. Merits and Shortcomings

The contribution of Russian formalism to literary scholarship is undeniable. In the international scene, it participated successfully in the neo-Kantian revolt against positivism, and it opened the way to constructive developments in the structuralist front, initially in Czechoslovakia and Poland,[42] and then in France. Within its national boundaries, Russian formalism discredited symbolist metaphysics and crude sociologism, and by advancing the fruitful ideas of the futurists it laid down the foundations of a scientific approach to literary phenomena.

These impressive achievements, however, fell short of resulting in a comprehensive aesthetics and a complete theory of literature. The most that Russian formalists can be credited with is their input in the rising of a new mode of awareness of literary creation, and their illumination of some of its fundamental aspects. In sum, the focus of the formalists on the internal organization of a literary work and on the functional relationships between its individual parts elevated literary criticism from an often impressionistic undertaking to a coherent scientific endeavor.

The shortcomings of Russian formalism should be first of all viewed within the framework of this movement's historical limitations. This practice is followed by Julia Kristeva who in a sketchy appraisal of the work of the Russian formalists, stresses that they did not go beyond the confines of a "mechanical idealism" because they were not equipped with the insights of Freudian discoveries and modern linguistics, being restricted by the philosophical presuppositions of Husserl and Heidegger. In Kristeva's words, this mechanical idealism is evident in "those numerous attempts to constitute a *poetics* in the form of a discourse with no object, an extra-temporal extra-spatial Logos speaking to itself in an endless creation of models which, being themselves carried over from linguistics or from an elementary system of logic, are then applied without justification. . . ." This way, Kristeva continues, the literary text is reduced to linguistic categories and theories "with no grasp of the individual character of the literary object in the history of modes of meaning, nor of the fact that this treatment disorganizes the 'poetic' discourse, since it is an inventory and a self-trial rather than objective knowledge."[43]

Kristeva maintains also, that the formalists' emphasis on the synchronic study of the internal dynamics of a literary structure was due to their adherence to structural linguistics and to the futurists' emphasis on "the linguistic raw material and the rules for turning it into the 'work of art'."[44] As for the formalists' inability to develop a satisfactory poetics and a theory of literature, Kristeva attributes it to the pressure put on them by the Marxists after the Revolution, and especially by Trotsky who urged that they limit themselves to the linguistic examination of literary works.

The outcome was devastating for the formalist movement because the various linguistic theories and categories preoccupied with the definition of the scientific object, overshadowed the real object of study: "literature as a particular mode of meaning, considered within the domain of the speaker, with his topology, history and ideology." Hence, Kristeva goes on, formalism which started with the purpose of placing emphasis on the literary object itself, "turned out and still turns out to be a discourse on nothing or on something which does not matter."[45]

It is a fact that Russian formalism did not have the opportunity to grow and to further reflect on its problems, even though their presence was felt quite strongly, as indicated for example by the joint Tynjanov-Jakobson statement of 1928, which views the distinction between synchrony and diachrony as a serious fetter to the overall advantages of linguistic analysis:

> The sharp opposition of synchronic (static) and diachronic cross sections has recently become a fruitful working hypothesis, both for linguistics and for the history of literature; this opposition reveals the nature of language (literature) as a system at each individual moment of its existence. At the present time, the achievements of the synchronic concept force us to reconsider the principles of diachrony as well. The idea of the mechanical agglomeration of material, having being replaced by the concept of system or structure in the realm of synchronic study, underwent a corresponding replacement in the realm of diachronic study as well. The history of a system is in turn a system. Pure synchronism now proves to be an illusion: every synchronic system has its past and its future as inseparable structural elements of the system: (a) archaism as a fact of style; the linguistic and literary background recognized as the rejected old-fashioned style; (b) the tendency in language and literature recognized as innovation in the system. The opposition between synchrony and diachrony was an opposition between the concept of system and the concept of evolution; thus it loses its importance in principle as soon as we recognize that every system necessarily exists as an evolution, whereas, on the other hand, evolution is inescapably of a systemic nature.[46]

This warning that more attention should be paid to the socio-historical, philosophical, etc. relations of literature, not by enumerating and classifying its stylistic devices but by adequately analyzing its structure,[47] was proven ineffective. Mere statements could by no means remedy the formalist fallacies. Shklovsky, for example, went so far as to employ the formalist notion of the 'motivation of the device' in order to explain "away the contradictions between Don Quixote's 'madness' and 'wisdom' as a mere technical expedient," and not as a problem with philosophical implications.[48]

In its effort to combat the genetic fallacy of the extrinsic approach, Russian formalism reached the other extreme and it is to the credit of the Prague structuralist circle that it attempted to avoid such one-sided extremism. We can mention the case of Jan Mukarovsky who accepts that a work of literature is a "sign which may indicate the characteristics and the state of society, but it is not an automatic by-product of its structure."[49] In any case, the late sensitivity of some formalist theoreticians about the socio-historical dimension of literature cannot alter the fact that the fundamental attitude of the movement was ahistorical.

On a general level then the partiality of the formalists is manifested in their scandalous neglect of the individual artist, his audience, the surrounding universe, as well as their own relation to the work, being exclusively interested in the latter 'in itself'. Even within their particular field of operation however their limitations are quite serious, one of them being their lack of evaluative standards resulting from their extreme aesthetic *relativism*, maintained by the Prague structuralists as well.[50]

In their criticial studies emphasis is placed on the inventiveness of the artist—regardless of whether he is mediocre, great or bad—and their main criterion of evaluation is often personal judgment. As K. Pomorska points out, the formalists "seem to accept silently the principle announced by Croche: that our evaluation of art is always and necessarily intuitive." Or, "that in every culture artistic phenomena objectively . . . are accepted as such owing to the common background of the criteria created by this culture."[51]

Even such a fruitful concept as that of a defamiliarization, in the framework of Russian formalism, becomes a fetter. Fredric Jameson observes, when he distinguishes between defamiliarization and Brecht's theory of the 'alienation effect' (in simple words, Brecht's artistic strategy to make his audience aware of the dynamic historical changes which a society, its institutions, its values, etc. undergo), that Shklovsky's doctrine of 'making strange' ends up "turning diachrony into mere appearance and undermining any genuine historical awareness of the changing of forms."[52]   As for the notion of "abrupt discontinuities" or "ruptures" in literary history—mentioned earlier as one of the formalist insights—we can agree with István Mészáros who regards it as a "myth that needs dispelling."[53]

Shklovsky's as well as the other formalists' passion for literary devices and against the meaningful content of literary works, reminds us of Flaubert's ultimate wish to write "a book about nothing,"[54] a book which would make style its sole purpose. We can suggest that this 'nothingness' is but the 'something-thingness' of deeply rooted idealist ideology. Hence, Trotsky's severe criticism of the formalist school from his materialist standpoint is well taken:

> Just as Kantian idealism represents historically a translation of Christianity into the language of rationalistic philosophy, so all the varieties of idealist formalization, either openly or secretly, lead to a God, as the cause of all causes. . . . The Formalist school represents an abortive idealism applied to the questions of art. The Formalists show a fast ripening religiousness. They are followers of St. John. They believe that 'In the beginning was the Word'. But we believe that in the beginning was the deed. The word followed, as its phonetic shadow.[55]

NOTES

[1] For the best account in English of Russian formalism, Cf. Victor Erlich, *Russian Formalism: History—Doctrine* (2nd ed.; The Hague; Mouton and Co., 1965).

[2] *Ibid.*, p. 35.

[3] *Ibid.*, p. 36.

[4] *Ibid.*, p. 41.

[5] Quoted in *Ibid.*, p. 44.

[6] Quoted in *Ibid.*, p. 44.

[7] Boris Ejxenbaum, "The Theory of the Formal Method," in L. Matejka and K. Pomorska, eds. *Readings in Russian Poetics: Formalist and Structuralist Views* (Massachusetts: The MIT Press, 1971), pp. 6, 7.

[8] *Ibid.*, p. 19.

[9] *Ibid.*, p. 34.

[10] Quoted in *Ibid.*, p. 8.

[11] Quoted in Erlich, *op. cit.*, p. 90.

[12] Roman Jakobson, "The Dominant," in Matejka and Pomorska, eds., *op. cit.*, p. 85.

[13] *Ibid.*, p. 82.

[14] *Ibid.*, p. 82.

[15] *Ibid.*, p. 84.

[16] *Ibid.*, p. 85.

[17] Richard Sherwood, "Victor Shklovsky and the Development of Early Formalist Theory on Prose Literature," in Stephen Bann and John E. Bowlt, eds. *Russian Formalism, op. cit.*, p. 39.

[18] Quoted in Ejxenbaum, *op. cit.*, p. 9.

[19] Erlich, *op. cit.*, p. 73.

[20] Quoted in Ejxenbaum, *op. cit.*, p. 11.

[21] Cf. Jurij Tynjanov, "Rhythm as the Constructive Factor in Verse," in Matejka and Pomorska, eds., *op. cit.*, pp. 126-135.

[22] Quoted in Erlich, *op. cit.*, p. 213.

[23] Quoted in *Ibid.*, p. 213.

[24] *Ibid.*, p. 218.

[25] *Ibid.*, p. 225.

[26] *Ibid.*, p. 225.

[27] O. M. Brik, "Contributions to the Study of Verse Language," in Matejka and Pomorska, eds., *op. cit.*, p. 125.

[28] Jan Mukarovsky, "Standard Language and Poetic Language," in Adams, ed., *op. cit.*, p. 1051.

[29] *Ibid.*, p. 1053.

[30] Erlich, *op. cit.*, p. 171.

[31] *Ibid.*, p. 187.

[32] Victor Shklovsky, "The Resurrection of the Word," in Bann and Bowlt, eds., *op. cit.*, pp. 41, 42.

[33] Victor Shklovsky, "The Connection Between Devices of Syuzhet Construction and General Stylistic Devices," in Bann and Bowlt, eds., *op. cit.*, p. 53.

[34] Cf. Erlich, *op. cit.*, p. 197.

[35] Both excerpts quoted in *Ibid.*, p. 77.

[36] Victor Shklovsky, "Art as Technique," in Lee T. Lemon and Marion J. Reiss, transl. *Russian Formalist Criticism: Four Essays* (Lincoln: University of Nebraska Press, 1965), p. 12.

[37] Cf. Erlich, *op. cit.*, pp. 178, 179.

[38] Fredric Jameson, *The Prison-House of Language* (Princeton: Princeton University Press, 1972), p. 52.

[39] Shklovsky, "The Connection Between Devices of Syuzhet Construction and General Stylistic Devices," *op. cit.*

[40] Erlich, *op. cit.*, pp. 188, 189.

[41] K. Pomorska, "Russian Formalism in Retrospect," in Matejka and Pomorska, eds., *op. cit.*, pp. 275-276.

[42] Cf. Erlich, *op. cit.*, pp. 154-168.

[43] Julia Kristeva, "The Ruin of a Poetics," in Bann and Bowlt, eds., *op. cit.*, p. 103.

[44] *Ibid.*, p. 103.

[45] *Ibid.*, p. 104.

[46] Jurij Tynjanov and Roman Jakobson, "Problems in the Study of Literature and Language," in Matejka and Pomorska, eds., *op. cit.*, pp. 79-80.

[47] Cf. *Ibid.*, p. 79.

[48] Erlich, *op. cit.*, p. 197.

[49] Quoted in *Ibid.*, p. 209.

[50] Cf. *Ibid.*, pp. 279-290.

[51] K. Pomorska, *op. cit.*, p. 275.

[52] Jameson, *The Prison-House of Language, op. cit.*, p. 59.

[53] István Mészáros, "From 'The Legend of Truth' to a 'True Legend': Phases of Sartre's Development," *Telos*, no. 25 (Fall, 1975), p. 116.

[54] Gustave Flaubert, "On Realism," in George J. Becker, ed., *Documents of Modern Literary Realism* (Princeton: Princeton University Press, 1963), p. 90. Despite Flaubert's wish, even a book just on style and about 'nothing' could not possibly be devoid of significant meaning. It seems that style and meaning are inseparable from each other. Cf., for example, Stephan Ullman, *Meaning and Style* (New York: Barnes and Noble, 1973).

[55] Leon Trotsky, *Literature and Revolution*, transl. by Rose Strunsky (Ann Arbor: The University of Michigan Press, 1971), p. 183.

SEVEN

RANSOM: THE PHILOSOPHER OF AMERICAN NEW CRITICISM

The term 'new criticism' was introduced by John Crowe Ransom in 1941 to characterize the work of a group of literary critics which manifested "some unity of method."[1] Eight years later, Mark Schorer writes in *The Hudson Review:*

> Modern criticism, through its exacting scrutiny of literary texts, has demonstrated with finality that in art beauty and truth are indivisible and one. . . . Modern criticism has shown us that to speak of content as such is not to speak of art at all, but of experience, and that it is only when we speak of the achieved content, the form, the work of art as a work of art, that we speak as critics. The difference between content, or experience, and achieved content, or art, is technique. When we speak of technique, then, we speak of nearly everything. For technique is the means by which the writer's experience, which is his subject matter, compels him to attend to it; technique is the only means he has of discovering, exploring, developing his subject, of conveying its meaning, and finally, of evaluating it.[2]

Schorer was scolded for his absolutism by Cleanth Brooks— an eminent new critic himself—who, nevertheless, referring to this particular excerpt, states: "I subscribe to all that is said here. It is an admirable summary of what modern criticism has achieved."[3]

We can suggest that the case of American new criticism is much more complicated than Schorer's description and Brooks' approval of it seem to imply, for three fundamental reasons: first, the foundations of this criticism are diverse and often in conflict; second, the points of disagreement among the major representatives of new criticism are so numerous that the uniform classification of these critics into a general category would necessarily have to omit the elements that divide them, those which constitute their individual particularity; and third, the viewpoints of new criticism evolved with time and circumstances and certain changes brought about significant qualitative transformations.

To avoid a possible mispresentation of this movement then we propose the following procedure: first, to present its origins from the most distant in time to the nearest; second, to focus on the work of John Crowe Ransom, who set the path for the whole movement, shaping its dominant tendencies and initiating its successive steps; and third, after pinpointing those features that were more or less shared by its main spokesmen, to conclude with some critical comments.

1. *Origins and Influences*

Cleanth Brooks, regards new criticism as a response to an increasing dissatisfaction with the Victorian insistence on the moral, social, political and religious significance of literary works, as well as to the insufficient linguistic education that the educational institutions offered to American youth.[4] Hence, Brooks claims that "The rise of modern criticism is part of a general intensification of the study of language and symbolism."[5]

In effect, the roots of new criticism go back to romanticism and symbolism. On one level, new criticism was a reaction against the romantic mystification of the artist which culminated in its doctrine of the *impersonality* of artistic creation. On another level, new criticism represents an "inversion" of romanticism's relation to its surrounding socio-historical reality: "In relation to the dominant social forms, the structural reality at the heart of romanticism was tension, negation; at the heart of modern critical theory, it is identification, affirmation."[6] The relationship between romanticism and new criticism has a positive side too: they both glorify *tradition*, raising it to the status of an authority and an objective ideal.

Symbolism is the other important source of origin of new criticism, having influenced the latter in a positive way, particularly through its French representatives, i.e. Baudelaire, Laforgue, Mallarmé, Verlaine, and Rimbaud. The symbolist passionate search for a poetic language bequeathed to the new critics such a concern with poetic expression that language came to be regarded as an autonomous and self-important entity. This fetishisation of language was extended to the literary text itself. In addition, new criticism is negatively related to impressionistic criticism to which is counterposed a rigid methodologism, as well as to the new humanism of Irving Babbitt and Paul Elmer More, which, even though anti-romantic, was found by the new critics "to be narrow and reductive, usually because of its emphasis on ethical content and external canons of judgment."[7]

To the new humanism of Babbitt and More the new critics counterposed the idea that both the morality and value of a literary work are related only to its intrinsic qualities. The reaction however of new criticism to romanticism, symbolism, impressionism and new humanism was not direct, in a chronological and philosophical/theoretical sense, but largely mediated by the ideas of three individuals: T. E. Hulme, T. S. Eliot, and I. A. Richards.

T. E. Hulme had a real abhorence for romanticism which he regarded as no less than a sickness. In his famous essay "Romanticism and Classicism," he announces the death of romanticism and the revival of classicism: "I want to maintain that after a hundred years of romanticism, we are in for a classical revival. . . ."[8] In essence, Hulme rejects "The view which regards man as a well, a reservoir full of possibilities," and he adopts the view which sees man "as a very finite and fixed creature."[9] He also distinguishes between "communal" language for everyday use and poetic language which alone can produce "dry, hard, classical verse."[10] What should be emphasized however is that ultimately Hulme dismisses the romantic view that man is good by nature and he adheres to an anthropology which professes that man "is intrinsically limited, but disciplined by order and tradition to something fairly decent."[11]

The principal source of origin of the new criticism's stress on language was the symbolist problematic, subsequently filtered and modified by T. S. Eliot[12] and I. A. Richards, who above all created the framework within which the new criticism developed. Ransom declares: "Discussion of the new criticism must start with Mr. Richards. The new criticism very nearly

began with him."[13]   It seems, though, that what marked deeply
the path which the new criticism was to follow was before
anything else Eliot's seminal essay "Tradition and the Individual
Talent" (1917), published much earlier than Richards' *Principles
of Literary Criticism* (1924).

Eliot's essay is a strong attack against the romanticist
idea of the *originality* of a poem being primarily the creative
outcome of the poet's *personality*. The poet, Eliot maintains,
is simply a medium that mediates between the work of the
dead poets and his own poetry, between the artistic richness
of the past and the artistic activity of his present, between
tradition and his *individual talent*, but after he has acquired
an historical consciousness and has learned "by great labor"
everything that tradition has to teach him.[14]   And unlike the
Russian formalists, for example, Eliot argues that a poet's significance does not lie in his "difference from his predecessors," but
on the contrary in "his relation to the dead poets and artists,"[15]
therefore, his work should be judged by comparison to the poetic
achievements of the past, that is, "by the standards of the
past."[16]

For Eliot, then, the poet "lives in what is not merely
the present, but the present moment of the past,"[17] by virtue
of his historical consciousness which appears to be blind to the
future. The necessary condition for the development of this
kind of consciousness by the poet is a "continual self-sacrifice,
a continual extinction of personality;" the successful graduation
of the poet from this depersonalization process will qualify his
art "to approach the condition of science,"[18] namely, scientific
neutrality. Eliot's theory of the *impersonality of poetry* aims
at two targets which are historically conditioned: first, to dis-
qualify the personality cult of the romantics; and second, to
shift emphasis from "the poet to the poetry," which, from his
perspective, "is a laudable aim."[19]

Poetry for Eliot is a double escape: "an escape from emotion" and "an escape from personality."[20]   It should be made
clear however that this escape takes place primarily on the
level of form and not of content, and it is an escape only to
the extent that the former affects the latter. This can be sub-
stantiated by the fact that Eliot does not oppose the expression
of emotion through poetry; he just tries to determine its mode
of presentation. He suggests that the "only way of expressing
emotion in the form of art" is by the use of an *objective cor-*

relative, which he vaguely defines as "a set of objects, a situation, a chain of events which shall be the formula of that *particular* emotion."[21]

In the light of his perception of poetry as impersonal, and of tradition as a supreme value, we can see that the desired function of an objective correlative is that of a technical device aiming at the presentation of a poem as completely objective, preferably as a scientific proposition, that is, as a non-poem. This tension in Eliot's thinking can be attributed to his philosophical and theoretical limitations: his inability to view reality not as consisting of pairs of opposites, i.e. subjective emotion/personality vs. poetic objectivity/impersonality, but in terms of the complex dialectical interrelationships of its elements which interpenetrate and interact with one another.

Eliot deals again with the problem of emotion and feeling in poetry but from a different angle, expressing it with his influential term *dissociation of sensibility*. This term marks the difference between an intellectual and a reflective poet, and it was meant to underline the former's inability to "devour any kind of experience," as, according to Eliot, the examples of Milton and Dryden indicate. In their poetry, "while the language became more refined the feeling became more crude."[22] Of course, Eliot eventually admitted the inadequacy of this concept to account for such a complicated problem as the change of aesthetic expression preconditioned by changes of a cultural, intellectual, psychological, etc., order. However, when Eliot began to have second thoughts about this concept, it had already become "a fixed star in the constellation of modern theory."[23]

Besides romanticism, Eliot had another target: impressionism and the literary criticism which stemmed from it. Impressionistic criticism is interested exclusively in the individual responses and sensitiveness, while its only ambition is to present, in Anatole France's famous formulation, "the adventures of the soul among the masterpieces." In Eliot's anti-impressionistic point of view, literary criticism, like poetry, should attain the status of an objective fact by liberating itself totally from emotion. Consequently, he rejects the impressionistic critic to whom he counterposes the 'perfect critic', that is, an emotionless critic: "A literary critic should have no emotions except those immediately provoked by a work of art—and these . . . are, when valid, perhaps not to be called emotions at all."[24] It is hoped that such a critic will reach something outside of himself, something "which may provisionally be called truth."[25]

This approach to poetry should be undertaken on the basis of the critic's focus on language, the medium by which poetry is expressed. Eliot's position on this matter is crystal clear. For example, in the preface to the 1928 edition of *The Sacred Wood*, he states: "In criticizing poetry, we are right if we begin, . . . with poetry as excellent words in excellent arrangement and excellent metre."[26]   Given that Eliot views literary criticism as an aesthetic legislator of society, its foremost function being "the elucidation of works of art and the correction of taste,"[27] this function is further extended to be the guardian of poetic language. As we shall see shortly, however, it was I. A. Richards who pushed to the extreme the emphasis on language.

Eliot's influence on new criticism stems from his insistence on "the integrity of poetry," and his consideration of it first of all "as poetry and not another thing."[28]   Richards' own influence on the new critics derives from a similar stand towards poetry. In an overall assessment of his contribution to new criticism, Cleanth Brooks states: "The net effect of his criticism has been to emphasize the need of a more careful reading of poetry and to regard the poem as an organic thing."[29]

Richards was a psychologist and semanticist, and we can distinguish two phases of his interest for poetry: one psychological, the other predominantly philosophical starting at the time of his *Coleridge on Imagination* (1934); the first, perceives of poetry as emotion; the second, as a kind of knowledge. During the long phase of his psychological perspective on poetry, he considers the poem as located in the reader's response to it: in the experience that it stimulates. In this view, the value of a poem is determined by the reader's right response to it.

This approach, however, created insoluble problems in respect to the actual study of the structure of the reader's experience, to the variety of experiences generated in different readers, etc. Therefore, it was rejected by the new critics as inadequate. Ramson, for example, notices that for Richards, "the real values of art are not cognitions at all, but the affective states which art induces and expresses," and he rejects the British psychologist's attempt to subordinate "the cognitive element in the experience to the emotive, and the emotive to the conative."[30]

Notwithstanding the inacceptability of his psychological criticism, Richards' influence on new criticism was immense, as already mentioned. It starts with his stress on the poetic use of words. In *Poetries and Sciences* (1926), he writes: "The chief characteristic of poets is their amazing command of words. . . . It is not the quantity of words a writer has at his disposal but the way in which he disposes of them that gives him his rank as a poet."[31]   But the ultimate significance of this book for the new critics derives from its extraordinary emphasis on the role of poetry, as well as from Richards' general philosophical view of the state of the world after the changing status of science and religion.

In short, Richards refers to the crisis of the world as originating, on the one hand, in the declining authority of religion and of the magical view of the world that comes with it, and on the other, in the ascent of science which is unable to explain "the nature of things in any *ultimate* sense. It can never answer any question of the form: *What* is so and so? It can only tell us *how* such and such behaves."[32]   Richards claims that science's inability to "tell us what we are or what this world is," has resulted in "a biological crisis," and since neither religion nor philosophy can help us any more, we should confront it by ourselves and "decide for ourselves, partly by thinking, partly by reorganizing our minds in other ways."[33]

The gap created by religion and science, he goes on, can only be filled up by poetry which can play a therapeutic role: "Our protection, . . . is in poetry. It is capable of saving us from confusion and frustration. The poetic function is the source, and the tradition of poetry is the guardian, of the supra-scientific myths."[34]   Subsequently, he distinguishes between scientific *statements* and poetic *pseudostatements*, their main difference consisting in their particular relation to verification.[35] Yet, however different, both kinds of statements are necessary, even though the significance of poetic pseudostatements vs. scientific statements for the very life of humans is overemphasized. In this sense, the scientific function is separated from the poetic, and eventually the latter is further separated from the function of any other kind of linguistic communication. Richards states: "It is the privilege of poetry to preserve us from mistaking our notions either for things or for ourselves. Poetry is the completest mode of utterance."[36]

Richards' interest in language is great, specifically the

workings of language on the human mind, regarding the latter primarily as an "instrument for communication," and the arts, "the supreme form of the communicative activity." Therefore, in his *Principles of Literary Criticism* (1924), he defines the double basis of literary criticism as "an account of value and an account of communication."[37]   Moreover, in his *Practical Criticism* (1929), he insists on the supremacy of that side of literary criticism which is concerned with communication.

This book was written during his strong commitment to psychology, and it emphasizes that the essential thing for literary criticism is to reveal "perfectly, the experience, the *mental condition* relevant to the poem;" as for valuation, it is a question which "nearly always settles itself; or rather, our own inmost nature and the nature of the world in which we live decide it for us."[38]   The main contribution of *Practical Criticism* for the new critics, however, was its being a demonstration itself of the close analysis of a number of poems. In addition, it calls for the systematic study of language which should be the fundamental task of literary criticism as it explores its poetic manifestations. In *Coleridge on Imagination*, Richards maintains that literary criticism must "recall that poetry is the supreme use of language, man's chief co-ordinating instrument, . . . and to explore, with thoroughness, the intricacies of the modes of language as working modes of the mind."[39]

2. *The Input of John Crowe Ransom*

Richards' ideas on religion, science and poetry, as well as on textual analysis and the study of language, reoccur in different formulations in many new critical writings. American new criticism underwent three distinct phases—the *fugitive*, the *agrarian* and the *new critical*—in all of which Ransom, the philosopher of the movement, played the leading role.

The fugitive phase, which marks the beginning of new criticism, developed by a group of poets in Nashville, Tennessee, between 1922-1926. Besides Ransom, one might include among its members Allen Tate, Robert Penn Warren and the latecomer Cleanth Brooks. The group acquired its name from the magazine it was publishing for four years, *The Fugitive* (1922-1926), and it soon attracted the interest of many American scholars, poets and writers, most of whom contributed to what is called the "Southern Literary Renaissance."[40] The principal characteristic of the fugitives was their feeling of alienation from the way of life of the Old and the New South, and they can be defined by their "concern with metaphysics, with poetic production, with literary criticism, and with their location in the South in a period whose driving impulse was 'progress'."[41]

Ransom's first book, *God Without Thunder* (1930), reflects the conception of man's place in the contemporary world of the fugitives and the agrarians (the movement which the fugitives evolved into). Religion and science were the dominant themes colored by the historical reality of the twenties. The purpose of this book was "to explain . . . , the function of myths in human civilization,"[42] and it takes the form of a passionate attack against modern life in America's advanced industrial society. One of its concrete targets was the practice of modern Christianity, protestant rationality in particular, which demystified myths and made them look like lies, abandoning man to the mercy of the limited scientific explanation of the world.

God Without Thunder, expresses a deep disillusionment with and disgust for production, consumerism, alienation from nature and the soil, instrumental reason, etc. Industrialism and the reason on which it is based, Ransom claims, condemns man "to live a life more animal than that of animals,"[43] and he counterposes an "esthetic theory of life," that is, both a critique and negation of "industrial progresss" and its reason, the key term of this theory being *sensibility*.

Concretely, in contrast to industrialism, the fixed aim of which is the increase of production and the maximization of productivity, that is, in contrast to capitalist rationalization, Ransom advocates an aesthetic attitude towards life based on Kant's concept of "desirelessness." He refers to this aesthetic attitude as "the most objective and the most innocent attitude in which we can look upon the world, and it is possible only when we neither desire the world nor pretend to control it."[44] Ransom seems to be convinced that industrialism and its theory of life will be defeated after this attitude is adopted. He states: "In order to be human, we have to have something which will stop action, and this something cannot possibly be reason in its narrow sense, I would call it sensibility."[45]

Ransom even has a distinct economic theory, which, while

allowing for the production of those goods that will be considered necessary, will not seek to dehumanize labor. This theory demands no less than a return to an agricultural mode of production and it sets the foundation of agrarianism. He writes: "All labor should be effective without being arduous; and with that general proviso the best labor is the one which provides the best field for the exercise of sensibility—it is clearly some form of pastoral or agrarian labor. . . . In agrarian societies. . ., agriculture was not necessarily the only labor, but agriculture was the most respected of the forms of labor, and its example affected all the other forms."[46]

While the agrarian phase of new criticism was under way, a shift in emphasis was taking place: from the isolationist position of the fugitives, to the admiration of the way of life of the Old South, that is, to the adoption of a clear traditionalist view by the agrarians. The publication of *I'll Take My Stand: The South and the Agrarian Tradition* (1930), a collection of articles written by twelve southerners—among them Ransom—announced the agrarian standpoint, amounting to a demand for the abolition of industrialism and the adoption of agriculture as the main mode of material production. In the introduction of this book, the agrarians go as far as to criticize the "Communist menace" not as a "Red one" but as a bad example for America which is forced to compete with the Soviet Union for industrial development.[47] In all, in their hate of industrialism the agrarians turned to "the plantation culture of the old South,"[48] in sweet nostalgia, that is, to the culture which was based on slavery. In *I'll Take My Stand: The South and the Agrarian Tradition*, Ransom writes: "Slavery was a feature monstrous enough in theory, but, more often than not, humane in practice."[49]

The utterly reactionary agrarian theory was of course never tested in practice. What was severely tested during the thirties, however, was the American economy as a whole. The administration's response to the depression was more and better rationalization, and this development, on the level of practice, might have something to do with a new change that occured in Ransom's perception of reality. Thus, in his new book, *The World's Body* (1938), he attacks science again but from an artistic angle instead of a religious one. Ransom's *The World's Body,* presents his ideas on poetry and literary criticism, while with the last essay of this book, namely, "Criticism, Inc.," the third phase of new criticism really commences.

To begin with, Ransom wishes to establish art as science,[50] and like all new critics he emphasizes the cognitive function of art, stressing that poetry provides us with true knowledge of objects in their entirety, in contradistinction to the compartmentalized knowledge that science offers. He also deals with the problem of poetic form, urging the poet to pay special attention to it: "Given an object, and a poet burning to utter himself upon it, he must take into account a third item, the form into which he must cast his utterance. (If we like, we may call it the body which he must give to his passion)."[51] The point to be made is that whereas Russian formalism views form as a revolutionary element in the hands of the poet, Ransom regards it as a conservative device. In his formulation: "The aesthetic forms are a technique of restraint. . . . They stand between the individual and his natural object and impose a check upon his action."[52]

Ransom's "Criticism, Inc.," is largely an attempt toward the application of capitalist scientific rationalization for an approach to literature, which should thus acquire a status of its own, i.e. as a distinct scientific activity. He is unsatisfied with both the poet-critic and the philosopher-critic, and he turns to university professors—that is, to the professionals of the establishment—and asks them to make literary criticism their business. He argues in the following way: "Criticism must become more scientific, or precise and systematic, and this means that it must be developed by the collective and sustained effort of learned persons—which means that its proper seat is in the universities. . . . I should think the whole enterprise might be seriously taken in hand by professionals. Perhaps I use a distasteful figure, but I have the idea that what we need is Criticism Inc., or Criticism Ltd."[53]

Evidently, the adoption of what the fugitive and agrarian Ransom rejected, namely, capitalist reason and even the very terminology of the business world, is complete and striking. The *new critic* Ransom is after a rationalized and wholly *aesthetic* criticism which he understands as "the attempt to define and enjoy the aesthetic or characteristic values of literature."[54] In effect, what Ransom leads to is an intrinsic criticism, which by the close analysis of a work's structure will reveal its artistic properties. In this framework, he accuses the English department of American universities that even though it "is charged with the understanding and the communication of literature, an art, yet it has usually forgotten to inquire into the peculiar constitution and structure of its product."[55]

What Ransom demands of literary criticism is: a) to be objective and "cite the nature of the object rather than its effects upon the subject;"[56] b) to exclude synopsis and paraphrase; c) to leave out matters of an historical interest, e.g. an account of the socio-historical environment, the artist's biography, etc.; d) to avoid engaging in linguistic puzzles, e.g. the meaning of uncommon, foreign or archaic words, because "Acquaintance with all the languages and literatures in the world would not necessarily produce a critic;"[57] to distinguish morality from criticism, and e) to disregard some special studies, e.g. legal, biological, etc., which might somehow be related to a text. And, Ransom concludes that the scientific literary criticism he envisages should also take into account the following:

> Studies in the technique of art belong to criticism certainly. They cannot belong anywhere else, because the technique is not peculiar to any prose materials discoverable in the work of art, nor to anything else but the unique form of that art. A very large volume of studies is indicated by this classification. They would be technical studies of poetry, for instance, the art I am specifically discussing, if they treated its metric; its inversions, solecisms, lapses from the prose norm of language, and from close prose logic; its tropes; its fictions, or inventions, by which it secures "aesthetic distance" and removes itself from history; or any other device. . . . Poetry distinguishes itself from prose on the technical side by the devices which are, precisely, its means of escaping from prose. . . . The critic should regard the poem as nothing short of a desperate ontological or metaphysical maneuver.[58]

According to Ransom, the chief elements of a poem are its *structure*, i.e. the idea on which it is based, or "the prose of the poem," and its *texture*, i.e. the image that is created by the poet as he contemplates the idea; the texture can "be of any real content that may be come upon." Consequently, "it is an *order* of content, rather than a *kind* of content, that distinguishes texture from structure, and poetry from prose."[59]

In a poem, the texture always dominates the structure, there-fore, it is *the* element to which the critic must pay very close attention and approach it as an ontological entity that cannot be accounted for scientifically.

These ideas are developed in *The New Criticism* (1941) in which Ransom lays down the foundations for an ontological criticism based on the sharp differentiation of structure from texture. He states: "The differentia of poetry as discourse is an ontological one. It treats an order of existence, a grade of objectivity, which cannot be treated in scientific discourse."[60] His unqualified stress on the aesthetic study of a poem's texture, however, contributed to an analytical fever among the new critics at the expense of any attempts towards a subsequent synthesis on the level of structure. Thus, subscribing to Ransom's general guidelines for an *ontological* approach, that is, a criticism that will treat a poem as an autonomous entity, independent from both the poet and its surrounding socio-historical environ-ment, the new critics more or less disregard their numerous differences and agree to look upon poetry as poetry and to exclude and fight all ideas associated with the extrinsic ap-proaches to literature, especially the Marxist, notwithstanding the latter's very weak presence in the American literary scholar-ship of the 1930's and the 1940's.

Cleanth Brooks, for example, in his *The Well-Wrought Urn*, examines a number of poems belonging to different his-torical periods, feeling "anxious to see what residuum, if any, is left after we have referred the poem to its cultural matrix."[61] Brooks' main target is what he refers to as the relativistic temper of our time, and he sets forth to investigate "whether a poem represents anything more universal than the expression of the particular values of its time."[62] This question Brooks pro-poses to approach "by making the closest possible examination of what the poem says as a poem."[63] In the course of his study, he attacks forcefully the heresy of paraphrase. At a certain point he criticizes the practice of Y. Winters[64] and states: "The 'prose-sense' of the poem is not a rank on which the stuff of the poem is hung; . . . it does not represent the 'inner' struc-ture or the 'essential' structure or the 'real' structure of the poem. . . . We must not mistake [statements about what a poem says] for the internal and essential structure of the building itself."[65]

What this position implies is the possibility for some absolute standards of literary evaluation in contrast to the critical relativism of the Russian formalists.   The exclusion of any extrinsic considerations, however, was fully endorsed by Robert Penn Warren and acceptable only with qualifications by Allen Tate[66] and Ransom in his late phase.

The preoccupation with an intrinsic criticism resulted in a kind of reaction against this exclusively technical study of poetry which, after debates and transformations within the camp of new criticism, culminated in the acceptance, at least by some new critics, of the partial consideration of extra-literary elements related to a poem's idea.   Ransom is again in the vanguard of this transition. Writing about Richard Blackmur's *Language as Gesture* (1953), he declares:

> I do not know what is meant nowadays by a "new critic," and I will not call him* that; I will call him a close critic, or an intensive one, by all means a linguistic one. . . . But it is remarkable how technical all his studies are; the poems are examined along linguistic lines, strategical lines; whatever may be the gravity of the content. There is no ideological emphasis; the social or religious ideas are looked at shrewdly, but they are appraised for their function within the work; even though they may be ideas from which, at the very moment, out in the world of action, the issues of life and death are hung.[67]

This approval of Blackmur's critical practice is in essence Ransom's self-criticism, yet it could not possibly have any real repercussions.   The hayday of new criticism had already passed and its mark on American literary history identifies it as a movement that fought for the scientific analysis of poems as poems: for a highly technical, intrinsic literary criticism.

3. *An Overview of American New Criticism*

A systematic assessment of the American new criticism in

---

*Ransom refers to Blackmur

terms of its epistemological and philosophical principles, its diverse and often vaguely defined concepts and propositions as well as its changes of orientation, would have met innumerable obstacles and would require a full-length study. On the one hand, there are so many variations in intellectual tools, ideas and emphasis among the new critics that their detailed elaboration would keep us away from our specific objective; and on the other, the new critics have not offered any distinct theory on the basis of which they could be scrutinized.

What seems to unite the new critics is their common American heritage and their stand against certain literary doctrines. Moreover, like Kant, they believed that the knowledge one can acquire through a poetic work cannot be achieved by the assistance of science. Actually, their philosophical debt to Kant is sometimes openly acknowledged,[68] and the connection between new criticism and Kantian thought is discussed in specific studies.[69] The American new critics are rightly characterized as 'formalists' because they are profoundly interested in the form and techniques of poetic works. It is due to this perspective that they examine a poem, 'reading' it as closely as possible. In all, as W. Handy states, what they all have in common is the conviction that *"The specific symbolic formulation of language which characterizes the literary work is unique in its ability to represent a part of man's experience that cannot be represented adequately by the abstractions of logic."*[70]

The contribution of new criticism to American literary studies is paramount for three reasons: first, it infused American literary scholarship with a dynamism unprecedented in the history of the country; second, it alone placed emphasis on poems as singular artistic achievements, ontologically autonomous; finally, it discredited those approaches to literature that are crudely concerned with historical, moral, sociological, etc. factors. In short, new criticism gave to America the best this country could expect to produce in the area of literary criticism during that particular period of time, given its limited national intellectual tradition and its historical specificity.

On the debit side, the list could be much longer, boiling down to two major shortcomings of the new criticism: first, its lack of a comprehensive theory, as already pointed out, and second, its turning to the other extreme than that which it undertook to combat. From a general viewpoint then, as far as its formalism is concerned, American new criticism could be reproached for those limitations that were criticized in respect to Russian formalism. The almost exclusive concern with poetry, which is a common characteristic of both formalist movements, must have something to do with their oversensitivity to matters pertaining to form. The 'organistic' approach to poetry of such eminent critics as Cleanth Brooks[71] and Robert Penn Warren resembles the formalist-structuralist methodology, developed by Russian formalism and Prague structuralism, whereas the influence of functionalism (i.e. Malinowski) on the new critical practice seems to be a fact.[72]

Unlike the Russian formalists, however, who were anti-establishment and anti-authoritarian, many new critics were reactionary intellectuals who mixed their critical practice with philosophical, political, economic, etc. statements that were often theoretically unsound. The most important new critics believed in the supreme mission of religion in the world,[73] and their ideas were channeled through *The American Review* (1933-1937), which was supported by the agrarians and by such groups as the "Distributionists," the "Neoscholastics," etc. Some well-known names in American letters—among them T. S. Eliot—were members of these groups and they also contributed to *The American Review*.[74]   Moreover, viewing reality mostly from the context of the American South many new critics believed in the unique power of private property, which they regarded as the indisputable basis of the social order.

Unlike the Russian formalists, these American formalists had both the time and the adequate means (i.e. magazines, part of the American Academic establishment, etc.) to develop fully their ideas and consequently to exhaust their potential. Today, there is hardly mention of them outside the United States, as lately the interest of the literary world is focused on some other 'new critics,' in France, who despite basic differences with their American counterparts also share a passion for the distinctly literary and for the close study of language.

For some of the Russian formalists the watchword was *innovation*; for some of the American new critics, it was *tradition*; but for the French new critics—the structuralists—*structure* is the keynote as we shall see in the next chapter.

NOTES

[1] John Crowe Ransom, *The New Criticism* (Norfolk, Conneticut: New Directions, 1941), p. x.

[2] Quoted in Cleanth Brooks, "Modern Criticism," in Clarence A. Brown, ed., *The Achievement of American Criticism* (New York: The Roland Press Company, 1954), p. 678.

[3] *Ibid.*, p. 678.

[4] *Ibid.*, p. 681.

[5] *Ibid.*, p. 682.

[6] John Fekete, *The Critical Twilight* (London: Routledge and Kegan Paul, 1978), p. 3.

[7] Adams, ed., *op. cit.*, p. 791.

[8] T. E. Hulme, "Romanticism and Classicism," in *Ibid.*, p. 767.

[9] *Ibid.*, p. 768.

[10] *Ibid.*, p. 772.

[11] *Ibid.*, p. 768.

[12] The influence of symbolism on Eliot is admitted by him as he comments on Arthur Symons', *Studies in Elizabethan Drama*. He writes: "if we can recall the time when we were ignorant of the French symbolists, and met with *The Symbolist Movement in Literature*, we remember that book (Symon's book) as an introduction to wholly new feelings, as a revelation. After we have read Verlaine and Laforgue and Rimbaud and return to Mr. Symons' book, we may find that our own impressions dissent from him." (T. S. Eliot, "The Perfect Critic," in *The Sacred Wood* (London: Methuen & Co. Ltd., 1964), p. 5.)

[13] Ransom, *The New Criticism, op. cit.*, p. 31.

[14] T. S. Eliot, "Tradition and the Individual Talent," in *Selected Essays* (New York: Harcourt, Brace and Company, 1950), p. 4.

[15] *Ibid.*

[16] *Ibid.*, p. 51.

[17] *Ibid.*, p. 11.

[18] *Ibid.*, p. 7.

[19] *Ibid.*, p. 11.

[20] *Ibid.*, p. 10.

[21] T. S. Eliot, "Hamlet," in *Ibid.*, pp. 124-125.

[22] T. S. Eliot, "The Metaphysical Poets," in *Ibid.*, p. 247.

[23] Fekete, *op. cit.*, p. 24.

[24] T. S. Eliot, "The Perfect Critic," *op. cit.*, p. 12.

[25] T. S. Eliot, "The Function of Criticism," in *Selected Essays, op. cit.*, p. 22.

[26] T. S. Eliot, *The Sacred Wood, op. cit.*, p. ix.

[27] T. S. Eliot, "The Function of Criticism," *op. cit.*, p. 12.

[28] T. S. Eliot, *The Sacred Wood, op. cit.*, p. viii.

[29] Cleanth Brooks, *The Well-Wrought Urn* (London: Dennis Debson, 1968), p. 60.

[30] Ransom, *The New Criticism, op. cit.*, pp. 12, 15.

[31] I. A. Richards, *Poetries and Sciences* (London: Routledge and Kegan Paul, 1970), p. 43.

[32] *Ibid.*, p. 54.

[33] *Ibid.*, pp. 55-56.

[34] *Ibid.*, p. 78.

[35] *Ibid.*, p. 60.

[36] I. A. Richards, *Coleridge on Imagination* (3rd ed.; London: Routledge and Kegan Paul Ltd., 1962), p. 163.

[37] I. A. Richards, *Principles of Literary Criticism* (4th ed.; London: Kegan Paul, Trench, Trubner and Co. LTD., 1930), pp. 25, 26.

[38] I. A. Richards, *Practical Criticism* (New York: Harcourt, Brace and Company, 1964), p. 10.

[39] I. A. Richards, *Coleridge on Imagination, op. cit.*, p. 230.

[40] John M. Bradbury, *The Fugitives: A Critical Account* (Chapel Hill: The University of North Carolina Press, 1958), p. 3.

[41] Fekete, *op. cit.*, p. 57.

[42] John Crowe Ransom, *God Without Thunder: An Unorthodox Defense of Orthodoxy* (Hamden, Connecticut: Archon Books, 1965), p. x.

[43] *Ibid.*, p. 188.

[44] *Ibid.*, p. 173.

[45] *Ibid.*, p. 190.

[46] *Ibid.*, pp. 193, 194.

[47] *I'll Take My Stand: The South and the Agrarian Tradition*, by Twelve Southerners (New York, 1930), pp. xiii-xiv.

[48] Walter Sutton, *Modern American Criticism* (New Jersey: Prentice-Hall, Inc., 1963), p. 109.

[49] *I'll Take My Stand: The South and the Agrarian Tradition, op. cit.*, p. 14.

[50] John Crowe Ransom, *The World's Body* (Port Washington, N.Y.: Kennikat Press, Inc., 1964), p. 53.

[51] *Ibid.*, p. 40.

[52] *Ibid.*, p. 31.

[53] *Ibid.*, p. 329.

[54] *Ibid.*, p. 332.

[55] *Ibid.*, p. 335.

[56] *Ibid.*, p. 342.

[57] *Ibid.*, p. 34.

[58] *Ibid.*, pp. 346-347.

[59] John Crowe Ransom, *The New Criticism, op. cit.*, pp. 280-281.

[60] *Ibid.*, p. 281.

[61] Cleanth Brooks, *The Well-Wrought Urn, op. cit.*, p. vi.

[62] *Ibid.*, p. vi.

[63] *Ibid.*, p. vii.

[64] *Ibid.*, p. 163-164.

[65] *Ibid.*, p. 162.

[66] Cf. for example, Allen Tate, "Literature as Knowledge" in *Essays of Four Decades* (Chicago: The Shallow Press, Inc., 1968), pp. 72-105.

[67] John Crowe Ransom, *Poems and Essays* (New York: Vintage Books, 1955), pp. 103, 104.

[68] *Ibid.*, p. 159.

[69] Cf. William J. Handy, *Kant and the Southern New Critics* (Austin: University of Texas Press, 1963)

[70] *Ibid.*, p. 8.

[71] Cleanth Brooks, *The Well-Wrought Urn, op. cit.*, p. 163.

[72] Cf. Fekete, *op. cit.*, p. 35.

[73] Sutton, *op. cit.*, p. 110. The new critics were not members of the same church. For example, J. C. Ransom was a Greek Orthodox, A. Tate a Catholic and T. S. Eliot an Anglican.

[74] *Ibid.*, pp. 109-110.

EIGHT

BARTHES: THE CROWN PRINCE OF FRENCH STRUCTURALISM

1. *Kantian and Linguistic Basis*

Kant's influence on the establishment of aesthetics as a distinct discipline is indisputable.[1] His distinction between aesthetic judgments concerned with the *beautiful* and aesthetic judgments concerned with the *sublime*[2] —originating in Edmund Burke's *Philosophical Inquiry into the Origin of our Ideas of the Sublime and Beautiful*—is, according to Hegel, interesting "despite all prolixity and the premised reduction of all categories to something subjective, to the powers of mind, imagination, reason, etc."[3]

Hegel himself, of course, uses Kant's distinction in order to propound the power of the mind to grasp sublimity, that is, the infinite. But for our purposes here, it is enough to stress the "reduction to subjective," which the first part of Kant's *Critique of Judgment* makes explicit. Indeed, his initial differentiation between "judgment of taste" and "cognitive judgment"[4] makes it clear that aesthetic judgments are only to be understood subjectively with the use of the imagination. Aesthetic judgments, however, should be distinguished from feelings of pain and pleasure. Both aesthetic judgments and these feelings are subjective; yet, while the first are universal and *disinterested*,[5] the latter are purely personal.

The cornerstones of Kant's aesthetic theory are his "four moments." The first moment refers to the *quality* of aesthetic judgment to be totally disinterested: *"Taste* is the faculty of estimating an object or a mode of representation by means of a delight or aversion *apart from any interest*. The object of such delight is called *beautiful.*"[6] The second moment is that of *quality* and it stresses that aesthetic judgment is subjective and universal. In the second moment, the beautiful is defined as "that which, apart from a concept, pleases universally."[7] The third moment is of special importance for our consideration here because it demonstrates that for Kant aesthetic judgment is solely concentrated on the formal qualities of objects. Thus, Kant rejects the idea that any aesthetic judgment can be based on either a subjective or an objective end—an aesthetic is clearly different from a cognitive judgment—and he presumes the universality of aesthetic judgment, that is, that the pleasure derived from it is "valid for everyone." He writes:

> The sole foundation of the judgment of taste is the FORM OF FINALITY of an object (or mode of representing it). Whenever an end is regarded as a source of delight it always imports an interest as determining ground of the judgment on the object of pleasure. Hence the judgment of taste cannot rest on any subjective end as its ground, but neither can any representation of an objective end, i.e. of the possibility of the object itself on principles of final connection, determine the judgment of taste, and, consequently, neither can any concept of the good. . . . We are thus left with the subjective finality in the representation of an object, exclusive of any end (objective or subjective)—consequently the bare *form of finality* in the representation whereby an object is *given to us so far as we are conscious of it—as that which alone is capable of constituting the delight which, apart from any concept, we estimate as universally communicable, and so of forming the determining ground of the judgment of taste.*[8] (My italics).

Hence, Kant identifies the beauty of an object with the latter's *outer form*: "*Beauty* is the form of *finality* in an object, so far as perceived in it apart *from the representation* of an end."[9] In the fourth moment Kant defines the beautiful as "that which, apart from a concept, is cognized as object of a necessary delight."[10]

The point to be made here is that Kant treats art systematically as *autonomous*. He distinguishes it from "sensualism and its reduction of art to pleasure," also from "moralism, intellectualism and didacticism."[11] His emphasis on *form* is based on his general epistemological position as it is developed

in the *Critique of Pure Reason*. Thus, for Kant, only the knowledge of appearances is accessible to us; we cannot possibly know
the "things-in-themselves."[12]

Finally,   since the first moment—directed against the
empiricists—establishes the disinterested nature of aesthetic
judgment, it should be remembered that the latter is *pure* and
should not be confused with *empirical* aesthetic judgment.
In the case of the pure aesthetic judgment (judgment of taste
proper) the pleasure and displeasure originating in an object
derives from its form; in the case of the empirical aesthetic
judgment (empirical judgment of taste) the pleasure or displeasure originates in an object and derives from its matter.[13]
It is in the distinction between *formal* and *material* aesthetic
judgments—and the emphasis on the primary importance of the
first, as well as some aspects of his epistemology—that Russian
formalism, American new criticism and French formalistic
structuralism are connected with Kant.

The second common characteristic of these three forms
of intrinsic criticism is that they approach directly and solely
the literary works themselves.   And, since all literature, both
oral[14] and written is manifested through language, the study
of language, its component units, i.e. words, sentences, the
infinitely possible combinations of words, as well as matters of
vocal sound, rhythm, metre, style, construction of images,
symbolism, etc., is of primary concern to all three of them, but
to the extent that it is demanded by each one's special priorities
and objectives.

Languages can be defined—if one wishes to avoid some
strictly technical definitions[15]—as "that which pertains to the
human tongue."[16]   More specifically, language, the basis of
human communication, can be defined as a sign system expressed
through vocal sounds, *phonemes*, which comprise certain patterns, *morphemes*, pertaining to linguistic form, and *tagmemes*,
pertaining to arrangement.

Linguistics is the science of language.   Therefore, those
approaches to literature which focus on the forms taken by
words comprising a literary work, as well as the meanings of
the words, are closely related to linguistics.   The use of the
linguistic method by the formalists is evident in their practice
to approach literature beginning with the patterns of sound,[17]
and then to proceed with the consideration of the structure of
metre, arrangement, style—in a word, with form.[18]   As for

structuralism, it is not only claimed that it is based on linguistics —especially semiology—but it is often identified with the latter. This, for example, is stated by the major structuralist representative in the field of literary studies, Roland Barthes.[19]

Our brief introduction to linguistics requires reference to the revolutionary work of the Swiss linguist Ferdinand de Saussure.[20] His *Course in General Linguistics* (1915) had a tremendous influence not only within but also outside the boundaries of linguistics. Saussure's work distinguishes: i) *Language (langage)*, which includes all human capability—both actual and potential— for expression and communication through speech; ii) *Language (langue)*, as the entire *language-system* developed and used by society at any given point in time—a collective phenomenon; and iii) *Parole*, that is, the *langue* as it is manifested through the particular speech of an individual—the concrete act of speaking.

According to Saussure, *langue*, that is, the actual language-system, is the object of linguistics. A *langue*, however, can only be studied through the analysis of what is available for direct communication: *paroles*. In effect, the basic unit through which a language-system should be approached is the *sign*. Semiology is founded on the basis of the need for the study of signs.[21]

For Saussure, this fundamental unit of communication, the sign, is not a symbol, i.e. in general sense a representation: "The linguistic sign unites, not a thing and a name, but a concept and a sound-image."[22] He points out that while a concept *and* a sound-image make up a sign, the latter often leads to confusion. This happens because one usually disregards the fact that a sound-image is perceived as a sign when it contains the relevant concept. For the avoidance of such a mistake, Saussure proposes "to retain the word sign . . . to designate the whole and to replace *concept* and *sound-image* respectively by *signified* . . . and *signifier*."[23] In his own example,[24] the sound-image *arbor* is the signifier, that is, the actual sound which we hear as we listen to someone or to ourselves pronouncing that word. The concept *tree* is the signified, that is, the particular image which this sound creates in the listener's mind.

A basic principle of Saussure's theory is that there is no rule or norm (not to mention law) which relates a sound-image and a concept, a signifier with a signified. For him, the relationship between the two is *arbitrary*. He regards meaning as two-sided; as an arbitrary relationship between two equally important participants which comprise the linguistic sign: the signifier and the signified. Of course, by calling this relationship —that is, the linguistic sign—arbitrary, Saussure does not mean what this term indicates at a first glance, i.e. that the speaker chooses in any given case the signifier of his absolute preference. He specifically means that the signifier "is unmotivated, i.e. arbitrary, in that it actually has no natural connection with the signified."[25]

This doctrine had important consequences for the establishment of the idea of men's capability not just to speak but to develop signs as well (i.e. the invalidation of the conception of language as natural in origin). The study of signs is the object of the general science of *semiology* part of which is linguistics: "*A science that studies the life of signs within society* is conceivable . . . I shall call it *semiology*. . . . Linguistics is only a part of the general science of semiology; the laws discovered by semiology will be applicable to linguistics, and the latter will circumscribe a well-defined area within the mass of anthropological facts."[26]   To grasp fully the wider implications of Saussure's linguistic doctrine, one would have to situate it historically and take a closer look at some of its basic assertions.[27]

In attempting to define the object of linguistics, Saussure compares it with other sciences and he pinpoints a number of difficulties pertaining to the former because linguistic phenomena are manifested in the form of dualities. Syllables, for example, manifest the duality of *sounds* and *vocal organs*; speech (not just a meaningless sound) is the combinatory result of the duality of a *sound* and an *idea*; speech also consists of another duality with an *individual* and a *social* aspect; finally, speech again is the manifestation of a third duality, that of a *well-established system* and an *evolution*. In all these cases, the study of the linguistic phenomenon itself seems problematical, because if one begins the investigation of each duality from either one of its sides, the possibility exists that the importance of the other might be undermined. The difficulty then is that one cannot locate the object of linguistics within these dualities. Also, if one attempts to approach them from outside, e.g. to study speech by trying to relate it to various extraneous elements, points of view, etc., the result for the science of linguistics will be a confusion.[28]

The study of a linguistic phenomenon cannot begin from *langage*, because the latter lacks "inner unity and validity as an autonomous system."[29] This is why, to surpass this difficulty, Saussure designates *langue* as the object of linguistics.[30] In contradistinction to *langage* which is "many-sided," "heterogeneous" and non-classifiable, *langue* "is a self-contained whole and a principle of classification."[31]

Finally, the third Saussurean idea with important consequences inside and outside of linguistics (i.e. structuralism) is the focus on the *synchronic* study of language (*langue*) at the expense of *diachronic* considerations. Making the distinction between the two linguistic approaches, Saussure explains that the object of synchronic linguistics is the language-system perceived in the collective mind as co-existing terms interrelated in a logical and psychological manner. The object of diachronic linguistics is not the language-system but successive *language states* outside the perception of the collective mind.[32] What Saussure stresses is that it is "absolutely impossible to study simultaneously relations in time and relations within the system."[33] Therefore, the opposition between the synchronic and diachronic approaches "is absolute and allows no compromise."[34]

The differentiation between the evolution of language, its history, and the language-system at any given point in time is clear. As Volosinov argues, Saussure's attitude toward history is influenced by the idea of irrationality, because historical (diachronic) concerns could distort "the logical purity of the language system."[35] This introduction can be closed by adding that being interested only in the internal relations between signs, Saussure distinguishes two kinds of such relations: the *syntagmatic*, expressed as *presences*—structure—, (i.e. a word's position and its relationship to other words in a sentence), and the *paradigmatic* (associative), expressed as *absences*, (i.e. a word's relation with words which are not included in the sentence but with which it is related on the basis of some rule, for example, meaning).[36]

Notwithstanding its achievements, the shortcomings of Saussure's problematic have resulted in its surpassing by the linguistic approach developed by some new contributors to that field, especially Noam Chomsky. Since, however, Saussure's own ideas have directly influenced literary criticism,[37] the following up of the developments in linguistics after Saussure is beyond our particular interest. Hence, returning to our main subject, we can say that the structuralist approach to literature—

following Saussure's footsteps—is a synchronic analysis of the structure of its language.   Here we specifically refer to the structuralism of Levi-Strauss who agress with Saussure's distinction between synchrony and diachrony, in contradistinction to the Prague structuralist school which, adopting the standpoint taken by Jakobson and Tynjanov in 1928,* rejects Saussure's exclusive preference for the synchronic approach.

After these brief remarks about the Kantian[38] and linguistic basis of the main forms of intrinsic criticism in general and structuralism in particular we can now turn to some aspects of the work of the latter's Grand Pope: Claude Levi-Strauss.

2. *Levi-Strauss: The Hidden Structure*

During the second world war, Levi-Strauss was working in the New School for Social Research together with Roman Jakobson, and it is partly due to this encounter that the science of linguistics was introduced to Anthropology.[39]   In effect, when Levi-Strauss decided to re-examine some anthropological problems from this new angle, the concept of 'structure' took a different meaning from the traditional one attached to it by the British anthropologists (especially Radcliffe-Brown[40]), and by their French counterparts (Durkeim, Mauss, etc.).[41]

The newly acquired meaning of this concept cannot be expressed by a single definition because it varies from one structuralist writer to another, and from one of their books to the next.   For example, definitions made up by Levi-Strauss himself help little in the clarification of the problem.   Concretely, structure might refer to the numerous relationships between the various elements of a phenomenon *and* to the relationship of these elements (parts) to the phenomenon as a whole (totality).[42]   Structure is also defined, again by Levi-Strauss, as a "non-meaning" which is "behind all meaning,"[43] and this increases the difficulty of its comprehension.

A fruitful suggestion is that the meaning of this concept

---

*Cf. chapter six, pp. 214-215.

should be constructed in relation to the three characteristics of structure: *polysemantics, contextuality* and *permeability*. This implies that one has to keep in mind the possibility that the concept of structure varies according to the context in which it is employed as well as to the interchanges between hetero-geneous (i.e. scientific and non-scientific) descriptions of it.[44]

The basic premise of Levi-Strauss' epistemology is that reality is not what we see and observe. Reality is beneath the appearance of phenomena: it is *hidden*. This invisible reality is organized according to a logical scheme, an order operating everywhere, a *structure* which is the key for the understanding of the essence of reality. The task of the anthropologist and sociologist, then, is neither the 'description' of socio-cultural phenomena as they manifest themselves to the observer (phe-nomenology), nor their explanation on the basis of one's 'lived experience' (existentialism). Their task is to unveil the deeply concealed structure and establish its meaning by decoding it in a scientific and objective manner.

What Levi-Strauss does in fact is to regard all socio-cultural phenomena as sign systems—as a *langue* is a sign system itself—organized into systems of structures which are distinct from the concrete and observable experience of everyday life: they are indeed located in the human mind. Levi-Strauss accounts for such a sign system, as for example the kinship system, by per-ceiving it not as the result of the blood ties established among people but as something existing in their minds. He writes: "A kinship system does not consist in the objective ties of descent and consanguinity between individuals. It exists only in human consciousness; it is an arbitrary system of representa-tions, not the spontaneous development of a real situation."[45]

Because of the similarity attributed by Levi-Strauss to socio-cultural and language phenomena—both regarded as sign systems of the same type—he arrived at the conclusion that the same method should be able to account for both equally well: structural linguistic analysis.[46]   When he theorizes on the correlation between culture and language, however, he simply states the obvious: " . . . between culture and language there cannot be *no* relations at all, and there cannot be 100 per cent relations either."[47]   But to establish the existing correlations one has to go after the respective structures of the two systems. Levi-Strauss explains, for example, that the object of compara-tive structural analysis is the comparison of certain structures

wherever they can be found: in cooking and economic trans-
actions, religious practices and musical performances, artistic
creations and literary products.[48]   From this point of view
"the question is not to substitute one particular content for
another or to reduce one to the other, but, rather, to discover
whether the formal properties present homologies . . . contradictions . . . or dialectical relationships. . . ."[49]

Levi-Strauss' relationship with the Russian formalists is
not only through Roman Jakobson.   Vladimir Propp's *Morphology of the Folktale*[50] presented a challenge to the French
anthropologist who decided to transform its formalist approach
into a structuralist one.   To this effect, Levi-Strauss criticizes
Propp's analysis as based on the antinomy between form and
content.   Propp, as a formalist, views content as absolutely
secondary; but also his notion of form is so abstract that it
hardly signifies anything.   Levi-Strauss argues that content and
form are not opposed to each other and that emphasis should
be given to the relationship between myth and its social context.
This demonstrates his primary concern for the signifier—the
myth—which he regards as a sign system with universal properties: "Whatever our ignorance of the language and the culture of
the people where it originated, a myth is still felt as a myth by
any reader anywhere in the world.   Its substance does not lie
in the style, its original music, or its syntax, but in the *story*
which it tells.   Myth is language, functioning on an especially
high level where meaning succeeds practically at 'taking off'
from the linguistic ground on which it keeps on rolling."[51]

Generally speaking, it is at this point that the structuralist
approach began to diverge from formalism.   What attracted
the literary critics mostly was the precise like mathematics
linguistic method by which a story can be explained.   Thus,
the revealing and decoding of the hidden structures became the
central objective of structural analysis in the sphere of literary
criticism, despite some serious theoretical problems which make
the scientific validity of such an exercise questionable.

In an article written together by Roman Jakobson and
Levi-Strauss in which a structural analysis of Baudelaire's 'Les
Chats' is attempted, the authors state that "In poetic works
the linguist discerns structures which present a striking analogy
with those that the analysis of myths reveals to the ethnolo-
gist."[52]   Nevertheless, the organizing principle of these structures
(i.e. phonetic, syntactic, semantic, etc.) seems to be choosen

arbitrarily, the ultimate purpose being the establishment of just any correlations and some kind of order behind the amorphous mass of elements composing a poem.[53] These elements are considered in their relationships within the limits of the poem while all extrinsic relations are completely disregarded. Therefore, there is no point of reference to verify the findings of a poem's or a text's structural analysis, and the supposedly objective linguistic approach runs the risk of becoming no more than a subjective enterprise. Levi-Strauss, who considers his own analyses objective and validated in some unspecified way, comments about the structuralist approach to literature as follows: "The fundamental vice of any literary criticism with structuralist pretensions comes from its amounting too often to a play of mirrors, wherein it becomes impossible to distinguish the object from its symbolic reverberation in the consciousness of the subject. The work studied and the analyzer's thoughts reflect themselves in each other, and we are denied any means of discerning what is simply received from the former and what the latter puts there. One is trapped in a reciprocal relativism which can afford subjectivity certain charms; but we do not see what type of external evidence it could be referred to."[54]

The hidden structure of language, like every social structure is for Levi-Strauss independent of human consciousness. Therefore, the human mind cannot be revealed by its open statements but by an invisible entity, the system of binary oppositions contained within itself. In his desire to make an "inventory of mental patterns"[55] and thus to systematize human knowledge, Levi-Strauss infers that human beings are not just in a position of no control of this hidden structure but they are themselves manipulated by it. He writes: "I claim to show, not how men think in myths, but how myths operate in men's minds without their being aware of the fact."[56] The implication here is that man is completely decentered from the meanings he creates since the hidden structure and it alone makes socio-cultural and historical phenomena intelligible. In fact, man's role in the making of history is negligible and history is considered by Levi-Strauss as nothing else but a succession of atemporal, discontinuous structures.[57]

3. *Roland Barthes: Linguistic-Structuralist Criticism*

Structuralism, a tendency rather and a method than a movement or a school, resists the confinements of a definition, hence the obscurities and disagreements both in its practice[58] and its description.[59]   Here, it suffices to quote Barthes' statement that structuralism is "essentially an activity, i.e. the controlled succession of certain number of mental operations."[60]

Barthes, follows Saussure's views in regard to semiology— he even wrote a book entitled *Elements of Semiology* in which he presents this discipline—and he is in general agreement with certain ideas developed by Levi-Strauss. He can by no means be considered, however, as a 'representative' of structuralism because each individual structuralist differs from another in procedure and intention, and each one is related to something distinct.   Tzvetan Todorov, for example, is mainly associated with a theory of reading, when 'reading' (a *systematic* commentary) is that activity of structuralist poetics which focuses on concrete literary works regarded as autonomous entities.[61]

For Barthes too, reading is an extremely important activity, but the key term of his literary criticism is *code*: he regards human experience, that is, any context which the human mind understands as pre-coded and organized by language. Barthes is given preference here because he is considered the leading theoretician and practitioner of the new criticism in France, as well as one of the most brilliant and provocative post-World War II literary critics.

a. *Against Academic Criticism*

In an essay entitled "The Two Criticisms," Barthes makes the distinction between *academic* criticism which continues to employ the positivist Lansonian approach (objective method) and non-academic, *interpretive* criticism which is ideological in nature (Marxist, existentialist, psychoanalytic, phenomenological).   The aim of academic criticism is the establishment of the objective "facts" of literary texts, i.e. biographical, literary, historical, sociological, etc., which Barthes accepts as a useful contribution.   This concession, however, is made on condition that academic criticism leaves the interpretation of these facts to ideological criticism. This could be an ideal "division of labor" but it does not materialize because academic (positivist) criticism also is ideological.

In the first place, academic criticism is one-sided as being concerned only with the external factors ("circumstances") of a work, without any immediate interest in its nature and *raison d'être*. According to Barthes, this indifference reflects the time old attitude that literary works express the feelings of their authors, which reveals the contradiction of the rejection of historical experience, for example, by historical criticism itself. This experience shows that a "timeless essence of literature" is but a myth, and that literature is merely "a process of very different forms, functions, institutions, reasons and projects whose relativity it is precisely the historian's responsibility to discern,"[62] in order for the pertinent facts to be explained.

The second manifestation of the ideological nature of academic criticism is the "postulate of analogy"[63] by means of which literary texts are always examined in analogical relation to something outside of them, to an external model. This results in the inability of academic criticism to discover the "functional meaning" of literary facts to the extent that their truth is missed. For Barthes, "It is the work which is its own model; its truth is not to be sought in depth, but in extent; and if there is a relation between the author and his work . . . (it is) . . . a relation between the *entire* author and the *entire* work, a relation of relations, a homological and not an analogical correspondence."[64]

In its acceptance of Freudian psychoanalysis, academic criticism still relates literary works to an external factor: the psychology of their author. This is the ultimate denial of the possibility that literary works can be interpreted in terms of their internal functions. Thus, academic criticism rejects the phenomenological explication of literary works, the thematic reconstruction of their metaphors, and also "structural criticism (which regards the work as a system of functions)." What is required then is a radical shift from "a criticism of determinations to a criticism of functions and significations."[65]

b. *The Case of Structuralist Criticism*

Barthes concentrates on the camp of interpretive criticism and tries to establish the supremacy of structuralism in his essay "What is Criticism?" Concretely, he avoids existentialism by characterizing Sartre's study of Genet "splendid," and he does away with Marxist criticism as sterile and mechanical. Only Goldmann's "fruitful" method is partially approved. He also seems to dismiss Freudian criticism with the exemption of what he calls "marginal" psychoanalysis which, with its emphasis on *substances* and *images* and not on the literary works themselves, appears to be promising, e.g. Bachelard, Poulet, Starobinski, Richard. When he zeros in on structuralism—or "formalism" as he writes with disapproval of this term—he fully acknowledges the influence of Saussure, Levi-Strauss and Jakobson.

According to Barthes, the attainment of "truth" is not a prerequisite for the validation of critical practice. The being of criticism is directly related to the being ("psyche and history") of the critic. Therefore, both the writer and the critic have the same objective: creation. This point is made crystal clear. Criticism reflects simultaneously on the work *and* on itself. Negatively, "Criticism is not at all a table of results or a body of judgments;" positively, criticism "is essentially an activity, i.e. a series of intellectual acts profoundly committed to the historical and subjective existence (they are the same thing) of the man who performs them."[66]

Despite that it is not the purpose of critical activity to achieve "truth", it nevertheless has to respond to other necessities. The writer speaks about the world which is the object of literature in general. The object of criticism, however, is not the world but the writer's discourse about the world. In this sense, literature is *language*, and criticism is a *metalanguage*. The critical task then is double: to account for the relation between itself and the language of literature, and to account for the relations between the latter and its object, namely, the world.

In the light of this argument, the aim of this metalanguage which is criticism "is not at all to discover 'truths,' but only validities." This derives from the assumption that "In itself, a language is not true or false, it is or is not valid: valid, i.e. constitutes a coherent system of signs." Hence, the task of criticism is formal, and it is in a *logical* sense that structuralism is a formalism not in an *aesthetic* one. In Barthes words—indicating a significant shift from the structuralist approach advocated by Levi-Strauss—the goal of the critic is "not to 'discover' in the work or the author something 'hidden', 'profound', 'secret' which hitherto passed unnoticed. . . , but only to adjust the language his period affords him (existentialism, Marxism, psychoanalysis) to the language, i.e., the formal system of logical constrains elaborated by the author according to his own period."[67]

The goal of the criticism Barthes advocates cannot be the revealing of a work's meaning because such a meaning does not exist. Certainly, every literary work generates meaning but not just one particular meaning. The literary work signifies something which is not clear: it is a *"suspended"* meaning. This meaning "offers itself to the reader as an avowed signifying system yet withholds itself from him as a signifying object." Thus, the goal of criticism—and consequently the objective of structuralist poetics—is "the reconstruction of the rules and constrains of that meaning's elaboration. . . ."[68] Ultimately, the poetic study of a literary work co-creates a meaning for the latter.

Literature, for Barthes, is simply a sign-system, a language, and its being cannot be found "in its message but in this 'system'." The critic, therefore, should not engage in the reconstruction of this message but in the reconstruction of this system. As a metalanguage, however, criticism can be "both objective and subjective, historical and existential, totalitarian and liberal." This is so because the critic chooses the language most appropriate to him and determined by various factors, including ideological ones. In other words, criticism is a dialogue between the history and subjectivity of the writer and the history and subjectivity of the critic. A dialogue, which focuses on the present, not on the past: "Criticism is not an 'homage' to the truth of the past or to the truth of 'others'—it is a construction of the intelligibility of our own time."[69] The understanding of this perception of the relationship between the writer and the critic is imperative for an appraisal of Barthes' structuralism.

c. *The Writer, the Critic and the Text*

It is Barthes' position that literary works are in essence "forms" waiting to be filled with meaning. In addition, he perceives the time of literary creation as double in nature: the time during which a work is written, and the time(s) during which the initial activity of writing is recollected. The first, the writer's time is a form to be filled by the second, the time of the critic. In reality, the critic himself is a writer engaged in "indirect discourse."

Writing, is both a sign system and a system of forms. To the extent that it takes a position, expresses an ideology, etc., a piece of writing has a *content*; but to the extent that it contains a theme it has a *form*. A work's theme, however, should never be confused with its content, that is, with the open and obvious statements of the writer in respect to certain issues. The theme is the product of the dialogue between the writer and the critic. And, as every individual critic participates in a different dialogue, the aim of criticism is "less to give a meaning to the enigmatic work than to destroy those meanings by which it is immediately and forever encumbered."[70]

Barthes takes a close look at the activity of writing maintaining that it is not the expression of an idea; it is rather a projection and the fulfillment of a task which has itself as its object. Hence, from the writer's point of view, the process of writing is far more important than the result. This is why certain literary works are "nothing but their own project,"[71] the writer being more faithful to form than to content and, consequently, unwilling to give a definite meaning to his work. In effect, the moment writing becomes a present it is already a past, from which the writer wishes to detach himself.

In the light of this analysis, the being of literature—the literariness of a text—emerges from the "conditions of variation" of a direct, initial message; conditions, which "refer only to the *originality* of the second message." This originality which transforms an immediate message to an indirect one, is for Barthes the basis of literary production. He writes: "In literature as in private communication, to be least 'false' I must be most 'original', or if you prefer, most 'indirect'."

For a writer to be original and consequently attractive to the reader, he must send his message indirectly by means of a connotation, which, instead of transmitting a meaning, will simply make possible the construction of a meaning. Writing, therefore, is not the establishment of a language, but the creation of certain conditions for the expression of the language of others. In essence, writing is not a content, but a form, "an activity of variation and combination" which demonstrates that writers are not "creators" but "combinators."

Furthermore, to write is to make a commitment and take a stand towards the various aspects of human reality: towards the "named." The named is the writer's primary material, and his task is to extract a new language from the various languages which he already finds in the world. In other words, the writer must tune his activity according to a pre-existing code. Thus, the aim of literature is not "to *express the inexpressible*" but to *"unexpress the expressible,"* to kidnap from the world's language, which is the poor and powerful language of the passions, another language, an exact speech.[72] This can only be achieved by the use of one of the numerous literary techniques, i.e. rhetoric, articulation, irony or recitence.

Writing is also an attempt for the establishment of a code containing the writer's own "I." This "I," which in novels for example is masked under numerous third persons, is established as a sign. The critic, on the contrary, cannot transform his own "I" into a sign. The critic's "I" is not located in his speech but in his silence, that is, in the discontinuity of his own discourse. Clearly then, the writer's "I" is presented as a part of a code, while the critic's "I" remains hidden and outside of the code of literature. In the final analysis, the critic's "I" is hidden under the "I" of the writer as the critic takes an indirect course to deal with the writer's direct discourse: "The critic is a writer, he wants to be believed less because of what he writes than because of his decision to write it; but unlike the writer, he cannot *sign* that desire; he remains condemned to error—to truth."[73]

What, of course, connects the codified "I" of the writer with the imprisoned "I" of the critic is the text itself. To evaluate a text, Barthes argues, one should focus on its function not in relation to any scientific rule or ideological standpoint, i.e. moral, aesthetic, political, etc., but in relation to the activity of writing. In this sense, texts can be evaluated positively if they can be rewritten: the "writerly;" and they can be evaluated negatively if they can just be read: the "readerly."[74]

Readerly texts reduce the reader to a pathetic consumer

of literature; on the contrary, writerly texts elevate the reader to an active producer.   Barthes regards the writerly text as a permanent present, as the reader practicing writing: "The writerly is the novelistic without the novel, poetry without the poem, the essay without the dissertation, writing without style, production without product, structuration without structure."[75]   The readerly texts are nothing but ready-made products, and they represent the bulk of literature.

The comparative evaluation of the mass of readerly texts can only be made on the basis of an additional activity: interpretation.   To interpret a readerly text, however, is not to give it a meaning but "to appreciate what *plural* constitutes it"[76]— plural indicating simply a polysemous text.   What is required here is a criticism of *connotation* (secondary meaning), not one of *denotation* (primary meaning).   The philologists, who view the text as the embodiment of an objective truth, give priority to denotation; the semiologists, on the contrary, consider connotation as much more significant because they regard the raw material of denotation, language, as one system among others.

For Barthes, connotation is the key to the polysemy of the readerly (classic) texts, and he explains it on ten levels: definitionally, topically, analytically, topologically, semiologically, dynamically, historically, functionally, structurally and ideologically.   Connotation should not be confused with the association of ideas because it has nothing to do with the ideological system of a subject.   Connotation is always something internal to the text, it is "an association made by the text-as-subject within its own system."[77]

One of the most interesting and central parts of Barthes reasoning refers to the activity ("operation") of reading.   Here, to read a text is not tantamount to reveal the properties of an object.   In point of fact, plural texts are mainly written *after* their reading, because the reader, before even opens up a text, is himself "a plurality of other texts, of codes which are infinite. . . ."[78]   Thus, Barthes regards the *subjectivity* of the reader as the mere awakening of pre-existing codes, and his *objectivity* as another imaginary system which misleads the reader's self-awareness.

To the extent that a text is regarded as an object expressing a definite meaning, reading is vulnerable to risks emanating from the imaginary systems of objectivity and subjectivity. Nevertheless, reading is not the mere reaction to a pre-existing

object: the text. Reading is a creative activity itself, "a lexeo-
logical act" based on a "topological" method. This means
that the reader is not establishing his own meanings, or the
meanings suggested by others, but he establishes meanings
"by their *systematic* mark: there is no other *proof* of a reading
than the quality and endurance of its systematics; in other words
than its functioning."

To read is to establish a meaning, then forget it and then
establish a new one. This way the text moves constantly, its
meaning being always in the making, an endless approximation.
To *forget* a plural text's meaning is a plus of the perpetual
operation of reading and not a liability because plural texts
do not have one objectively given meaning. To forget the meanings of a plural text "is an affirmative value, a way of asserting
the irresponsibility of the text, the pluralism of systems. . . : it
is precisely because I forget that I read."[79]

Every element of a text is, according to Barthes, the signification of an underlying structure, while every single text
is not representative of all texts but it is literature itself. An
individual text is not a key to a model but a door leading to
a network with numerous doors. In this framework, to study
a text means to study, step-by-step, its details, its major structures, its meanings and its codes by means of small units of
reading, the *lexias*. Each lexia does not have more than three
or four meanings and it is composed by a few words or many
sentences.

To study a given text we divide it into, what Barthes calls,
"zones of reading" and then we observe the moving of meanings and the sprouting of codes. One should not forget, however, that lexias do not aim to construct a text's "truth" but
to establish its "plurality." Consequently, not just one but
many kinds of criticism are possible, in terms of their potential
contribution to the establishment of a text's meanings: psychological, psychoanalytical, thematic, historical, structural. Obviously, each one of the criticisms will pursue its own objective,
and it will brake the continuity of the text in order to comment
and make its own "voice heard, which is the hearing of one of
the voices of the text." The ultimate purpose here is the sketch-
ing of "the stereographic space of writing." This is why the
text may be interrupted and broken, regardless of the natural
divisions imposed by its author: "What is thereby denied is not
the *quality* of the text . . . but its *'naturalness'*."[80]

Evidently, with Barthes—as with Todorov in "Comment lire?"—the activity of reading takes on an enormous importance. When the question of the required number of readings arises, he distinguishes between the reader who simply wishes to enjoy a good story and the reader who is determined to establish the plural of the text. In this second case, a plural reading is unavoidable, and re-reading is advocated as a must: to multiply the significations of a text and free the text from the constrains of its conventional time. From Barthes' point of view, to re-read a text is not to consume it but to engage in play. What the reader deals with is not an object, "the *real* text, but a plural text: the same and new."[81] The determining role of reading is a fundamental principle of the structuralist activity.

d. *The Structuralist Activity*

For Barthes, even the realist texts of what is considered as 'great' literature, e.g. the major works of Balzac, are based on a pre-existing code, and for this reason every literary work should be analyzed on the basis of its *functioning*. It is this function which defines the goal of the structuralist activity. A goal, which aims exclusively at the reconstruction of an object so as its "rules of functioning" can be manifested. This is why Barthes defines structure as a "simulacrum" of the object: "a directed, *interested* simulacrum, since the imitated object makes something appear which remained invisible, or . . . unintelligible in the natural object."[82]

The result of the structuralist activity is the decomposition and recomposition of the text, until "something new" is produced, something which is now intelligible. In effect, "the simulacrum is intellect added to the object." As for this series of mental operations, labelled the structuralist activity, it is not a creative or reflective exercise but an *imitative* one like literature itself. This *mimesis*, however, should not be related to an analogy between contents; it is rather an analogy between functions. Art then is defined not by the substance of the imitated object (realist thesis) but by man's artistic reconstruction of the object. Alike the Russian formalists, Barthes regards *technique* as "the very being of all creation." It is the recomposition of the object which reveals its functions; it is "the way that makes the work."[83]

The structuralist activity consists of two standard operations. The first is *dissection*, that is, the identification of those fragments of a text from which a meaning can be extracted. The second is *articulation*, that is, the establishment of the rules by which these fragments (units) are interrelated. Barthes, adopting the linguistic terminology calls these rules, *forms*. He maintains that the construction of the object's structure, its simulacrum, causes the changing of the object by showing a new category of it "which is neither the real nor the rational, but the functional. . . ." In other words, the reconstruction of the object gives it a new meaning, a process indicating a new approach or a new "poetics" the objective of which is "less to assign completed meanings to the objects it discovers than to know how meaning is possible. . . ." Therefore, "The object of structuralism is not man endowed with meanings but man fabricating meanings. . . ."[84]

When he reflects on the structuralist activity, Barthes takes a relativistic perspective viewing it just as another historical form which sooner or later will have its eclipse. During the period of its functioning structuralism is trying "to link to history" both the "contents" and the "forms" of the world, the "material and the intelligible," the "ideological" and the "esthetic." This is the way for structuralism to experience its temporary validity—not its truth—as it is bound to be superceded by another form, another language.

At this point let us clarify the structuralist concept of *meaning* and try to see the reader's role in this light. Thus, we can agree with Jan M. Broekman who characterizes this meaning as functional itself in the sense that "the meaning of a literary element consists in the possibilities for function which we give that element." Consequently, a text's unit, be it a word or a paragraph, takes its meaning from its association with the other units of the text. The interpretation of the text then is a function of the reader's personal choice "who picks the element out of the whole context and fits it into a new system (such as an economic, ideological, historical, or biological system) thus asserting it according to his own standards. If this functional conception limits the number of possible meanings of the text-element. . . , the number of possible interpretations remains in principle, however, unlimited."[85] In this respect, the main consequences of Barthes' literary criticism are three: the insistence on the relativity of the content of any text, the viewing of literature as a process of fulfillment of meanings and the perception of meaning in a new dynamic way.[86]

4. *An Assessment of Barthian Criticism*

In Barthes' view, any approach to literary works should be synchronic because they are by nature unhistorical.[87] This is justified by the fact that the activity of reading (i.e. the activity of fabricating meaning) is synchronic itself; second, because the literary works are susceptible to every interpretation possible since their meaning is constantly in the making; and thirdly, because in modern writing (that is, writing after Flaubert), words have a total, unhistorical content, as they are "reduced to a short of zero degree, pregnant with all past and future specifications."[88] Such a perception of the word is not surprising since, according to Barthes, a word can take all the meanings that numerous successive readings can ascribe to it.

Sensitive to criticism against the unhistorical nature of structuralism (especially from the Marxists) Barthes decides to address the question of the relationship between history and literature directly in his book *On Racine*.[89] Thus, he argues that the "continent" of the study of history and the "continent" of the study of literature develop autonomously, and that what is known as "history of literature" is pure nonsense.

In order to demonstrate that an "historical approach" to literature can tell us nothing of "what is happening inside an author at the moment he is writing," Barthes refers to Loucien Febvre's 'formula' for such an approach which includes: a) the study of the milieu; b) the author's public; and c) the level of intellectual development of both the writer and his public. Barthes rejects this formula on the grounds that it is impossible to have at our disposal studies and data accurate enough to rely on them for so much information. Consequently, the focus primarily on the author himself is bound to fail. He writes: "It is only on the level of literary *functions* (production, communication, consumption), that such an history can be written, and not on the level of the individuals who have exercised them."[90] It is this level then which should be the object of knowledge. As already explained, any attempt for an objective approach aspiring to relate a literary work to a source, to a reality which the work somehow reflects, is also doomed to fail.

These ideas of course, suggest a new definition of literature, and Barthes formulates it as follows: "Literature is that ensemble of objects and rules, techniques and works, whose function in the general economy of our society is to institutionalize subjectivity."[91] Therefore, the task of the literary historian is different from the task of the literary critic. The literary historian should study the "techniques, rules, rites and collective mentalities," while the literary critic, if he really wants "to install" himself "inside" the author, he must become systematic and "reveal himself as an utterly subjective, utterly historical being."[92] In this framework, the questions to be asked at this point are the following: a) What is the significance of Barthes' approach to literature? b) What are its main characteristics? And, c) How do they affect the structuralist critical activity?

To begin with, the first striking feature of structuralism is its *epistemological relativism.*[93] Barthes' own adherence to unrestrained relativism—at least on the level of theory—is manifested in his attitude towards the various kinds of criticism, each one of which is welcomed as "one of the voices of the text," that is, as long as the plural meaning of the text is constituted. Yet, distinct meanings are established not only because different aspects (or dimensions) of the text are dealt with by each particular criticism, but also because the text is approached from different epistemological, philosophical, theoretical and methodological perspectives. The various kinds of criticism which Barthes mentions, establish the meaning(s) of a text in dissimilar, often mutually exclusive, ways. Of course, there are psychological, historical, thematic, etc., meanings of a text, but they should all be established from the same angle. The meanings established by various criticisms, however, are not always commensurable in relation to a text. And since a semantic common measure is lacking, how these supposedly various "voices of the text" relate to one another? Barthes himself, avoids such relativism in his *practical* criticism, e.g. in his *S/Z*.

A similar phenomenon is manifested in Barthes' attitude towards reading. Relativism is the position taken towards the various readers of the same text *and* towards the different readings of a text by one and the same reader, indiscriminately.

For example, in his dispute with professor Picard over Racine,
Barthes states that "his book on Racine is several years old and
that his views may have changed in the meantime."[94]   The
partial change of a reader's view of a text is certainly possible.
But when relativism is adopted as a fundamental epistemological
principle, almost every signification is permissible, while the
establishment of relatively enduring knowledge of a text becomes
impossible. This is not to suggest a *fixed* view on literary works;
it is to point out that there are certain limits to relativism—both
synchronic and diachronic—which cannot be overlooked.

Every text has some objective elements. The most important of these elements is the text's language which, from the
writer's point of view, has a specific meaning—save for the case
of purposeful ambiguity. Contrary to Barthes' standpoint, the
critic cannot afford to ignore this objective meaning, no matter
how many additional meanings (or the fresh implications of
these objective statements in the light of new conditions) successive readings of the text will manage to establish. Ignored or
acknowledged by the critic, the writer's conscious meaning of
his text—which is different from the latter's objective significance
—still exists and, as Lucien Goldmann maintains, it should be
considered as at least one "suggestive element among others."*
The critic, of course, can only determine an approximation of
a text's objective (intended) meaning because, among other
things, the writer's meaning of a text is a dialectical relationship
between the said and the unsaid, the full identity of which
escapes the critic's awareness. Other objective elements are a
text's intellectual context, literary tradition, stylistic devices,
etc., none of which can be ignored by the critic without a price:
the limitation of his view of the text. Even accepting that
literary history and literary criticism are sharply distinct intellectual specialties, none of the two can neglect to be fully in-
formed about the activity of the other.

The second characteristic of Barthe's structuralism is its
indifference for the diachronic dimension for reasons already
mentioned. Thus, while the structuralist critic can achieve his
narrowly prescribed objective by Barthes (demonstrating his

---

*Cf. chapter three, pp. 68-69.

ability to describe the organization of sign-systems with exceptional rigor[95]), at the same time he fails to link the whole of a literary work to the greater whole of the society and history of which it is but a small part. As Fredric Jameson rightly observes, the structuralist approach prevents "the ultimate return of the socialized intellectual discipline to that concrete social and historical situation in which it is of necessity grounded."[96]

In the first place, it is the structuralist critic's passionate quest to explore the possibility of new significations and to "construct the intelligibility of our own time," or better, his uncontrollable ambition to liberate the writer lying still inside himself—the critic is a writer postponed—which renders any diachronic considerations irrelevent. And in the second place, it is perhaps due to his regret that man's historical being is repressed, that the structuralist refuses to consider history. In his book, *Writing Degree Zero*, Barthes seems to deplore the fact that "every man is the prisoner of his language,"[97] regarding the modern writer as striving "to create a colorless writing, freed from all bondage to a pre-ordained state of language,"[98] with the hope that an unalienated, classless, "homogeneous social state"[99] will be reached, and that the conditions of necessity will be transcended by conditions of freedom. This structuralist wish, however, is more or less similar to those utopias which the mind can build when it desperately tries to escape the hardships of historical reality.[100]

It has already been mentioned that, according to Barthes, all human experience is pre-coded and pre-shaped by language. This codification is manifested in such aspects of reality as food, fashion, furniture, etc., where both syntagmatic and paradigmatic relationships can be found. Literary texts too are codified, and this means that they are devoid of a truly *original* context. Every context is pre-coded, while the author—even the realist author—merely uses such codes. The third characteristic of Barthian structuralism is its conviction that literary texts can best be approached in terms of certain codes.

Barthes himself, engages in an exhaustive analysis of Balzac's novella *Sarrasine* by means of five principal codes under which all the signifiers of the text can be grouped. The *hermeneutic* code pertaining to the unknown factors of the story; the *thematic* code under which all themes are classified; the *symbolic* code organizing the text's main ideas; the *proairetic* code pertaining to the story's actions; and finally, the *cultural* code indicating the particular category of knowledge, i.e. literary, historical, etc., employed in the text.

The organization of *Sarrasine* on the basis of these five codes which transcend the traditional literary categories of plot, setting, character, etc., demonstrates the dynamism and innovativeness of structuralist criticism. But one should be cautious about its potential. *Sarrasine* is a thirty-page story, while Barthes' study of it, *S/Z*, is about two hundred and fifty pages. A lengthier story would probably present enormous difficulties both to the organization of the material and its detailed commentary. The second, and perhaps far more serious problem has to do with the method itself: these codes are the products of a personal and arbitrary choice. Barthes, of course, was able to produce a brilliant study. But no one can be certain about the performance of other critics dealing with other stories. The question here is, to what extent this method can be generalized. Thus, we can agree with Robert Scholes who suggests that in the debit side, Barthes' approach needs improvement before it is used again. This could be a rewarding undertaking because this method "has the great virtue of bringing the semantic dimension of narrative into the field of structuralist criticism in a vigorous and productive way."[101]

For Barthes, the object of structuralism is "man fabricating meaning" and not the meaning itself. Yet, from another standpoint, the arbitrary ways in which the meaning and significance of literary works are established lead structuralism not simply outside of the accepted notions of scientific endeavor (unlike its linguistic basis) but even beyond art; into the realm of total relativism where anything contains the possibility of signifying everything. This, apparently unlimited relativism, faithful to itself, is also relative. Concretely, while the philosophical position of structuralism's Grand Pope, Claude Levi-Strauss "fluctuates considerably, from a revised materialism to Kantianism . . . a genuine 'structuralist philosophy' is not to be found."[102] What is to be found, is an ultimate epistemological point of reference in which all structuralists seem to seek occasional refuge.

Literature might be viewed as a sign-system incorporated into another: language. The one, however, cannot be fully decoded by the other, and the decoding of both is often left to something which can even be beyond our knowledge. Fredric Jameson, writes: "in practice, all the structuralists: Levi-Strauss with his idea of nature; Barthes with his feeling for social and ideological materials; Althusser with his sense of history; *do* tend to presuppose, beyond the sign-system itself, some kind of ultimate reality which, unknowable or not, serves as its most distant object of reference."[103]

NOTES

[1]Cf. Joseph Margolis, ed. *Philosophy Looks at the Arts* (New York: Scribner's, 1962), pp. 506.

[2]For Kant, the beautiful has a form and thus it is limited; the sublime, on the contrary, is unlimited.

[3]G. W. F. Hegel, *Aesthetics: Lectures on Fine Art*, transl. by T. M. Knox (London: Oxford University Press, 1961), p. 41.

[4]Immanuel Kant, *The Critique of Judgment*, transl. by J.C. Meredith (London: Oxford University Press, 1961), p. 41.

[5]*Ibid.*, pp. 42-44. Rene Wellek suggests that Kant's characterization of aesthetic judgments as "disinterested" implies the autonomy of art and not the doctrine of art-for-art's sake. Kant merely wants "to distinguish the object of our investigation from morality, pleasure, truth, and utility." (*A History of Modern Criticism: 1750-1950*, I, *op. cit.*, pp. 229-230).

[6]Kant, *op. cit.*, p. 50.

[7]*Ibid.*, p. 60.

[8]*Ibid.*, p. 62.

[9]*Ibid.*, p. 80.

[10]*Ibid.*, p. 84.

[11]Wellek, *A History of Modern Criticism: 1750-1950*, I, *op. cit.*, p. 230.

[12]For a discussion cf., Lucien Goldmann, *Immanuel Kant*, transl. by Robert Black (London: NLB., 1972), pp. 133-136.

[13]Kant, *op. cit.*, p. 65.

[14]Wellek and Warren, *op. cit.*, p. 142.

[15]Leonard R. Palmer, *Descriptive and Comparative Linguistics* (London: Faber and Faber, 1972), pp. 13, 81.

[16]Mario Pei, *Invitation to Linguistics* (New York: Doubleday and Company, Inc., 1965), p. 1.

[17]Wellek and Warren, *op. cit.*, p. 159.

[18]Wellek, *Concepts of Criticism, op. cit.*, p. 276.

[19]Cf. Jonathan Culler, *Structuralist Poetics* (London: Routledge and Kegan Paul, 1975), pp. 3, 6.

[20]This account is based on Ferdinand de Saussure, *Course in General Linguistics*, transl. by Wade Baskin (London: Peter Owen, 1964)

[21]*Ibid.*, p. 16.

[22]*Ibid.*, p. 66.

[23]*Ibid.*, p. 67.

[24]*Ibid.*, p. 67.

[25]*Ibid.*, p. 69.

[26]*Ibid.*, p. 16.

[27]Cf. for example, Volosinov, *op. cit.*, especially, pp. 57-58.

[28]Saussure, *op. cit.*, pp. 8-9.

[29]Volosinov, *op. cit.*, p. 59.

[30]Saussure, *op. cit.*, p. 9.

[31]*Ibid.*, p. 9.

[32]Saussure, *op. cit.*, pp. 99-100.

[33]*Ibid.*, p. 81.

[34]*Ibid.*, p. 83.

[35]Volosinov, *op. cit.*, p. 61.

[36]Saussure, *op. cit.*, pp. 122-124.

[37]Cf. Fredric Jameson, *The Prison-House of Language* (Princeton: Princeton University Press, 1972), p. 39.

[38]For a systematic account of the Kantian origins of the Russian and the Western varieties of formalism, cf. Ewa M. Thompson, *Russian Formalism and Anglo-American New Criticism* (The Hague: Mouton, 1971). Also, as noted in the previous chapter, the relation between Kant and the American new critics is discussed in William J. Handy, *Kant and the Southern New Critics, op. cit.*

[39]Mark Poster, *Existential Marxism in Postwar France* (Princeton: Princeton University Press, 1975), p. 307.

[40]Cf. A. R. Radcliffe-Brown, *Structure and Function in Primitive Society* (London: Cohen and West, 1952), p. 10.

[41]Cf. Glucksmann, *Structuralist Analysis in Contemporary Social Thought, op. cit.*, p. 31.

[42]Cf. *Ibid.*, p. 40.

[43]"A Confrontation," *New Left Review*, no. 62 (July-August, 1970), p. 64.

[44]Jan M. Broekman, *Structuralism* (Dordrecht: D. Reidel Publishing Company, 1974), pp. 6-10.

[45]Claude Levi-Strauss, *Structural Anthropology*, transl. by C. Jakob-

son and B. G. Schoept (New York: Basic Books, 1963), p. 50.

[46] *Ibid*., p. 34.

[47] *Ibid*., p. 84.

[48] *Ibid*., p. 85.

[49] *Ibid*., pp. 85-86.

[50] Vladimir Propp, "Morphology of the Folktale," *International Journal of American Linguistics*, vol. 24, no. 4.

[51] Levi-Strauss, *Structural Anthropology, op. cit.*, p. 210.

[52] Transl. and quoted by James A. Boon in *From Symbolism to Structuralism* (New York: Harper Torchbooks, 1973), p. 38.

[53] *Ibid*., p. 41.

[54] Transl. and quoted by Boon in *Ibid*., pp. 54-55.

[55] Claude Levi-Strauss, *The Raw and the Cooked*, transl. by J. and D. Weightman (New York: Harper Torchbooks, 1969), p. 10.

[56] *Ibid*., p. 62.

[57] Claude Levi-Strauss, *The Savage Mind* (Chicago: The University of Chicago Press, 1966), p. 256.

[58] Examples of the disagreements among various structuralists can be found in Richard Macksey and Eugenio Donato, eds. *The Languages of Criticism and the Sciences of Man: The Structuralist Controversy* (Baltimore: The John Hopkins Press, 1970).

[59] Cf. Jacques Ehrmann, ed. *Structuralism* (New York: Anchor Books, 1970), p. ix. Also, Robert Scholes, *Structuralism in Literature* (New Haven: Yale University Press, 1974), pp. 107. And, David Robey, ed. *Structuralism: An Introduction* (London: Oxford University Press, 1973), pp. 1-2.

[60] Roland Barthes, "The Structuralist Activity," in *Critical Essays*, transl by Richard Howard (Evanston: Northwestern University Press, 1972), p. 214.

[61] Cf. Tzvetan Todorov, "Comment lire?" in his *Poetique de la prose* (Paris: Seuil, 1971).

[62] Barthes, "The Two Criticisms," in *Critical Essays, op. cit.*, p. 251.

[63] *Ibid*., p. 251.

[64] *Ibid*., pp. 252-253.

[65] *Ibid*., p. 254.

[66] Barthes, "What is Criticism?", in *Ibid*., p. 257.

[67] *Ibid*., pp. 258-259.

[68] *Ibid*., p. 259.

[69] *Ibid*., p. 260.

[70] Barthes, "Preface," in *Ibid*., p. xiii.

[71] *Ibid*., p. xiii.

[72] *Ibid*., pp. xvii-xviii.

[73] *Ibid*., p. xxi.

[74]Roland Barthes, *S/Z*, transl. by R. Miller (New York: Hill and Wang, 1974), p. 4.

[75]*Ibid.*, p. 5.

[76]*Ibid.*, p. 5.

[77]*Ibid.*, p. 8.

[78]*Ibid.*, p. 10.

[79]*Ibid.*, p. 11.

[80]*Ibid.*, p. 15.

[81]*Ibid.*, p. 16.

[82]Barthes, "The Structuralist Activity," *op. cit.*, pp. 214-215.

[83]*Ibid.*, p. 216.

[84]*Ibid.*, p. 218.

[85]Broekman, *op. cit.*, p. 73.

[86]*Ibid.*, pp. 78, 79.

[87]Serge Doubrovsky, *The New Criticism in France*, transl. by D. Coltman (Chicago: The University of Chicago Press, 1973), pp. 29-31.

[88]Roland Barthes, *Writing Degree Zero*, transl. by A. Lavers and C. Smith (London: Jonathan Cape, 1967), p. 54.

[89]Roland Barthes, "History or Literature" in *On Racine* (New York: Hill and Wang, 1964), pp. 153-172.

[90]*Ibid.*, p. 161.

[91]*Ibid.*, p. 172.

[92]*Ibid.*, p. 172.

[93]Cf. Broekman, *op. cit.*, pp. 10-11.

[94]"Crisis in Criticism: The Picard-Barthes Debate," *T.L.S.*, (London: Oxford University Press, 1967), p. 169.

[95]Cf. Doubrovsky, *op. cit.*

[96]Jameson, *The Prison-House of Language, op. cit.*, p. 211.

[97]Barthes, *Writing Degree Zero, op. cit.*, p. 87.

[98]*Ibid.*, p. 82.

[99]*Ibid.*, p. 93.

[100]Cf. Poster, *op. cit.*, pp. 332-333.

[101]Cf. Scholes, *op. cit.*, p. 156.

[102]Broekman, *op. cit.*, p. 87.

[103]Jameson, *The Prison-House of Language, op. cit.*, pp. 109-110.

NINE

ASPECTS OF THE PHENOMENOLOGICAL APPROACH

Phenomenological writings on art and literature are greatly diversified, highly idiosyncratic and peculiar to each individual phenomenologist. Instead of proceeding then with an exposition of the contribution of the various phenomenologists on this subject, we will organize our discussion around the issue of subjectivity which now cautiously, now strongly, is regarded by leading phenomenologists as the fundamental element of both literary works and of the very approach to literature itself.

There are instances, in which artistic creativity appears to be related to both subjectivity and objectivity. For example, in his essay "Art and Phenomenology," Fritz Kaufmann writes that "The originality of the artistic expression has both a subjective and an objective bearing,"[1] but this statement rather means that the subjectivity of a given work has general validity.[2] For our purposes here, we can begin with a brief introduction of the characteristic examples of Gaston Bachelard and Georges Poulet who, by adopting the phenomenological perspective, emphasize the element of subjectivity in literary creations themselves as well as in the critical activity.

1. *Bachelard and Poulet: The Primacy of Subjectivity*

An historian and philosopher of science at the Sorbonne, Bachelard left his mark for his contribution to the study of poetic imagination. His attempt to penetrate the secrets of the creative act by the use of the phenomenological method have influenced a number of French philosophers and writers, as well as some phenomenological critics, e.g. Georges Poulet and Jean-Pierre Richard[3] —although he has also been rejected as an alchemist and magician.[4]

Bachelard's celebrated book *The Poetics of Space* is the culmination of the philosopher's effort to deal with the realm of the imaginary. The introduction to this book emphasizes his disappointment with the scientific study of poetic imagination where "the cultural past doesn't count,"[5] and with the causal explanations of psychology/psychoanalysis which focus exclusively on the author. Bachelard maintains that in contrast to the psychoanalyst, the phenomenologist concentrates on the work, being primarily concerned about the poetic act.

A *poetic image* is for Bachelard the ultimate that a man's soul can express. Therefore, his main objective is the study of the ontology of this image, on the level of which "the duality of subject and object is irridescent, shimmering, increasingly active in its inversions." He relates the duality poem/image to the duality mind/soul as follows: "To compose a finished, well constructed poem the mind is obliged to make projects that prefigure it. But for a simple poetic image, there is no project; a flicker of the soul is all that is needed." Bachelard is convinced that "Forces are minifested in poems that do not pass through the circuits of knowledge," and he believes that the critical (judicial) attitude destroys everything that the poetic image is able to generate.

From Bachelard's point of view, only a phenomenology of the imagination can adequately examine the strange being of the poetic image, and only the phenomenological reader is able to identify completely with the original creator. The phenomenological reader is an active participant in the creative process, and as if he "were the writer's ghost" his enjoyment of reading reflects the enjoyment of writing.

Bachelard dismisses completely the rational inquiry prescribed by the scientific method as well as the psychological/psychoanalytic approaches. Moreover he regrets that being trained in the philosophy of science he was initially excluding the purely "personal" approach to poetic image. Even a personal interpretation, however, would not be enough by itself, and he insists that "Only phenomenology—that is to say, consideration of the *onset of the image* in an individual consciousness—can help us to restore the subjectivity of images and to measure their fulness, their strength and their transubjectivity." He further maintains that the phenomenological reader is fundamentally different from the professional literary critic: "A literary critic is a reader who is necessarily severe. . . . I only read and re-read what I like . . . in reading we are re-living our temptation to be a poet." The similarity of Bachelard's position in respect to the relationship between writer and reader with Barthes' attitude toward the same subject is striking.

As with Barthian structuralism, Bachelard's phenomenology is ahistorical too. Bachelard is convinced that "for a phenomenologist, the attempt to attribute antecedents to an image, is a sign of inveterate psychologism." Therefore, he states, "The imagination separates us from the past as well as from reality; it faces the future."

Bachelard examines the poetic image with admiration, perhaps with some kind of passion, and he claims that "nothing prepares a poetic image, especially not culture in the literary sense, and especially not perception, in the psychological sense." In this frame of mind he comes up with an extraordinary conclusion: "*A man's work stands out from life to such an extent that life cannot explain it.*" (My italics).

Finally, according to Bachelard, phenomenological reading is an art in itself, while literary criticism is intended to become in its turn literature. Together with an exclusive emphasis on the uniqueness of the subjective (personal) approach to literary works, this is a general characteristic more or less shared by all phenomenologists concerned with art and literature, and Georges Poulet is not an exception.

A close examination of Poulet's essay, "The Phenomenology of Reading" will be useful in two respects. First, it will give us the opportunity to take another look at the way of thinking of phenomenological critics, since it presents the main ideas of notable figures belonging to this tradition; and second, it will throw additional light upon phenomenology's weaknesses as Poulet himself attempts to make his own contribution to the general body of phenomenological literary criticism.

Poulet's essay demonstrates his opposition to an objective (scientific) approach to literature. For him, books are objects radically different from all others, because their materiality is transformed by the act of reading during which they acquire a new existence in the reader's "innermost self."[6] In this sense, a book is the meeting ground of the subjectivity of the reader, who is being possessed on two levels: the level of his "objective thought" and that of his "very subjectivity." Of course, the reader is conquered by his subjectivity, and for this reason Poulet does not deny the relative usefulness of "a mass of biographical, bibliographical, textual and general critical information" for the understanding[7] of literary works. He underlines, however, that "this knowledge does not coincide with the internal knowledge of the work," and he points out that "Nothing external to the work could possibly share the extraordinary claim which the work now exerts on me."[8]

Further, Poulet argues that during the act of reading, the writer and the reader "start having a common consciousness" even though the importance of the two is by no means equal. The writer's consciousness is "active and potent" related to "its own world" and to "its own objects." The consciousness of the reader is "passive" and despite Poulet's conviction that "reading does not interrupt my activity as subject," he adds: "I am a consciousness astonished by an existence which is not mine, but which I experience as though it were mine." As for the consciousness of the critic, Poulet agrees that the extent of its identity with the consciousness of the writer affects decisively the degree of success of literary criticism. Consequently, "the variation of . . . this relationship" manifested in the work of leading phenomenological critics, attracts Poulet's attention.[9]

When no identification takes place—Jacques Riviere's case—literary criticism is "destined to failure" because understanding does not go beyond surfaces. In contrast to this, namely in the case of total identification—this is achieved, for example, by Jean-Pierre Richard who is generally influenced by Bachelard—literary criticism remains incomplete, because the critic-subject is entirely abolished. In the opposite pole is found the abolition of the work-object by dint of a "hyper-critical consciousness" engaged in a process of abstraction and intellectualization; Maurice Blanchot is a case in point. Poulet concludes that either *extreme identification* with the writer's consciousness, or *extreme detachment* from it, results in unsatisfactory literary criticism.[10]

Poulet argues that these two extremes are not completely disadvantageous. Thus, extreme identification is able "to move at once to the heart of the work," and extreme detachment "to confer on its objects the highest degree of intelligibility." On the one hand, then, Poulet speaks of a "penetration by the senses," and on the other, of "penetration by the reflective consciousness." The synthesis of these two extremes, Poulet maintains, will result in the most efficient practical literary criticism. He believes that the phenomenological critic Jean

Starobinski has already achieved this synthesis, because his own method is flexible enough and able to move from an *initial intimacy* to a *final detachment* to the effect that the reader identifies with the writer without losing the critic. Yet, notwithstanding its merits, even Starobinski's critical method is not free of error. Poulet states: "The sole fault with which I might reproach such criticism is the excessive ease with which it penetrates what it illuminates. . ., under its action, literary works lose their opacity, their solidity, their objective dimension. . . ."[11]

In effect, Starobinski's criticism leaves the work's *form* unexamined. This failure is overcome by the literary criticism of Marcel Raymond and Jean Rousset, the creators of the so-called Geneva School, with which Poulet himself identifies. What Raymond and Rousset actually suggest is the approach of the writer's consciousness (subjectivity) through the work's objective and formal elements (objective dimension), while they recognize "the precedence of the subject over its objects."[12] For the Geneva School, then, the object of the work mediates between the subject of the critic and the subject of the writer. The proper way of approaching literary works can be expressed by the formula subject $\longrightarrow$ object $\longrightarrow$ subject, which is essentially similar to the formula subject $\longrightarrow$ subject $\longrightarrow$ object.[13]

Poulet's account of phenomenological literary criticism ends here, from which point on he attempts to make his own input. He argues that the criticism of the two leading figures of the Geneva School is adequate for the understanding of just *one part* of a writer's subjectivity, concretely, "the part played by the subject in its interrelation with objects." The remaining part of the writer's subjectivity, however, has a peculiar relationship to the objective dimension of the work, since it is *"present"* in the work, and yet it "stands alone" within it: it can only be seized by the critic's *intuition*. Right at the end of his essay, Poulet discloses his own thoughts in relation to this part of a writer's subjectivity which is untouched, as he maintains, by all other phenomenological critics. Given the relative complexity of the subject, a long quotation seems to be necessary here. Poulet writes:

> all subjective activity present in a literary work is not
> entirely explained by its relationship with forms and
> objects within the work. There is in the work a *mental*

activity profoundly engaged in objective forms; and there is, at another level, forsaking all forms, *a subject which reveals itself to itself (and to me)* in its transcendence relative to all which is reflected in it. At this point, no object can any longer express it; no structure can any longer define it; it is exposed in its ineffability and in its fundamental indeterminacy. Such is perhaps the reason why the critic, in his elucidation of works, is haunted by his transcendence of mind. *It seems then that criticism, in order to accompany the mind in this effort of detachment from itself needs to annihilate, or at least momentarily to forget, the objective elements of the work, and to elevate itself to the apprehension of a subjectivity without objectivity.*[14]

Poulet's essay was presented in a symposium on structuralism and in the discussion which followed he emphasized that the first stage of literary criticism should be "absolute adherence,"[15] and that criticism should remain totally dissociated from science. He committed himself as follows: "to my own mind, very clearly, very definitely, criticism has the character of knowledge, but it is not a kind of scientific knowledge, and I have to decline very strongly the name of *scientist*. I am *not* a scientist and I do not think that any true critic when he is making an act of criticism can be a scientist." And after a few phrases he ended by saying that during the act of criticism "my hope" is to arrive "at something which I call *absolute subjectivity*."[16] (My italics). To Lucien Goldmann's question —who also participated in that symposium—concerning "the criterion of falsity" of this knowledge, when, for example, a particular judgment is made on a given literary work, Poulet answered that the sole criterion would be his own personal acceptance or not of that judgment.[17]

In view of Poulet's position it is evident that the phenomenological literary criticism he advocates can "elevate itself to the apprehension of a subjectivity without objectivity" by means of the critic's *intuition*. Thus, instead of engaging in a commentary on Bachelard's and Poulet's[18] ideas on the level of their general and abstract formulations, and before we go into the examination of the foundations—epistemological and philosophical—of the kind of literary criticism they are subscribing to, in the light of which the validity of their viewpoint will be shown, it is necessary to discuss the method of intuition or *verstehen.*

2. *The Method of Verstehen*

Phenomenology, psychoanalysis, existential psychology, the critical theorists of the Frankfurt School, Lukács in *History and Class Consciousness* and Goldmann in *The Human Sciences and Philosophy*, all have one concern in common: to understand the *subjectivity* of an human actor, that is, the *intended meaning* which an actor gives to his own behavior and activity, including his own understanding of external events and phenomena.

To achieve this objective, phenomenology in particular depends upon the methodological procedures established in the nineteenth century as a reaction to the spirit of the Enlightenment assuming the universality of the scientific method for the arriving at objective and empirically verifiable knowledge. This spirit, based on the methodological unity of the natural and the social sciences, was manifested in positivism and subsequently advanced by empiricism, naturalism, behaviorism and vulgar materialism attached to the idea of universal natural and historical laws.

Specifically, as Peter Hamilton states, "the method of phenomenological analysis becomes . . . the interpretational method of *verstehen.*"[19] Given that Max Weber was an ardent advocate of *verstehen* as an indispensable methodological tool of the human sciences (especially sociology), it will be helpful to present some ideas deriving from his systematic methodological investigations,[20] without ignoring the fact that the Weberian *verstehen* has been *re-defined and modified in some of its subsequent phenomenological formulations.*

Weber's starting point was Kant's distinction between the world of natural and the world of socio-cultural phenomena. Natural phenomena belong to "the world of human experience,"[21] while socio-cultural phenomena include Kant's "practical reason,"[22] human values and purposes. The fundamental difficulty which prevents the construction of a single cognitive system able to deal with both the natural and the socio-cultural worlds consists in that the latter is concerned with evaluations, purposes, meanings and motives, which are not only found in the investigated phenomenon (i.e. a literary work), but also in the investigator himself (i.e. a literary critic).

This peculiarity of socio-cultural phenomena was noted by Wilhelm Windelband who distinguished the "natural" from "historical" sciences, and who characterized the first as "nomothetic" and the second as "idiographic."[23] Heinrich Rickert, following this distinction, suggests that if empirical reality is examined for the purpose of the formulation of "general laws" it belongs to the sphere of the natural sciences; but if it is examined as consisting of particular and unique events, it belongs to the sphere of the cultural sciences.[24] Nevertheless, the idiographic (descriptive, focusing on unique events) and nomothetic (establishment of general laws) methods can be used simultaneously by both the natural and cultural sciences, because the description of unique phenomena is not the sole privilege of the cultural sciences.[25]

To return to Max Weber, we can point out that through his methodology, he tried to give to the propositions of the social sciences the nomothetic and objective nature which were essential for the propositions of the natural sciences as based on the principle of *causality*. According to Weber, then, the investigation of socio-cultural phenomena could not avoid the use of the category of causality when it was aiming at general propositions. However, in the formulation of these propositions the investigator also uses his own evaluations and judgments. Therefore, the question to be asked is how is it possible to arrive at the objective knowledge of social phenomena based on the principle of causality when the investigator incorporates in his study his own prejudices? That is, how is it possible for the investigator to be able to keep separate from his investigations his own preferences and beliefs in order to honour an essential scientific demand?

Weber, very much aware of this problem, used as the axis of his methodology the category of *verstehen* on condition that is was subseqently subjected to scientific verification. At any rate, an elaboration of the method of *verstehen* as advocated by Weber is necessary, and it will indicate some of the deficiencies of what becomes phenomenology's primary methodological tool, from the point of view of *scientific objectivity*. In addition, it will prepare the ground for an understanding of why Georges Poulet's demand for a literary criticism able to "elevate itself to the apprehension of a subjectivity without objectivity" implies not just the rejection of the scientific method—as Bachelard strongly emphasizes—but, first of all, a completely different way of approaching man, which is modified as the way of thinking influenced by phenomenology goes through a process of self-reflection.

Verstehen, which holds a central position in Weber's methodology, is usually translated as "understanding" or "interpretative understanding." Weber uses this concept in a specifically technical sense which cannot be expressed by an exact English term. Talcott Parsons explains: "Its primary reference . . . is to the observation and theoretical interpretation of the subjective 'states of mind' of actors. But it also extends to the grasp of the meaning of logical and other systems of symbols, a meaning which is usually thought of as in some sense 'intended' by a mind or intelligent being of some sort."[26]

The category of *verstehen* is directly related to the understanding of an actor's subjectivity, on the presupposition that the meanings which he attributes to phenomena and events are intended.* With this Weberian meaning of *verstehen,* the phenomenologist Alfred Schutz is in complete agreement. Schutz points out that even though *verstehen* is "subjective" in the sense indicated by Weber, nevertheless its critics "call it subjective, because they hold that understanding the motives of another man's action depends upon the private, uncontrollable, and unverifiable intuition of the observer or refers to his private value system." Hence, Schutz continues, the opponents of *verstehen* fail "to distinguish clearly between verstehen (1), as the experiential form of common-sense knowledge of human affairs, (2), as an epistemological problem, and (3), as a method peculiar to the social sciences."[27] The first two meanings of *verstehen* are of special interest to phenomenology.

That *verstehen* is a method, or an "operation"[28] which an investigator performs with the purpose of finding causal relationships among the behavior or actions of an actor and his motives, rationality, etc. was not suggested by Weber alone. It was not even a German idea originally. The first advocates of *verstehen* were Giambattista Vico and August Comte. Much later, it was considered a necessary tool of the social sciences by H.E. Cooley,

---

*This term has its special phenomenological meaning.

F. Znaniecki, P. Sorokin, R. M. Mc Iver, et al.[29]   In Germany,
the method of *verstehen* was introduced by the neo-Kantians
Windelband, Rickert, Simmel and Dilthey.[30]   Weber, borrowed
the idea of *verstehen* from Dilthey, after he had come—as H.
Stuart Hughes mentions—"close to the twilight relativism in
which Dilthey had dwelt . . .,"[31] and he developed it into a
powerful tool in the hands of the social scientist.   Hughes goes
on to suggest that *verstehen*, as understood by these German
thinkers, "was the effort to 'feel oneself into' a historical or
social action by putting oneself in the place of the actor or
actors.   It was a method of psychological sympathy. . . ."[32]

For our purposes here we need not engage in a detailed
discussion of *verstehen*.   However, it is useful to mention some
of the arguments against its validity which developed on the
basis of scientific thinking.   Theodore Abel, for example, examines the concrete steps of this method[33] and operationalizing
it in three different cases, he concludes:

> The operation of *verstehen* is performed by analyzing a
> behavior situation in such a way—usually in terms of
> general "feeling states"—that it parallels some personal
> experience of the interpreter.   Primarily, the operation
> of *verstehen* does two things: It relieves us of a sense
> of apprehension in connection with behavior that is
> unfamiliar or unexpected and it is a source of hunches,
> which help us in the formulation of hypotheses.   The
> operation of *verstehen* does not, however, add to our
> store of knowledge, because it consists of the application
> of knowledge already validated by personal experience;
> nor does it serve as a means of verification.[34]

Notwithstanding such criticisms, though, *verstehen*, as Hughes
writes "has passed over from the writings of history to become
an accepted part of social-science method."[35]

Weber was not unaware of the weaknesses of *verstehen*.
Of course, he accepted it as suggested by the neo-Kantians,
but at the same time—and here lies his difference with them
on this matter—he strongly emphasizes the dangers inherent
in this method, since the possibility was ever present that the
investigator's prejudices could be incorporated into his overall
investigation.   The securing of objectivity Weber entrusted to
the scientific method.   He writes: "*Verstehen* . . . must . . . be

controlled so far as possible by the . . . usual methods of causal imputation, before even the most evident interpretation can become a valid 'intelligible explanation'."[36]

Parsons, correctly reflects Weber's fear of the possibility of an inappropriate use of the operation of *verstehen* when he states that "our immediate intentions of meaning may be real and, as such correct. But their interpretation cannot dispense with a rationally consistent system of theoretical concepts. Only in so far as they measure up to such criticisms can intuitions constitute knowledge. And without such criticism the door is opened to any number of uncontrolled and unverifiable allegations. Weber had a very deep and strong ethical feeling on this point; to him the intuitionist position made possible the evasion of responsibility for scientific judgments."[37]

Weber's awareness of the limitations of the method of *verstehen* certainly did not shake his belief in its indispensability for the study of socio-cultural phenomena. He was a "methodological individualist,"[38] and, as G. W. Runciman rightly observes, he was convinced that "the task of the sociologist is to establish causal explanations of the social actions of individuals themselves."[39] In his discussion of the problems generated by the use of *verstehen*,[40] Weber indicates the supplementary methodological safeguards required for the achievement of objectivity and the drawing of valid conclusions. For example, the categories of *comparison*,[41] *causality*, and *value relevance*,[42] are particularly valuable in this respect. However, it is beyond the scope of this study to pursue an examination of the Weberian methodological categories, or to give the reasons which substantiate the argument that Weber's own attempts towards "value-free" social science were unsuccessful. In relation to this, we can quote István Mészáros who points out that "the instruments and methods of social analysis can never by radically neutral with regard to their object."[43] But before we end our brief discussion of *verstehen*, let us look at some of its critics' ideas more closely.

Theodore Abel, examines and criticizes the method of *verstehen* in its pure* form with the primary purpose of streng-

---

*When the investigator merely tries to 'put himself into' the subjectivity of the actor.

thening the cause of positivism. Indeed, one of our previous quotations from Abel's article* continues as follows: "The probability of connection can be ascertained only by means of objective, experimental and statistical tests." Weber, also, insisting on a value-free social science, falls into the same positivist trap as Abel, despite his reservations about positivism. His ultimate stand is that "science in general and social science in particular, need to be *Wertfrei* (value-free) so as to perform the task of exact empirical description. In so far as the scientist gives allegiance to religious, philosophical, political or artistic values, he does so in his personal capacity."[44]

Positivism, on the one hand, uses observations and experiments as passive tools (Abel's case), and on the other, it preaches the separation of facts from values, of theory from praxis, of man the scientist from man the active member of society (Weber's case). Thus, at worst, positivism demonstrates its contempt for everything human in individuals and societies, and at best, its incapacity to understand the special nature of human communication and interaction. In the final analysis, what positivism proclaims is useful to the maintenance of established social orders.

An alleged "objective" and "value-free" social science legitimates—under certain conditions—the division of society into antagonistic classes and interest groups, and/or the supression of entire national communities by powerful bureaucracies. In this sense, the striving for scientism and for measurable empirical facts (after the manner of the natural sciences) in the examination of man's complex reality without effective social controls, often conceals an attempt of those who benefit from a radically stratified society, to present themselves above the ugliness of the everyday struggle for human living and meaningful existence.[45]

Weber tried to free himself from both the crude assumptions of positivism (by stressing the necessity for the application of the method of *verstehen*), and the naive assertions of idealism (by maintaining that the scientific verification of the findings resulting from *verstehen* was possible; yet, he remained oscil-

---

*See, note no. 34.

lating between the two, leaving himself vulnerable to various attacks, as for example, that which emanated from the quarters of phenomenology, as we will see shortly.

In his interesting article, "The Problem of Reification and the *Verstehen-Erklären* controversy," the Yugoslavian philosopher Mihailo Marković suggests that it is misleading to assume that the objective (explanation) and subjective (understanding) methodologies are mutually exclusive. He reinterprets the methods of *Erklären* and *Verstehen*, perceiving them as "two special moments within *dialectic*, conceived as a method of critical social study characterized by both structural and historical, objective and subjective approach."[46]

3. *The Subjectivity of the Phenomenological Method*

Regardless of the credit which phenomenologists give to Max Weber for his contribution to the development of the method of *verstehen*, phenomenology itself took the task of making this method "fully intelligible" and thus the road opened for a criticism of the Weberian standpoint. What phenomenologists seem to hold against Weber is primarily the contradictory nature of his epistemology. On the one hand, Weber was fighting for the legitimation of the subjective approach to sociocultural phenomena, and on the other, he was trying to retain a scientific guise. Phenomenologists, then, had not only to make clear their own epistemological position, but also to define *verstehen* in the light of the latter.

In regard to epistemology, the fundamental phenomenological presupposition is that *Lebenswelt* (the life-world)—that is, the world of men's immediate experience—is the foundation of all knowledge. A basic premise of phenomenology is that the world of knowledge and social reality is based on the face-to-face everyday interaction among men, in other words, on intersubjectivity. This is obvious, for example, in Berger and Luckmann's attempt to develop a sociology of knowledge based on phenomenological principles, especially those laid down by Alfred Schutz, i.e. his theory about the stock of knowledge at hand: "Man in daily life . . . finds at any given moment a stock of knowledge at hand that serves him as a scheme of interpretation of his past and present experiences and also determines his anticipations of things to come."[47]

According to Schutz, this stock of knowledge at hand is shaped and structured by "the system of our practical and theoretical interest at this specific moment," and it is "in continual flux, and changes from any Now to the next one not only in its range but also in its structure."[48] Berger and Luckmann elaborate on Schutz's theory as follows: "I live in a world of signs and symbols every day. . . . I live in the commonsense world of everyday life equipped with specific bodies of knowledge. What is more, I know that others share at least part of this knowledge, and they know that I know this. My interaction with others in everyday life is, therefore, constantly affected by our common participation in the available social stock of knowledge. The social stock of knowledge includes knowledge of my situation and its limits."[49]

By the same token, scientific knowledge too derives from the social reality of our day-to-day experience. Hence, it is maintained that there is a point of unity between the natural and cultural sciences, but contrary to what has been suggested by the positivists, this unity is not due to their common methodological (i.e. the prevalence of the scientific method) and ontological (i.e. reductionism of all natural phenomena to simpler ones which can be accounted for by the science of physics) assumptions. Each one of these two categories of science has its own method, and neither physics nor psychology (as for example Jean Piaget suggests) is the basic science.[50]

Aron Gurvitsch writes that the natural and cultural sciences have another common point: "The first presupposition of the sciences proves to be the life-world itself, our paramount and even sole reality. Whatever unity obtains among the sciences derives from their common rootedness in the life-world. . . ."[51] On this basis, the precedence of the human over the natural sciences is proclaimed because phenomenology classifies sciences "in terms of priority of access."[52]

From the point of view of phenomenology, the unity between the natural and human sciences is very weak (limited to their common ties with the life-world), while the disagreements separating the two are serious.[53] An important difference between the two results from their different methods, and at this point phenomenologists simply borrow the idea put forward by the neo-Kantians, only providing some new terms. Alfred Schutz, for example, says that the natural scientist creates theoretical "constructs of the first degree," while the social scientist creates theoretical constructs "of the second degree." These second degree constructs are nothing else but the Weberian ideal types.[54]

Thus, there seems to have been not only a basic agreement between Windelband, Rickert, Weber, et al, and certain phenomenologists on what distinguishes the natural from the human sciences, but in addition, these phenomenologists seem to have continued the methodological investigations of the neo-Kantians, (as in the case, for example, of the relationship between Dilthey and Schutz).[55] This is why *verstehen* became the primary tool of the phenomenological approach. Nevertheless, as mentioned earlier, epistemological and other considerations led to a phenomenological rethinking of the whole issue of *verstehen*, the essentials of which will be presented in the following chapter. Here, it is necessary to give a general account of phenomenology itself.

The extreme diversity and vagueness characterizing the writings of leading phenomenologists, i.e. Husserl, Merleau-Ponty, et al, do not allow for a direct answer to the question of 'what is phenomenology.' In the introduction of his two-volume history of phenomenology, Herbert Spiegelberg rejects such notions as "school" or "system," and, explaining the difficulties involved in a definition of phenomenology, he chooses to call it a "movement."[56]

Spiegelberg distinguishes the phenomenological movement which was initiated by Husserl from: a) *extra-philosophical phenomenologies* (e.g. particular phenomenologies established by the natural sciences; and b) *philosophical phenomenologies* related to the works of Johann Heinrich Lambert, Kant, Hegel, Eduard von Hartmann, William Hamilton and Charles Sanders Pierce). Both (a) and (b) are unconnected to the Husserlian phenomenological movement, the background of which goes back to the nineteenth century.[57] Spiegelberg presents the ideas of all phenomenologists who have contributed to the movement, but he makes it clear that in order to define it, he can only speak for himself because the definition of phenomenology cannot be other than a "personal venture."[58]

The various differences between the major phenomenologists which result in "idealistic, realistic, and neutralistic phenomenologies," Spiegelberg asserts, do not facilitate the definition of the phenomenological movement according to "its

results," and he adds that what all phenomenologists seem
to agree about more or less is a common method.[59] He further
presents this method as a series of seven steps, the first three
of which are accepted by all phenomenologists, while the last
four are followed just by some of them.

The first step, namely, the "investigating of particular
phenomena," consists of three distinct operations: *intuiting,
analyzing* and *describing*.   The second, referred to as the "investigating of general essences," that is , universals, completes
the understanding of the already investigated particulars.   As
in the first step, the operations of *intuiting, analyzing* and
describing are performed distinctly from each other.   The third
step is called "apprehending essential relationships among essences."   And the fourth, which Spiegelberg pinpoints as an
original contribution of the phenomenological movement is
referred to as "watching modes of approaching" of particulars
and universals alike.   The fifth step is indicated as "watching
the constitution of phenomena in consciousness."   The sixth,
"suspending belief in the existence of the phenomena," is the
so-called *phenomenological reduction*, and the seventh, "interpreting the meaning of phenomena," brings into the picture
Heiddeger as well as a different phenomenology from the "descriptive" one, namely, *hermeneutic phenomenology*, which
will be discussed in the next chapter.

These seven steps of the phenomenological method taken
together are, according to Spiegelberg, unified by a common
idea: "On all levels the phenomenological approach is opposed
to explanatory hypotheses; it confirms itself to the direct evidence of intuitive seeing . . . it constitutes a determined attempt
to enrich the world of our experience by bringing out hitherto
neglected aspects of our experience . . . one might describe the
underlying unity of the phenomenological procedures as the
usually obstinate attempt to look at the phenomena and to
remain faithful to them before even thinking about them."[60]

Apart from this definition of phenomenology primarily
as a method, Spiegelberg also focuses on its relationship to subjectivity and he writes a special essay entitled "How Subjective
is Phenomenology?"   In this essay, he begins with an affirmation of Husserl's inclination "towards 'subjectivity' as the ultimate foundation for the new scientific rigour which he wanted
to bring to philosophy."[61]   Next, he underlines three particular
meanings of the term 'subjective': subjective as the "*merely*

personal"; subjective as that which is *"dependent upon the subject"*; and subjective as *"subject-related."* Further, Spiegelberg makes the distinction between "transcendental" and "non-transcendental" phenomenologies, and he points out that for the former "all phenomena were subjective in the sense of dependence . . . upon . . . the transcendental subject which (Husserl) tried to keep apart from the empirical subject," while the latter is subjective also, but in the sense of "subject-related."[62]

Spiegelberg argues that neither transcendental nor non-transcendental phenomenologies have in reality surrendered to subjectivity. In fact, he states that "Husserl's enterprise may well be characterized as the triumph of objectivity over subjectivity," and he gives the following explanation: "The main key to Husserl's solution has to be sought in his conception of a priori essences. For phenomenology is not the study of consciousness in all its empirical varieties, but that of the essence of consciousness, or of its essential structure. Insofar as this essential structure is the same for all consciousness, it seemed possible to Husserl to eliminate all personal varieties of the subject as accidental. Based on this identical essential consciousness, even the world constituted by several transcendental subjects could not fail to be identical."[63] Even so, the category of "a priori essences" does not secure objectivity for the reason that, in Spiegelberg's own words, "phenomenologists, non-transcendental as well as transcendental, seem all too often not to agree in their verdicts about essences. And *all of them* seem to base their claims as self-evident intuition of phenomena. *Thus it would seem that the subjective factor in the phenomenological approach lays it wide open to subjectivism.*"[64] (My italics).

To remove the danger of falling into subjectivism and its consequences, Spiegelberg warns the serious phenomenologist to be careful not to be deceived by the "lazy thinkers" who are attracted to the movement, and he adds that the intuitive method needs "self-discipline and vigilance." He also proposes that no phenomenological study should be accepted "until the claimant to self-evidence can give himself and others proof that he has made every effort to deactivate his personal and institutional biases. . . ."[65]

Finally, Spiegelberg, in his eagerness to safeguard phenomenology from subjectivism, maintains that the subjective phenomenological method is the most adequate one, since, the alternative, namely the scientific method of positivism cannot prove the objectivity of its data "in the sense of public." The only way of achieving objectivity is, according to Spiegelberg, by recording and summing up a great number of individual "direct experiences." And confident that he has demonstrated the absolute superiority of the intuitive method (as well as amazingly ignorant of the tremendous possibilities offered by the dialectical method) he concludes: "All objective experience is really intersubjective experience, i.e. a solution from subjective experiences. This makes subjective experience even more indispensable. There is then no escape from subjectivity. . . . I conclude that all phenomenology is subjective in the sense that it makes phenomena completely subject-dependent."[66]

Subjectivity then is a central category of the phenomenological approach, and the upper limit of the expectations of phenomenologists like Spiegelberg is not to transcend it but to reduce it to "proper proportions." In reference to his claim that "the only care for subjectivisitic subjectivity is more and better subjectivity,"[67] we can say that, apart from playing with words, such a recipe can hardly affect the practice of phenomenology.

In regard to phenomenological literary criticism, for example, we can say that the critic's own subjectivity (either in the form of a partial or a total dependence upon the subject) approaches a literary work—with the primary aim of understanding the subjectivity of its author—without actually resorting to what Spiegelberg calls "comparing of notes," that is, to the sum-total of the individual impressions and judgments of as many subjectivities as possible (i.e. the standpoints of other phenomenological critics) before a conclusive statement is released. But even if such a practice was possible, in which case one could speak of collective criticism, the average of many subjective positions might and might not have been able to result in (scientific) objectivity, unless the epistemological premise of phenomenology about the "common-sense" foundation of all knowledge is fully accepted.[68]

Is there then no way out of the deadlock of subjectivism into which the phenomenological approach may easily lapse? This problem, in addition to that of phenomenology's *abistorical character*, has generated severe criticism and has caused a great deal of trouble to phenomenologists who eventually tried seriously to overcome. To follow developments in this direction, we have to move out of Husserl's descriptive phenomenology and enter the field of hermeneutics, skillfully expounded in Hans-Georg Gadamer's *Truth and Method*.

NOTES

[1] Fritz Kaufmann, "Art and Phenomenology," in Maurice Natanson, ed. *Essays in Phenomenology* (The Hague: Martinus Nijhoff, 1960), p. 144.

[2] Cf. *Ibid.*, pp. 145, 150.

[3] Cf. for example, Poulet's preface to Jean-Pierre Richard's *Littérature et sensation* (Paris, 1954), pp. 10-11.   Also, Jean-Pierre Richard's *Poésie et profondeur* (Paris, 1953), p. 10.

[4] Cf. C. G. Christofides, "Gaston Bachelard's Phenomenology of the Imagination," *The Romanic Review*, vol. 52-53 (February 1961), p. 36.

[5] All quotations in reference to Gaston Bachelard's work are from the introduction to his book, *The Poetics of Space*, transl. by E. Gilson (Boston: Beacon Press, 1970).

[6] Georges Poulet, "Criticism and the Experience of Interiority," in Macksey and Donato, eds. *op. cit.*, p. 57. This essay was initially presented as a paper in a symposium on structuralism at the John Hopkins Humanities Center and subsequently published under the title "The Phenomenology of Reading," in Adams, ed. *op. cit.*, p. 1213.

[7] Poulet explains this term as follows: "To understand a literary work . . . is to let the individual who wrote it to reveal himself to us *in* us. It is not the biography which explicates the work, but rather the work which sometimes enables us to understand the biography." ("Criticism and the Experience of Interiority," *Ibid.*, p. 61).

[8] *Ibid.*, p. 62.

[9] *Ibid.*, p. 63.

[10] Cf. *Ibid.*, pp. 66-67.

[11] *Ibid.*, p. 69.

[12] *Ibid.*, p. 71.

[13] *Ibid.*, p. 72.

[14] *Ibid.*, p. 72.

[15] *Ibid.*, p. 76.

[16] *Ibid.*, pp. 77, 78.

[17]*Ibid.*, pp. 84, 85.

[18]Cf. for example, J. Hillis Miller, "The Literary Criticism of Georges Poulet," in *Modern Language Notes*, vol. 78 (December 1983), pp. 471-488.

[19]Peter Hamilton, *Knowledge and Social Structure* (London: Routledge and Kegan Paul, 1974), p. 137.

[20]Cf. Alfred Schutz, "Phenomenology and the Social Sciences," in Joseph J. Kockelmans, ed. *Phenomenology* (New York: Doubleday and Company, Inc., 1967), p. 371.

[21]Talcott Parsons, ed. *Max Weber: The Theory of Social and Economic Organization* (New York: The Free Press, 1964), p. 8.

[22]By *practical reason* it "is meant (reason) in as much as it illuminates the activity . . . (which) produces no changes in the outer world but only in the acting being itself." J. Grooten and G. Jo Steenbergen, *New Encyclopedia of Philosophy* (New York: Philosophical Library, 1972), p. 342.

[23]For definitions cf. George A. Theodorson and Achilles G. Theodorson, *Modern Dictionary of Sociology* (New York: Apollo Editions, 1970), p. 369.

[24]Hughes, *op. cit.*, p. 190.

[25]Cf. Ernest Cassirer, *An Essay on Man* (New Haven: Yale University Press, 1944), p. 187.

[26]Parsons, *op. cit.*, p. 87.

[27]Helmut R. Wagner, ed. *Alfred Schutz on Phenomenology and Social Relations* (Chicago: The University of Chicago Press, 1970), p. 274.

[28]Cf. Theodore Abel, "The Operation Called Verstehen," *American Journal of Sociology*, LIV (1948), p. 211.

[29]*Ibid.*, pp. 211-212.

[30]Hughes, *op. cit.*, pp. 190-200.

[31]*Ibid.*, p. 310.

[32]*Ibid.*, p. 311.

[33]Cf. Abel, *op. cit.*, pp. 215-216.

[34]*Ibid.*, p. 218.

[35]Hughes, *op. cit.*, p. 312.

[36]Max Weber, quoted in *Ibid.*, p. 311.

[37]Talcott Parsons, *The Structure of Social Action* (New York: The Free Press of Glencoe, 1961), p. 589.

[38]Generally speaking, "methodological individualism . . . is a prescription for explanation, asserting that no purported explanation of social (or individual) phenomena are to count as explanations . . . unless they are couched wholly in terms of facts about individuals." Steves Lukes, "Methodological Individualism Reconsidered," in Alan Ryan, ed. *The Philosophy of Social Explanation* (London: Oxford University Press, 1973), p. 122.

[39]G. W. Runciman, *A Critique of Max Weber's Philosophy of Social*

Sciences (Cambridge University Press, 1972), pp. 24-25.

[40] Cf. Weber's discussion of *versteben* in Parsons, ed. *op. cit.*, pp. 94-112.

[41] *Ibid.*, p. 97.

[42] The category of *value-relevance* indicates the connection which exists between a possible problem of investigation and a value which orients the concrete task of the investigator. Cf. Edward A. Shils and Henry A. Finch, eds. *Max Weber: The Methodology of the Social Sciences* (New York: The Free Press, 1968), p. 22.

[43] István Mészáros, "Ideology and Social Sciences," in Ralph Miliband and John Saville, eds. *The Socialist Register 1972* (London: The Merlin Press, 1972), p. 46.

[44] "Dialectical Methodology," *Times Literary Supplement* (March 12, 1970), p. 156.

[45] A look at Marx's and Engels' *The German Ideology* could be enlightening at this point.

[46] Mihailo Marković, "The Problem of Reification and the Verstehen-Erklären Controversy," *ACTA SOCIOLOGICA,* vol. 15 (1972), p. 28.

[47] Wagner, ed. *op. cit.*, p. 74.

[48] *Ibid.*, pp. 74, 75.

[49] Peter L. Berger and Thomas Luckmann, *The Social Construction of Reality* (New York: Doubleday and Company, Inc., 1967), p. 41.

[50] Lester Embree, ed. *Aron Gurwitsch: Phenomenology and the Theory of Science* (Northwestern University Press, 1974), p. 136.

[51] *Ibid.*, p. 139.

[52] *Ibid.*, p. 145.

[53] Cf. for example, Stephan Strasser, *Phenomenology and the Human Sciences* (Pittsburgh: Duquense University Press, 1974), pp. 5-6.

[54] Embree, ed. *op. cit.*, pp. 128-130.

[55] *Ibid.*, pp. 130-131.

[56] Cf. Herbert Spiegelberg, *The Phenomenological Movement: A Historical Introduction* (The Hague: Martinus Nijhoff, 1960), I, pp. 1-2.

[57] *Ibid.*, pp. 20-23.

[58] *Ibid.*, p. 23, and II, p. 654.

[59] *Ibid.*, p. 655.

[60] *Ibid.*, p. 700.

[61] Herbert Spiegelberg, *Doing Phenomenology* (The Hague: Martinus Nijhoff, 1975), p. 72.

[62] *Ibid.*, pp. 74, 75.

[63] *Ibid.*, p. 76.

[64] *Ibid.*, p. 77.

[65] *Ibid.*, p. 77.

[66] *Ibid.*, p. 78.

[67] *Ibid.*, p. 78.

[68] Husserl's *Lebenswelt* is not identical with the common sense world of the 'naive attitude' that it has become for Berger and Luckmann and, to some extent, Schutz.   Such differences among the various phenomenologists, however, are beyond our present concerns.   It will suffice to note here that Husserl's *Lebenswelt*, which refers to the pretheoretical and theoretical planes of the world of everyday life, is an ambiguous concept. Cf. Maurice Natanson, ed. *Phenomenology and the Social Sciences* (Evanston: Northwestern University Press, 1973), pp. 130-132.

TEN

HANS-GEORG GADAMER: *TRUTH AND METHOD*

1. *Gadamer's Hermeneutic Philosophy of History*

Gadamer's hermeneutics, an ambitious synthesis based on Husserl's phenomenology, Dilthey's historicism, and Heidegger's hermeneutic philosophy,[1] can be seen as an attempt towards the development of a complete ontology with a distinctive epistemology and methodology. This is stressed by Gadamer's repeated statements that his main concern is not the perfecting of the technique of understanding of traditional hermeneutics or the construction of an adequate method for the social sciences,[2] but primarily philosophical: "to discover what is common to all modes of understanding and to show that understanding is never subjective behavior toward a given 'object,' but towards its effective history—the history of its influence; in other words, understanding belongs to the being of that which is understood."[3]

Gadamer reproaches the scientific method for its domination of the human sciences, which he claims do not have a method of their own,[4] and for its inability to produce a satisfactory account of phenomena pertaining to man. He then views the difference between the natural and the human sciences not as methodological, but as derived from their diverse "objectives of knowledge."[5] His ultimate aim is "a discipline that guarantees truth,"[6] and he uses the term 'hermeneutics' in the sense given to it by the early Heidegger who perceived it not as "a methodical art, but as a theory of the real experience that thinking is."[7]

In rejecting the scientific method, Gadamer takes the following perspective: instead of being concerned like Weber about how to cloth *verstehen* with a scientific mantle and how to free it from the investigator's prejudices, he redefines the notions of *truth* and *objectivity* and makes *prejudice* a virtue rather than a vice of *verstehen*. The truth he is after is decidedly not scientific truth, but "that experience of truth that transcends the sphere of the control of scientific method wherever it is to be found. . . ." As Gadamer adds, "the human sciences are joined with modes of experience which lie outside science: with the experiences of philosophy, of art and of history itself. These are all modes of experience in which a truth is communicated that cannot be verified by the methodological means proper to science."[8]   The discovery of this truth is the task of hermeneutic *verstehen* as it attempts to transcend its Weberian counterpart.

a. *Artistic Truth*

Gadamer is convinced that artistic truth is essentially similar to the truth that the human sciences seek to find, thus he discusses hermeneutic theory after an elaboration of certain problems pertaining to aesthetics. Concretely, in the first part of his book, entitled, "The question of truth as it emerges in the experience of art," he prepares the way towards an approach to the human sciences' mode of understanding, not only because he believes that art offers "an excellent example," but also because he does not want simply to accept "the human sciences' own account of themselves."[9]

The subjectivisation of aesthetics by Kant,[10] and especially the idea of an aesthetic consciousness, come under Gadamer's attack. In his severe criticism of the latter he points out that "aesthetic differentiation,"[11] that is, the abstraction from the reality of an artistic work, its concrete content, socio-historical environment, etc., is "a self-contradictory process,"[12] even an impossible one.[13]   He holds the view that there cannot be a true experience of art apart from the understanding of a work's meaning. In other words, there cannot be such a thing as a timeless aesthetic experience outside or above history. He states: "It is necessary to adopt an attitude to the beautiful and to art that does not lay claim to immediacy, but corresponds to the historical reality of man."[14]

The transcendence of the Kantian position which relates "aesthetic judgment entirely to the condition of the subject,"[15] is according to Gadamer imperative, but not at the expense of the truth of aesthetic experience. It should not be over-looked, he points out, that despite their grounding on a sub-jective principle the aesthetics of Kant account satisfactorily for both aspects of the judgment of taste, "its empirical non-universality and its a priori claim to universality."[16]

This transcendence can only be achieved on the basis of the Hegelian concept of *world-view* by means of which, Gadamer stresses, "the truth that lies in every artistic experience is recog-nized and at the same time mediated with historical conscious-ness."[17] However, the overcoming of Kant's aesthetic subjec-tivism by Hegel's speculative idealism, that is, from the "stand-point of infinite knowledge,"[18] is unacceptable to Gadamer. Instead, he praises Heidegger's reproach of subjectivism from "the standpoint of finiteness," because it overcomes subjec-tivism by questioning it, i.e. by questioning the being of self-understanding which is thus transcended, and also because Heidegger's approach of being from a temporal perspective opens up new possibilities.[19] After these considerations, he rejects aesthetic consciousness as the proper object of investigation and concentrates on the mode of being of the work of art.

b. *The Mode of Being of Artistic and Literary Works*

Gadamer's discussion of the ontology of the work of art is based on the work's analogy with *play* which he frees from its subjective element, i.e. the attitude of the player. He argues that as self-representation is play's mode of being, representa-tion is the mode of being of the work of art.[20] Play has two aspects; one changing, the other permanent. In Gadamer's formulation, play is structure and structure is play, hence, in the place of aesthetic differentiation which he has rejected, he counterposes 'aesthetic non-differentiation' as an indispensable element of aesthetic consciousness.[21] Further, he replaces the notion of the variety of subjective conceptions of a work of art with the notion of the latter's possibilities of being.[22] This does not mean that a work of art loses its identity in the process of its representations; on the contrary, the aesthetic being is characterized by what Gadamer calls "contemporaneity" or "timelessness," that is, "a dialectical feature which arises out of temporality and in contrast with it."[23]

Since the work of art is play in the sense that its being is becoming only in representation, representation is part of its being and thus, despite all changing elements, the work of art maintains its unity and identity.[24] To illustrate this, Gadamer mentions the example of periodic festivals which even though they change they retain their sameness.[25] He also distinguishes between contemporaneity and "the simultaneity of the aesthetic consciousness" which refers "to the coexistence and the equal validity of different aesthetic objects of experience in the one consciousness." In the context of *Truth and Method* contemporaneity "means that a single thing that presents itself to us achieves in its presentation full presentness, however remote its origin may be."[26] As he explains, works of art, "as long as they still fulfill their function, they are contemporaneous with every age."[27]

Returning to our initial point we can say that Gadamer uses the concept of play to counterbalance and transcend the subjectivist attitude of modern aesthetics. According to his analysis, the picture as well as the plastic work of art are ontological events that cannot be examined as the objects of aesthetic consciousness. Hence, representation—the starting point of this approach—is "a universal ontological structural element of the aesthetic. . . ."[28]

The analysis of the work of art is also extended to the "borderline" case of literature. Gadamer begins by saying that the sole condition of literature is "its linguistic tradition and its being understood in reading," when reading refers to "a kind of reproduction and interpretation."[29] The literary work, i.e. the novel, he argues, cannot be approached through the reader's aesthetic experience, because it can only be understood as an ontological event materialized in reading.

From the work of literature, Gadamer generalizes for literature as a whole, the human sciences included, as well as for all texts of scientific research. As he writes, "An entire written tradition partakes of the mode of being of literature. . . ."[30] Of course, he takes into account differences in form and especially in the particular "claims to truth," yet he underlines that "literature is the place where art and science merge. The mode of being of literature has something unique and inseparable about it." Therefore, he concludes, "Nothing is so purely the trace of the mind as writing, but also nothing is so dependent on the understanding mind."[31]

Even so, as the being of a work of art emerges fully in representation, the being of a literary text emerges fully in reading which is understanding. Evidently, then, Gadamer maintains, the discipline of hermeneutics becomes of central importance for every form of literature, and understanding or hermeneutic *verstehen*, unlike its Weberian counterpart, "must be conceived as a part of the process of the coming into being of meaning, in which the significance of all statements—those of art and those of everything else that has been transmitted—is formed and made complete."[32]

c. *The Hermeneutic Task*

The last pages of the first part of *Truth and Method* deal with the question of the proper task of hermeneutics. On the one hand, the position of Schleiermacher is presented according to which the *reconstruction* and reproduction of a work's original purpose and the context of its surrounding world should be the hermeneutic task. Gadamer rejects Schleiermacher's approach because, as he rightly points out, it completely disregards the historicity of the being of the interpreter. On the other hand, Hegel's approach which makes *integration* the proper task of hermeneutics is referred to with approval.

Hegel considers the historical approach to the artistic works of the past as an "external," albeit necessary, activity, and by going beyond Schleiermacher's standpoint, he raises the whole problem of hermeneutics to a higher plane. For Hegel, Gadamer says, "the essential nature of the historical spirit does not consist of the restoration of the past, but in thoughtful mediation with contemporary life."[33] Therefore, in the second part of his study Gadamer extends his criticism of aesthetic consciousness, to historical consciousness as well.

At first, Gadamer gives a brief historical account of hermeneutics and criticizes Dilthey's effort to show that the human and the natural sciences aim at the same kind of objectivity.[34] Hence, he presents the concept of "life"—developed by Husserl and Graf Yorck in opposition to scientific objectivity—as phenomenology's epistemological point of reference, and he further outlines some of Heidegger's basic ideas on which his own hermeneutic theory is based.

What Gadamer fully endorses is Heidegger's outright rejection of the subjectivist and ahistorical nature of Husserl's eidetic phenomenology (distinguishing between fact and essence) which he confronts with his own "hermeneutics of facticity." Concretely, Heidegger demanded that "The facticity of there-being, existence . . . should represent the ontological basis of the phenomenological position," and that "being . . . was to be determined from within the horizon of time . . ." because for him "being itself is time." Thus, Heidegger transcended "both the concept of spirit developed by classical idealism and the thematic of transcendental consciousness, purified by phenomenological reduction."[35] Moreover, Gadamer continues, Heidegger conceived understanding in a radical way, as: "There-being's mode of being . . ." and "the act of understanding itself as the moment of transcendence, of moving beyond being," which indicates that "understanding is ultimately self-understanding."[36] Consequently, there exists a correspondence between the "interpreter and his object," while it becomes evident that "The general structure of understanding acquires its concrete form in historical understanding."[37] In other words, we can say that the historical context of the past and of the interpreter himself cannot be ignored.

Gadamer presents the major elements of the hermeneutic theory he sets forth to construct, beginning with an examination of Heidegger's "hermeneutic circle" which discloses the circular structure of understanding deriving from the temporality of there-being. He points out that this circle has an ontological and not just a methodological significance because it reveals how interpretation through understanding takes place. This circular process of interpretation starts with the interpreter approaching his object without any attempt to censor his prejudices because interpretation at all levels is grounded on understanding,[38] and the latter is inseparably connected with one's own prejudices originating in his own historicity. Gadamer perceives the relationship between interpretation and understanding as follows: "As understanding, Dasein projects its Being upon possibilities. . . . The projection of the understanding has its own possibility—that of developing itself. . . . This development of the understanding we call interpretation."[39] But what is the initial interpretative step?

In Heidegger's terminology, interpretation begins with the fore-structure of understanding, that is, with our fore-having, fore-sight and fore-conception:[40] it is primarily based on our fore-meaning of an object.[41] The final purpose is the enlargement of understanding and the improvement of interpretation until "objectivity"—different from scientific objectivity—is achieved. Gadamer explains that to understand a text is to *project* a meaning upon it and then *revise* it as many times as necessary according to the responses one gets from the text itself, until from projection to revision the meaning of the text is little by little determined. Thus, every revision will result in a new meaning which is in turn projected again, until the "unity of meaning" of the text becomes clear. The following quotation from *Truth and Method* includes the definition of hermeneutical 'objectivity' and the criterion of acceptance of a fore-meaning as valid:

> A person who is trying to understand is exposed to distraction from fore-meanings that are not borne out by the things themselves. The working out of appropriate projects, anticipatory in nature, to be confirmed 'by the things' themselves, is the constant task of understanding. The only 'objectivity' here is the confirmation of a fore-meaning in its being worked-out. The only thing that characterizes the arbitrariness of inappropriate fore-meanings is that they come to nothing in the working-out.[42]

Gadamer is against arbitrary interpretations and he quotes Heidegger who warns that as the movement of understanding and interpretation takes place the interpreter must "make the scientific theme secure by working out these fore-structures in terms of the things themselves."[43] As he explains, this "securing" only means that the interpreter must be constantly aware of his own prejudices and anticipatory ideas vis-a-vis the response of the text itself.

To be conscious of one's own prejudices and biases is, according to Gadamer, of basic importance because this is the only way one can distinguish his own projected fore-meanings from the meaning stemming out of the text. For this to be achieved a fundamental requirement has to be met: the interpreter must be permanently *open* to new meanings which might even completely contradict his projected fore-meanings and thus misunderstanding is precluded.

In effect, Gadamer makes one of the most crucial epistemo-logical/methodological points of his hermeneutic theory and argues that a hermeneutically trained interpreter can definitely avoid his misunderstanding of a text because instead of relying exclusively on his own fore-meanings he is prepared to listen to the text itself which will thus contribute to the formation of the next fore-meaning until objectivity is finally achieved. He states: "The hermeneutical task becomes automatically a questioning of things and is always in part determined by this."[44]   Thus, the hermeneutically defined objectivity is se-cured, and intuitive verification—in contrast to Weber's scientific verification—takes place on the basis of a dialectic of question and answer (after the model of the Platonic dialectic), that is, on the basis of an ongoing dialogue between prejudice and openness.   What Gadamer calls *legitimate prejudices* become not hindrances but the necessary preconditions of understanding, therefore he blames the Enlightenment for its "prejudice against prejudice itself."[45]

d. *Prejudices Re-examined*

The overcoming of the prejudice against prejudices, Gada-mer maintains, will result in a better understanding of ourselves and of our historical consciousness.   The idea of an absolute reason is a myth, the only valid reason being that determined by our historicity.   Consequently, hermeneutics cannot start with "self-reflection" and "autobiography" after the manner of Dilthey because history is not a private affair but something which encompasses man.   And Gadamer infers that the subjec-tive approach to human phenomena is unacceptable: "The focus of subjectivity is a distorting mirror.   The self-awareness of the individual is only a flickering in the closed circuits of historical life.   That is why the prejudices of the individual, far more than his judgments, constitute the historical reality of his being."[46]

To demonstrate the groundlessness of objectivism Gadamer inquires about the legitimacy of prejudices.   He refers to the *distinction* between prejudices due to *over-hastiness*, that is, to the misuse of one's reason, and prejudices legitimized by some *authority* in which case one's own reason remains unused.

This second kind of prejudice attracts all his interest, and he focuses on one form of authority, namely *tradition*, which romanticism, in its critique of the reason of the Enlightenment, suggested as something objective and of lasting value. Gadamer rejects the idea of an opposition between tradition and reason, and states: "Even the most genuine and solid tradition does not persist by nature . . . [but] It needs to be affirmed, embraced, cultivated [by] . . . reason. . . ."[47]

According to Gadamer, there is no way to free ourselves from tradition (this basic authority from which decisive legitimate prejudices emanate) and from its influence upon us: "we stand within tradition"[48] even when radical changes take place, e.g. in revolutionary times. Consequently, it is misleading to think of tradition and unprejudiced historical research as the poles of an antithesis. We should instead, Gadamer goes on, regard them as a unity, and in this sense historical consciousness is just "a new element within that which has always made up the human relation to the past."[49] The close examination of the relationship between tradition and historical consciousness enables Gadamer to give a more precise description of the process of hermeneutic *verstehen* in conjunction with the issue of subjectivity: "Understanding is not to be thought of so much as an action of one's subjectivity but as the placing of oneself within a process of tradition, in which past and present are constantly fused."[50]

Gadamer also rejects the nineteenth-century conception of the hermeneutic circle—expressing a formal relationship between the whole of a text and its parts—as being constituted by two distinct elements: one objective, one subjective. It is not necessary, he maintains, to know the author's state of mind but just the "objective validity" of his writings. In this sense, the movement of understanding cannot be based on the investigation of an author's individuality and subjectivity. Understanding "is not a mysterious communion of souls, but a sharing of a common meaning."[51] He speaks in similar terms of the objective element of this circle. For Gadamer, the attachment to the ideal of objectivity prevents "the concretion of historical consciousness in hermeneutical theory."[52]

This formal conception of the circular structure of understanding was overcome by Heidegger's existential account of the hermeneutic circle according to which understanding is constantly determined by the projection of fore-understanding.

An immediate implication was that instead of a complete understanding anticipated by the hermeneutical rule of part and whole,
Heidegger's hermeneutic circle anticipates only an endless improvement of understanding. This circle is not formal in nature.
Moreover, Gadamer maintains, it is "neither subjective nor
objective, but describes understanding as the interplay of the
movement of tradition and the movement of the interpreter."[53]
Participation then in a common meaning guides the process
of understanding; this meaning is continuously shaped by education which demonstrates that tradition is not something fixed
but rather something constantly reproduced. On this basis,
Gadamer insists that the hermeneutic circle is not methodological
in nature but ontological.

A prerequisite of understanding is what Gadamer calls the
"fore-conception of completion" by which he means that only
unities of meaning are intelligible, while the projected fore-
meaning must be always transcended. He further stresses that
what we primarily try to understand is not an author's specific
meaning, but the perspective or the overall content *encompassing*
this meaning. Therefore, fore-understanding becomes the basic
hermeneutic requirement. Gadamer writes of the importance
of self-understanding: "It is this that determines what unified
meaning can be realized and hence the application of the anticipation of completion. Thus the meaning of the connection with
tradition, i.e. the element of tradition in our historical, hermeneutical attitude, is fulfilled in the fact that we share fundamental prejudices with tradition."[54] However, a serious problem
arises since the interpreter cannot distinguish those of his prejudices which will eventually facilitate his understanding ("productive prejudices") from those which will mislead the investigation.
At this point, Gadamer introduces the notion of "temporal
distance" as a prerequisite for the evaluation of prejudices according to their significance for understanding.

The notion of the temporal distance unavoidably brings
to light the old problem of hermeneutics caused by the question
of which understanding of a text is "superior": that of the
text's own author or that of its interpreter. Gadamer states
that it is impossible for an author to know the total meaning
of his text (since the latter is open-ended) and he argues that
in this case understanding cannot be characterized as superior
or inferior but simply as different. The role played by temporal
distance then becomes evident. Consequently, time does not

separate a text from its interpretation (in Gadamer's view an erroneous assumption which aims to legitimize historical objectivism) but must be thought of as "a positive and productive possibility of understanding. It is not a yawning abyss, but is filled with the continuity of customs and tradition. . . ."[55]

The importance of temporal distance for understanding is twofold: it excludes the newly discovered sources of error, and as an unfinished process itself, it constantly provides new sources of understanding. Thus, only on the basis of temporal distance—i.e. during the endless process of understanding—the productive prejudices can be distinguished from those which are unproductive. This amounts to saying that the hermeneutical task includes historical consciousness in order for our own prejudices to be pinpointed and kept apart from a text's own meaning. Gadamer states that "The isolation of a prejudice clearly requires the suspension of its validity for us."[56] To achieve this, one should question his own prejudices, i.e. to question their legitimacy, which does not mean that he ignores them and only accepts what a text says as valid. This was the big mistake of historical objectivism. On the contrary, our own prejudice "is properly brought into play through its being at risk." In this framework, there is not such a thing as an objective historical object; one can just refer to a unity of the "reality of history" and the "reality of historical understanding." A new element then, namely the "effectivity of history," is an indispensable part of understanding, hence the latter "is, essentially, an effective-historical relation."[57]

e. *Effective-Historical Consciousness*

Gadamer's principle of effective-history connotes that the nature of our approach to a historical phenomenon has also been hammered out itself by the effects of this phenomenon on history, the particular history of our approach included. The interpreter himself has been subjected to the effective-history which denotes that, in the final analysis, historical consciousness bears within itself the effects of this effective-history. The awareness of this effective-history is imperative—notwithstanding that it can never be complete since the latter is an evergoing process—and what Gadamer calls "effective-historical consciousness," is already a determining factor in understanding.   For example, it influences the selection of an object, the questions to be asked, etc.

What Gadamer also wishes to emphasize (like Lucien Goldmann) is that in the human sciences the interpreter is part of his object, therefore it is impossible for him to adopt towards it an objective attitude.   He observes that even subjectivity itself, i.e. one's subjective meanings and attitudes, is strictly speaking based on the effects of effective-history (Hegel's "substance") and it is by no means a self-determined entity. At this point, Gadamer defines the aim of philosophical hermeneutics to "discover in all that is subjective the substantiality that determines it."[58]   Further, Gadamer defines the concept of 'situation' ("it represents a standpoint that limits the possibility of vision") part of which he considers the concept of 'horizon' ("the range of vision that includes everything that can be seen from a particular vantage point") and he explains that "to have an horizon means not to be limited to what is nearest, but to be able to see beyond it."[59]

The fallacy of historical objectivism, Gadamer proceeds, is that it distinguishes between two independent horizons: the horizon of the interpreter and that of his object.   His position is that there is only one single great horizon which encompasses historical consciousness in its totality.   When, from the point of view of historical hermeneutics, a *distinction* is made between these two horizons this is done momentarily for the sake of understanding and then they are immediately *recombined* and the great horizon becomes again one with itself.   This conscious distinction and recombination is the task of effective-historical consciousness: "In this process of understanding there takes place a great fusing of horizons, which means that as the historical horizon is projected, it is simultaneously removed."[60]   This, according to Gadamer, is the essential hermeneutical problem of *application*.

Gadamer regards hermeneutics as an unified process with three integral and internally connected parts: *understanding, interpretation* and *application*.   That the latter is an integral aspect of hermeneutics is recognized by theological, legal as well as literary hermeneutics.   It is Gadamer's position that understanding is application, and even though the true model of this is legal and theological hermeneutics, in literary criticism and the human sciences too, historical understanding performs also a task of application because the interpreter of a text of the past always tries to relate and apply it to his own situation.

Comparing the historian with the literary critic, Gadamer points out their fundamental differences. Notwithstanding their dissimilarities, however, he is convinced that "all reading involves application," and he refers to an inner unity between the two based on the act of application that both perform. By the same token, the historian and the literary critic understand themselves in their objects; in other words, effective-historical consciousness is present in the hermeneutical activity of both of them. Further, Gadamer clarifies that application here does not mean "the subsequent applying to a concrete case of a given universal that we understand first by itself, but it is the actual understanding of the universal itself that the given text constitutes for us. Understanding proves to be a kind of effect and knows itself as such."[61]

After establishing that effective-historical consciousness has itself an effect as an awareness of an historical phenomenon, Gadamer approaches its structure via the structure of an experience. He distinguishes two forms of experience, one positive, i.e. the confirmation of an anticipation, and one negative, i.e. the improvement of our knowledge of an object by negating our previous knowledge of it. This second form is, strictly speaking, a genuine experience since we can only have an experience *once*. It is dialectical, and it results in the acquiring of a new horizon by the experiencer. Gadamer writes: "In view of the experience that we have of another object, both things change, our knowledge and its object."[62]

Criticizing Hegel who anticipates the fulfillment of the dialectic of experience in absolute knowledge, Gadamer counterposes openness to new experience, and thus he relates experience to history. He analyses the structure of experience in general and then focuses on effective-historical consciousness, that is, on the hermeneutical experience which, as he claims, has the same elements as any experience. Effective-historical consciousness has the task of experiencing everything that tradition bears with it, where the latter is not something objective but being language itself "is a genuine partner in communication." Even so, in contradistinction to historical consciousness which does not take into account its own historicality, hermeneutic consciousness is characterized by openness and is fulfilled "not in its methodological sureness of itself, but in the same readiness for experience that distinguishes the experienced man by comparison with the man captivated by dogma."[63]

Further, Gadamer examines the logic of hermeneutical openness and maintains that it has the structure of a question, while the hermeneutic phenomenon as a whole has the structure of question and answer after the model of the Platonic dialectic. The latter, Gadamer goes on, as authentic conversation, manifests "the priority of question over the answer, which is the basis of the concept of knowledge,"[64] and it can be characterized as the art of seeking the truth through questioning.

The logic of question and answer, Gadamer proceeds, is also present in Hegel's dialectic as a philosophical method, "a monologue of thinking that seeks to carry out in advance what matures little by little in every genuine conversation."[65] The logic of question and answer, Gadamer argues, is also the logic of the human sciences and of literary criticism. We understand a text only if we understand the question to which it is an answer, and this, Gadamer says, is an axiom of hermeneutics referred to earlier as the "fore-conception of completion." However, he emphasizes, one should go beyond the writer's subjective ideas—which do not necessarily agree with historical reality— and focus on the meaning of the text.[66]

Thus, the attempt towards the understanding of an author's subjectivity Gadamer considers of limited importance. What seems to be significant, and this applies to both the historian and the literary critic, is the recognition of the inexhaustibility of the meaning of all texts, because each time they are "re-actualized in understanding" a new historical potentiality is revealed which is manifested as a different understanding. This is the effective-historical element of the hermeneutical experience and, according to Gadamer, there is not a viewpoint outside history, nor a positionless standpoint.

In the light of the dialectic of question and answer the nature of effective-historical consciousness is fully unveiled. Gadamer writes: "The anticipation of an answer itself presumes that the person asking is part of the tradition and regards himself as addressed by it." Hence, effective-historical consciousness "is the historically experienced consciousness that . . . is open to the experience of history," and it is realized in the form of the fusion of the horizons of understanding which mediates between a text and its interpreter. Since this fusion "that takes place in understanding is the proper achievement of language,"[67] the latter becomes the subject of the third part of *Truth and Method*.

f. *Language as the Universal Medium of Understanding*

Gadamer states from the outset that the process of understanding—that is, the coming to an agreement with an author on a subject and not 'entering' into his mind—is linguistic. Therefore, language is the universal medium of understanding, while the mode of realization of the latter is interpretation, with application being an integral aspect of the experience of meaning.[68] The central importance of language for hermeneutics is due to the fact that it determines the object of the latter, namely, literary tradition as well as the hermeneutic act itself. To illustrate this, Gadamer gives the example of the historian who despite his thirst for objectivity and his recourse to scientific method, ultimately subordinates "the alien being of the object to its own conceptual frame of reference."[69]

After an elaborate examination of the history of the concept of language, Gadamer considers it as the horizon of a hermeneutical ontology since the dialectical relationship between language and being reveals an essential ontological element of hermeneutics. Hence, he presents the close relationship between language and human experience on the basis of the ideas of Wilhelm von Humboldt. As he states, the great importance of von Humboldt as the founder of the philosophy of language consists in his insight that each specific language is a particular world-view. Nevertheless, he goes beyond von Humboldt's conception of language as a *form* and stresses the primary significance of its *content*. Yet, he praises as von Humboldt's great achievement the perception of the human world as linguistic in essence.[70]

Language goes hand in hand with man's freedom: it is the motive force of man's freedom from his habitat and of his acquiring a whole world. This does not simply mean that man is able to change his habitat by moving, but rather that "he has another attitude towards it, a free, distanced attitude, which is always realized in language."[71] As for the reality of language, it is created in conversation—the practice of understanding between people—in which alone the true being of language is achieved. Therefore, one can speak of every human community as a linguistic community.

The linguistic nature of our experience of the world provides hermeneutics with a wider horizon because the world of language encompasses the world of human experience. Of course, different linguistic, cultural or historical traditions result in varied world-views, nonetheless, Gadamer maintains, the world that is presented to us is always a human world, i.e. a world constituted by language and as such is open to our understanding regardless of our particular tradition. It is this great common tradition, that is, the linguistic human world, that constitutes the hermeneutic universal, and in this sense the notion of the relativity of the world is overcome. Gadamer writes: "In every view of the world the existence of the world-in-itself is implied. It is the whole to which the linguistically schematised experience is referred. The variety of these views of the world does not involve any relativisation of the 'world.' Rather, what the world is is not different from the view in which it presents itself."[72]

Thus, Gadamer subscribes to the view that the existence of the world is independent of the existence of language, even independent of the existence of man. The mode of presentation of the world to man is linguistic, but the world is not the object of language. Nevertheless, this presentation in itself is not relative but complete: "The experience of the world in language is 'absolute.' It transcends all the relativities of the positing of being, because it embraces all being-in-itself, in whatever relationships (relativities) it appears."[73] Moreover, Gadamer accepts that no matter which language is used, man can never go beyond a perspective of the world since, after all, the latter's being is constantly unfolding and its reality open-ended. At any rate, man's ability to penetrate different linguistic worlds does not present any special problem for Gadamer. His position is that man can enter another language-world without the need to renounce his own: "As travellers we return home with new experiences."[74]

In reference to sciences, Gadamer fully endorses Max Scheler's analysis demonstrating that their objectivity is "relative to a particular way of knowing and willing."[75] In addition, he says that sciences are limited by the fact that they cannot transcend their ontological horizon, hence they have knowledge of just a part of what exists (and consequently power over it):

that part of the world that can be experienced. In contrast to this, the world that is presented to man through language creates a different situation. Sciences give (wrongly) the impression that their world is a world of being-in-itself, an objective world: the true world that they are able to view from above. The linguistic world, however, cannot be seen from above, "for there is no point of view outside the experience of the world in language. . . ."[76] To have a language means to have a world. It becomes therefore evident that the notion of the "objectivity of science" has a different meaning from that of the "factuality of language."

Language, Gadamer maintains, is the speculative centre out of which our hermeneutical experience unfolds. It mediates between man as an historical, finite being and all other beings constituting the world. The world itself is essentially dialectical: on the one hand, it relates to the whole of lanugage by means of which it is a world; and on the other, every single world pulls, so to speak, the trigger of the whole which is language, and makes it reveal the world-view that it carries within it. In Gadamer's formulation, "Every word, in its momentariness, carries with it the unsaid, to which it is related by responding and indicating."[77]

On the assumption of the linguistic nature of man's experience of the world, Gadamer attempts an elucidation of the idea of "belongingness" of the interpreter to the interpreted text. The notion of belongingness between subject (interpreter) and object (text) aims to transcend the idea of objective understanding. Thus, hermeneutics makes language its starting point and views the dialogue of the interpreter with the text as a *happening* which is beyond the control of the interpreter's mind (his subjectivity) as well as beyond something that exists (objectively). The conversation of the interpreter with tradition is an *actual event* which transcends both the sphere of subjectivity and objectivity and results in a *new thing* which neither of the two partners contains in itself. Gadamer relates this hermeneutical event to language in the following way: "Language constitutes the hermeneutical event proper not as . . . grammar or lexicon, but in the coming into language of that which has been said in the tradition: an event that is at once assimilation and interpretation . . . this event is not an action upon the thing, but the act of the thing itself."[78]

g. *The Hermeneutic Dialectic: Beyond Subjectivism and
Objectivism*

The determination of the activity of the thing itself is
the seeking of the "true method"—in opposition to the modern
idea of subjectivity and objectivity—which manifests a basic
methodological agreement between hermeneutics, the Hegelian
dialectic and the dialectic of the Greeks. Gadamer maintains
that this dialectic of the thing means that "the thing does not
go its own course without our thinking being involved, but
thinking means unfolding the proper logic of the thing itself."[79]

Plato's dialectic—the art of conversing—is negative by
nature: it negates one's erroneous opinions and from negation to
negation it reveals the thing as it follows the latter's logic. Here,
"It is the thing itself that asserts itself." In Hegel's conception
of the dialectic, however, during the process of one's thinking
of a thing, the thing itself changes and becomes its opposite.
Despite this fundamental difference in the two conceptions
of the dialectic, Gadamer wishes to bring out a common element
extending to the hermeneutic dialectic (conceived from the
centre of language), the dialectic of Plato (conceived as the art
of conducting a conversation), and the Hegelian dialectic (conceived as the self-unfolding of pure thought seeking to free
itself from language in order to grasp the totality). This common
element, Gadamer calls the "speculative element," when "The
word 'speculative' here refers to the mirror relation . . . and it . . .
is the antithesis of the dogmatism of everyday experience."[80]

Notwithstanding their common speculative element, the
hermeneutical dialectic should not be confused with its Platonic
and Hegelian counterparts because it is essentially different
from both. To demonstrate this difference Gadamer refers to
Hegel's distinction between the speculative and the dialectical:
"The dialectical is the expression of the speculative, the representation of what is actually contained in the speculative, and
to this extent it is the truly speculative."[81] Nevertheless, Hegel
eventually removes this distinction because in reality it cancels
itself out. This shows first, Hegel's relationship to the Greek
concept of the dialectic to the extent that both subordinate
"language to the 'statement';" and second, the limit of both
conceptions of the dialectic, a limit which the hermeneutic
dialectic is able to overcome: "The concept of the statement . . .
is . . . in extreme contrast to the nature of the hermeneutical

experience and the linguistic nature of the human experience of the world." And Gadamer maintains that as Plato's dialectic is limited by not going beyond "the logic of the thing," the Hegelian dialectic "remains within the dimension of what is stated and does not attain the dimension of the linguistic experience of the world."[82]

Gadamer elaborates on the speculative nature of language in everyday speech, and identifies the speculative attitude first of all as a dialectical relationship between that which is said and an infinity of what remains unsaid. To speak speculatively, then, does not imply that one comes up with statements. Speculative speech is not a reflection of being, but it expresses "a relation to the whole of being." By the same token, the speculative nature of the linguistic event in poetic expression does not reflect what exists but it produces a "new sight of the world." Moreover, as mentioned earlier, in the hermeneutic situation too the linguistic event is speculative.

Hermeneutics and the Hegelian dialectics have different objectives: the first is trying to achieve the totality of meaning, but the aim of the second is to achieve the totality of truth. The Hegelian dialectic takes the form of a "rounded perfection," hence it is confronted with the insoluble problem of the beginning. Hermeneutics, however, does not face such a problem because it seeks its perfection in effective-historical consciousness which presupposes the "absolute openness of the meaning-event." Thus, as in the case of everyday and poetic speech, hermeneutic interpretation is speculative also because "the interpreting word is the word of the interpreter . . . (resulting in) a new creation of understanding . . . (which nevertheless) does not maintain any proper existence apart from the understanding process."[83] This, Gadamer argues, demonstrates that the interpreting word like every word is not objective but really speculative: "having no tangible being of its own and not yet throwing back the image that is presented to it."[84]

The last section of *Truth and Method* points to a universal ontological structure which constitutes the nature of everything that can be understood. This structure is language itself. "Being that can be understood is language," that is, self-presentation, which does not mean that through language a being acquires another being. What happens is that "The way in which a thing presents itself is, rather, part of its own being." Therefore, he asserts, "The speculative nature of language shows its universal ontological significance,"[85] since the coming into language of the meaning of a thing—its presentation—is part of the thing's being. In this framework, one cannot speak of aesthetic, historical or hermeneutical objects as fixed entities, but as objects mediated by historical consciousness with language being the universal medium of this mediation. Thus, hermeneutics, (based on the speculative center that language is, language which is unbreakably related to man's existential, finite and historical being), overcomes both the objectivism of the scientific ideal and Hegelian idealism preoccupied with the attainment of absolute knowledge.

Now that he has demonstrated the speculative character of being, Gadamer confesses that in his overall presentation of hermeneutics—resulting in a critique of the methodologism of the human sciences—he was guided by the Platonic idea of the *beautiful* and his metaphysics of *light*. At this point, he interjects a brief discussion of the beautiful as perceived by Plato, i.e. as having the unique property of mediating between its own *idea* and its own *appearance*. This property, namely *radiance*, constitutes the true being of the beautiful. Therefore, as Gadamer says, "Beauty has the mode of being of light."[86] This ontological structural element of the beautiful however reveals a universal ontological element of every being that can be understood. Concretely, as the realm of the *visible* is articulated in light, the realm of the *intelligible* is articulated in light too, albeit a different light from that of fire: the light of the mind, of *nous*, ultimately manifested in the *word*. This shows the close relationship between the metaphysics of light (Plato and Neoplatonists) and the Christian doctrine of the word. Light is the mode of being of the beautiful; the word is the mode of being of the intelligible.

At this point two things become clear. First, that both the mode of being of the beautiful and the mode of being of understanding have the character of something happening, of an event, which presupposes the finiteness of human life and experience. And second, that both the experience of the beautiful and the hermeneutical experience are genuine and immediate experiences, encounters "with something which asserts itself as truth." Subsequently, Gadamer tries to define the hermeneutical truth, and he argues that it should neither be identified with the scientific truth, nor with a subjectively determined truth, i.e. a truth arrived at through empathy. It is a truth independent of subjectivism and objectivism. Gadamer explains: "What we mean by truth here can best be determined again in terms of our concept of play. . . . What we encounter in the experience of the beautiful and in understanding the meaning of tradition has effectively something about it of the truth of play. In understanding we are drawn into an event of truth. . . ."[87] This is why he insists that there cannot be a *verstehen* free of all prejudices as the methodologism of the human sciences would have us believe. Nevertheless, Gadamer concludes his book positively and he asserts that the limitation of scientific method does not limit science itself: the truth that is unable to grasp can be guaranteed by the dialectical discipline of hermeneutics.

2. *An Assessment of Gadamer's Hermeneutics*

Gadamer's complex and multileveled hermeneutic-phenomenological work cannot be the subject of a thorough critical discussion here because this would lead us outside the scope of this study. We have seen that *Truth and Method* is not engaged with the development of a comprehensive theory of art and literature, but it is mainly preoccupied with the construction of a general theory of socio-cultural understanding. The main strategy of Gadamer's work is to make a selective synthesis of existing ideas with the purpose of transcending established categories and methods of approaching socio-cultural phenomena in order to arrive at a new conception of human reality.

After almost five hundred pages of presentations and critical discussions of issues pertaining to hermeneutics as it evolved in the course of Western thinking, Gadamer comes up with a new ontology with all its epistemological and methodological consequences. In this broad framework, we can pass over a detailed reference to numerous constructive ideas included in *Truth and Method* and its actual accomplishments.[88] Instead, our attention will be focussed on the overall effectiveness and adequacy of Gadamer's historical hermeneutics in the overcoming of the subjectivist as well as the objectivist approaches to artistic and literary products. To be able to make a balanced assessment, however, we will try to view Gadamer's construction in depth and in its entirety, and this partially explains the reason behind our previous elaborate account of it.

In the examination of the two basic modes of approaching socio-cultural phenomena—the one resulting in objectivism (the scientific method and Schleiermacher's historical objectivism), and the other in subjectivism (Kant and Husserl)—Gadamer's criticism is well taken.   It shows the limitations and shortcomings of these approaches for the artistic and literary realm as well as for that of the human sciences.   In this sense, and on the basis of a selective synthesis of ideas borrowed from Plato (the dialectic of question and answer), Hegel (integration), Dilthey (historical dimension), Husserl (phenomenological perspective: the concept of life) and Heidegger (Hermeneutic-existential philosophy), he appears to open up the way for a *third approach* to socio-cultural phenomena, qualitatively different from both the subjective and the objective modes.

With the skillful use of the concept of play as his mode, Gadamer regards the hermeneutic truth as representation (art), or as an ontological event materialized in reading (literature), or finally as a happening (socio-historical world) produced by the interplay of the movement of tradition and the movement of the interpreter.   Moreover, we should be reminded that Gadamer's hermeneutic circle is not simply methodological but above all ontological.   In other words, Gadamer's ultimate ambition is the revealing of the mode of being of all phenomena pertaining to man, hence, as Janet Wolff correctly observes, he is guilty of extending "methodology and epistemology into ontology."[89]

The basic question here is not merely whether or not Gadamer is actually able to go beyond the confines of subjectivism and objectivism—for example it will be argued shortly that he succeeds in transcending *only* the forms of objectivism he specifically considers in *Truth and Method* but not objectivism altogether—but also *how* his achievement is possible.   In other words, to what extent Gadamer's accomplishment can be regarded as a theoretical breakthrough and to what extent it is a capitulation?

We can state from the outset that Gadamer's achievement is, first, a simultaneous capitulation to a form of idealism the axis of which is not Plato's *ideas* or Hegel's *spirit*, but *language*. Indeed, Gadamer's claim implies that language is the motive force of history, since he regards language not only as the universal medium of understanding but also as a speculative center with universal ontological significance. Language for Gadamer determines man's consciousness of the world which itself is linguistically constituted; it also determines the being of man. However, it is one thing to take into account the close relationship between language and man's experience of the world, and another to consider the dialectical relationship between language and being as *the* determining relationship.

To put it differently, as Wolff points out, Gadamer seems to present language as "an independently existing, unalterable and primary entity;"[99] as the *idealist* basis of man's consciousness and of his being, considering that in language and in it alone the fusion of the horizons of understanding (the horizon of tradition and the horizon of the present) is achieved, which is but the realization of effective-historical consciousness. Our criticism here is twofold: first, that Gadamer neglects totally the material basis of man's existence and consequently the material basis of his consciousness; and second, that in addition he appears to revert into a form of deterministic and objectivistic view of man and history. To make this clear we should pay close attention to the hermeneutic circle and especially to the fore-structure of understanding as its most essential aspect.

Gadamer argues that in order for understanding to acquire its full potentiality the interpreter must first of all question the legitimacy of his own prejudices[91] (on condition that due to the effect of temporal distance, the distinction of productive from unproductive prejudices is possible. A discarding of prejudices (specifically his subjective fancies, biases, etc.) involves a kind of purification process which takes place during the successive revisions of the fore-projection of his fore-meaning, deriving from his repeatedly amended fore-understandings. After discarding those prejudices that will obscure his investigation, the investigator considers *just those of his prejudices which are caused by an authority and specifically by tradition, that is, just his "legitimate" or "objective" prejudices.* He also considers these in light of an ontological event of the hermeneutic truth revealed in the final revision. Therefore, if only these prejudices participate in the formation of the hermeneutic truth, namely, *prejudices exclusively determined by tradition*, then by implication, Gadamer seems to view the interpreter as a being devoid of any freedom, individuality and uniqueness.

Since, according to Gadamer, understanding is an ontological event and the interpreter a co-creator (though not the primary one), the conclusion can be reached that he regards artistic and literary creation itself from a deterministic perspective: as the product of unfreedom, given that, to live with his conception of human reality, the importance of even the original creator, i.e. the writer of a novel, lies in the objective significance of his work which derives straight out of his objective prejudices. This indicates that Gadamer has failed to pay the proper attention to the particularity of the artistic and literary mode of production. Furthermore, his reference to a work's objective significance should be differentiated from the Marxist concept of realism which, as already explained, refers to a standpoint or an artistic method resulting in the revealing of the essence of reality and has nothing to do with a deterministic perception of the artist's consciousness.

If the interpreter, as a partner in the ontological event of understanding, which is the hermeneutic truth (or the original creator himself as the 'interpreter' of the human and natural phenomena of his cosmos) is but a marionette in the omnipotent hands of his tradition, his effective-historical consciousness and his language: how is it possible for these determining factors to unfold, and grow, and change? In the final analysis, what is the interpreter's input in the interplay of his own movement with the movement of tradition? And what is the nature of this movement of the interpreter?

It has been emphasized that Gadamer is guilty of disregarding the material basis of man's existence. However, to speak of the man-interpreter is to speak primarily of a social being belonging to a specific social class. Hence, the prejudices of an individual interpreter cannot be blindly identified with the prejudices of society as a whole. The commonly shared prejudices due to the tradition or other factors should be always distinguished from an individual's class prejudices. Finally, to repeat the question we have asked in Lucien Goldmann's case, if man's being and consciousness are determined by his language, how is critical consciousness possible for Gadamer? In sum, how can social man have a future?

Gadamer's view of history and of the reality of human life and experience is an idealist construction full of holes and limitations. Certainly, *Truth and Method* has its merits; for example, it accounts for some factors pertaining to the realm of human necessity (tradition, man's finiteness, etc.) but it is insensitive to the realm of man's freedom and to its dialectical relationship with the former. Even when Gadamer does realize that the interpreter changes during the hermeneutic process, he remains one-sided: the change he talks about refers predominantly to the arithmetic of the interpreter's storage of knowledge, that is, to quantity.

In general, Gadamer seems to neglect that man's quantitative changes (i.e. the increasing storage of his legitimate prejudices and information) bring about qualitative transformations in his attitude and world view which cannot be explained mechanistically in terms of one-to-one relationships. One of Gadamer's greatest faults, however, is his failure to distinguish the primary importance of man's praxis and above all the latter's principal aspect, namely, human labor in the formation of man's experience and being. Jürgen Habermas rightly criticizes Gadamer's idealism and attempts to correct his theory by suggesting that not only language but also *work* and *authority* contribute to the formation of man's experience and life.[92]

In addition, Wolff refers to Emilio Betti's characterization of Gadamer's concept of objectivity as inadequate.[93] Indeed, we can accept that the hermeneutic objectivity resulting from the dialectic between openness and prejudice cannot become a substitute for the scientific concept of objectivity. Wolff, therefore, is right in concluding that Gadamer does not go beyond the Weberian notion of empirical verification, as the interplay between openness and prejudice that Gadamer suggests is rather a restatement of the same idea in different words. Thus, as Wolff correctly emphasizes, the location of objectivity in "speculative ontology" demonstrates Gadamer's epistemological shortcomings.

Focusing on literary criticism, we can say that in contrast to descriptive phenomenology, Gadamer's hermeneutic philosophy can account for the historical dimension of literary works as an horizon in fusion with the existential horizon of the interpreter (wrongly taken as the horizon of society in its entirety); it can also overcome the deadlock of subjectivism on the basis of the concept of play. Nonetheless, it can by no means provide by itself a solid basis for the development of a complete literary criticism. Gadamer's hermeneutics can primarily contribute to the advancement of the historical understanding of works of literature, but this contribution is limited as it does not properly consider the three factors which constitute the literary event from the point of view of both the writer and the reader: the sociological, the psychological and the aesthetic.

NOTES

[1] Hans-Georg Gadamer, *Truth and Method* (New York: The Seabury Press, 1975), p. xv.

[2] *Ibid.*, p. xiii.

[3] *Ibid.*, p. xix.

[4] *Ibid.*, p. 9.

[5] *Ibid.*, p. xvii.

[6] *Ibid.*, p. 442.

[7] *Ibid.*, p. xxiv.

[8] *Ibid.*, p. xii.

[9] *Ibid.*, pp. 147, 90.

[10] *Ibid.*, p. 40.

[11] *Ibid.*, p. 76.

[12] *Ibid.*, p. 80.

[13] *Ibid.*, p. 82.

[14] *Ibid.*, p. 86.

[15] *Ibid.*, p. 87.

[16] *Ibid.*, p. 40.

[17] *Ibid.*, p. 87.

[18] *Ibid.*, p. 88.

[19] *Ibid.*, p. 89.

[20] *Ibid.*, pp. 97, 104.

[21] *Ibid.*, p. 105.

[22] *Ibid.*, p. 106.

[23] *Ibid.*, p. 108.

[24] *Ibid.*, p. 109.

[25] *Ibid.*, p. 110.

[26] *Ibid.*, p. 112.

[27] *Ibid.*, p. 108.

[28] *Ibid.*, p. 141.

[29] *Ibid.*, p. 142.

[30] *Ibid.*, p. 144.

[31] *Ibid.*, p. 145.

[32] *Ibid.*, p. 146.

[33] *Ibid.*, p. 150.

[34] *Ibid.*, p. 213.

[35] *Ibid.*, pp. 225, 227, 228, 229.

[36] *Ibid.*, pp. 230, 231.

[37] *Ibid.*, p. 234.

[38] Martin Heidegger, *Being and Time*, transl. by J. Macquarrie and E. Robinson (New York: Harper and Row, Publ. 1962), p. 195.

[39] *Ibid.*, p. 188.

[40] *Ibid.*, p. 191.

[41] The relationship between understanding and interpretation is also underlined by Heidegger's definition of meaning: "Meaning is the 'upon-which' of a projection in terms of which something becomes intelligible as something: it gets its structure from a fore-having, a fore-sight, and a fore-conception." (*Ibid.*, p. 193).

[42] Gadamer, *Truth and Method, op. cit.*, pp. 236, 237.

[43] Quoted in *Ibid.*, p. 236.

[44] *Ibid.*, p. 238.

[45] *Ibid.*, p. 240.

[46] *Ibid.*, p. 245.

[47] *Ibid.*, p. 250.

[48] *Ibid.*, p. 251.

[49] *Ibid.*, p. 251.

[50] *Ibid.*, p. 258.

[51] *Ibid.*, p. 260.

[52] *Ibid.*, p. 260.

[53] *Ibid.*, p. 261.

[54] *Ibid.*, p. 262.

[55] *Ibid.*, p. 264.

[56] *Ibid.*, p. 266.

[57] *Ibid.*, p. 267.

[58] *Ibid.*, p. 269.

[59] *Ibid.*, p. 269.

[60] *Ibid.*, p. 273.

[61] *Ibid.*, p. 305.

[62] *Ibid.*, p. 318.

[63] *Ibid.*, p. 325.

[64] *Ibid.*, p. 328.

[65] *Ibid.*, p. 333.

[66] *Ibid.*, p. 335.

[67] *Ibid.*, p. 340.

[68] *Ibid.*, p. 350.

[69] *Ibid.*, p. 357.

[70] *Ibid.*, pp. 399-400.

[71] *Ibid.*, p. 403.

[72] *Ibid.*, p. 406.

[73] *Ibid.*, p. 408.

[74] *Ibid.*, p. 406.

[75] *Ibid.*, p. 408.

[76] *Ibid.*, p. 410.

[77] *Ibid.*, p. 416.

[78] *Ibid.*, p. 421.

[79] *Ibid.*, p. 421.

[80] *Ibid.*, p. 423. Gadamer explains the notion of 'specualative' in reference to the 'mirror relation' as follows: "Being reflected involves a constant substitution of one thing for another. When something is reflected in something else, say, the castle in the lake, it means that the lake throws back the image of the castle. The mirror image is essentially connected, through the medium of the observer, with the proper vision of the thing. It has no being of its own, it is like an 'appearance' that is not itself and yet causes the proper vision to appear as a mirror image . . ." (*Ibid.*, p. 423).

[81] *Ibid.*, p. 425.

[82] *Ibid.*, pp. 425, 426.

[83] *Ibid.*, p. 430.

[84] *Ibid.*, p. 431.

[85] *Ibid.*, p. 432.

[86] *Ibid.*, p. 439.

[87] *Ibid.*, p. 446.

[88] Cf. for example, Janet Wolff, *Hermeneutic Philosophy and the Sociology of Art* (London: Routledge and Kegan Paul, 1975), pp. 117, 118, 126, 133.

[89] *Ibid.*, p. 126.

[90] *Ibid.*, p. 124.

[91] Hans-Georg Gadamer, *Truth and Method, op. cit.*, p. 237.

[92] For a very interesting and elaborate exchange between Habermas and Gadamer on central aspects of the latter's *Truth and Method* cf. Karl Otto Apel et al., ed. *Hermeneutik und Ideologiekritik* (Frankfurt am Main: Suhrkamp Verlag, 1971). In English, Habermas' initial criticism of Gadamer's work, entitled "A review of Gadamer's *Truth and Method*," can be found in Fred R. Dallmayr and Thomas A. McCarthy, eds. *Understanding Social Inquiry* (Notre Dame, Indiana: The University Press, 1977). Also, cf. Hans-Georg Gadamer, "On the scope and function of hermeneutical

reflection," transl. by F. G. Hess and R. E. Palmer, *Continuum.*, vol. 8, nos. 1 and 2 (Spring and Summer 1970). And, Jürgen Habermas, "Summation and response," in *Ibid.*

[93] Janet Wolff, *Hermeneutic Philosophy and the Sociology of Art*, *op. cit.*, pp. 121-123.

ELEVEN

JEAN-PAUL SARTRE: THE DIALECTIC OF THE OBJECTIVE AND THE SUBJECTIVE

1. *Sartre's Literary Criticism*

Sartre writes that a totality is static, inert, an in-itself: the manifestation of past action. On the contrary, a *totalization* is always in the becoming, a living process: a *"developing* activity."[1] It is in terms of his concept of totalization that his over-all work should be understood[2] —philosophical, critical, literary, etc.—and, within it his literary criticism, as a totalization in-side a totalization, diffused in many of his writings. To para-phrase Sartre, his literary criticism carries within it the whole of his *oeuvre* "just as a wave carries the whole of the sea . . .,"[3] because as Benjamin Suhl accurately observes, it mediates be-tween his philosophical and his literary works.[4]

Sartre's criticism has raised great interest over the years and numerous studies have been devoted to its examination undertaken from different angles. The present exploration will be restricted to those aspects which are necessary for an under-standing of his methodological approach to literary creation in general and of its transcending of the objective and the sub-jective in particular. Our discussion, of course, will encompass his philosophical ideas, concepts and standpoints on specific issues concerning literature, but only to the extent that our objective is met. For example, Sartre's criticism considers a given literary work as the creation of an individual who chooses to become a writer, (and as the creator in turn of the same individual, since after all writing is but an enterprise in the field of possibles by which a writer produces his own life[5]). To that extent, and to the extent that the axis of his literary criticism is related to his larger philosophical project of under-standing man's fundamental activity and life process—in the realm of literary creation the main question is 'why does one write?'—to the same extent our exposition will include the relevant aspects of his philosophical problematic.

a. *Early Phenomenological Explorations and Criticism*

After an initial phase (1923-1931) during which Sartre's occasional writings do not represent more than pen-exercises, another phase follows (up to 1940) that results in the production of four phenomenological studies dealing with key psychological problems from a philosophical perspective. These studies interest us here because they influenced in a certain way the subsequent development of his literary criticism, from his two earliest articles on Faulkner (which provide him with the opportunity not only to define the critic's task as primarily philosophical, i.e. that it should seek to establish the relationship between a fictional technique and the writer's metaphysics,[6] but above all to make explicit his own conception of temporality[7]) to his critical *magnum opus* on Flaubert.[8]

The first, *The Transcendence of the Ego*, denies any content to consciousness—the latter being always consciousness of something *outside of it*—and consequently the existence of a transcendental ego. It concludes that the ego is outside consciousness, "in the world," not its owner but its object.[9] Evidently, the implication is a rejection of that kind of literature and criticism which deal with an alleged inner life. This was the first Sartrean blow to that psychological criticism which purports to scrutinize the depths of human personality.

The second, *Imagination*, firmly establishes the distinction between perception and imagination, concluding that an image is but a kind of consciousness, "a consciousness of some thing."[10] In this study, Sartre rejects the scientistic pre-phenomenological psychologies which do not separate perception from imagination. Instead, he is advocating the intuitive grasp of the phenomena produced by man's behavior and actions,[11] which can be achieved with the use of a psycholgical method based on phenomenology.

The third, *The Emotions*, introduced by Sartre as "an *experiment* in phenomenological psychology,"[12] demonstrates that "an emotion refers back to what it signifies."[13] According to this study, emotions are purposive behavior, which manifests that man is free, not subordinate to his feelings, and also that psychological causality should be rejected.

Finally, *The Psychology of Imagination*, demonstrates the limits of the phenomenological description of the imagination. The act of imagination can only take four forms,[14] all intending a nothingness, with real objects serving as *analoga* which are traversed by an intention. The perception of the analogon of a physical object does not present any particular problem. However, the analogon of a mental image is inaccessible to phenomenological description (adequate for the realm of the immediate and certain), therefore Sartre turns to experimental psychology[15] (suitable to the realm of the probable).

In this framework, a grasping of the relationship between the *real* and the *unreal* becomes possible, since as Sartre argues, "an image . . . is always *the world regarded from a certain point of view*," that is, from a *situation* defined as an immediate way "of apprehending the real as a world." What he wishes to stress here is that consciousness has the capacity to imagine precisely because it is situated in the world.[16] In the same study, Sartre refers specifically to literature and art. In the first place, reading is imagination caused by linguistic analogy, i.e. words, and the work of art itself is "an unreality."[17] Thus, the artist, i.e. a painter, just produces on canvas the analoga of his mental images—certain physical objects—on the basis of which everyone can constitute his own images. The latter are directed by feelings, yet as they negate and transcend reality—the actual painting—from the spectator's particular situation, they demonstrate the freedom of consciousness. Sartre makes it clear, though, that the spectator's aesthetic enjoyment is not imaginary but real. It is a way of apprehending the real object which is constituted imaginatively on the basis of the actual painting. Here Sartre locates the source of the Kantian notion of the disinterestedness of the aesthetic enjoyment and he observes that it has nothing mysterious about it. "What happens," he writes, "is that the aesthetic object is constituted and apprehended by an imaginative consciousness which points it as real."[18]

During the same period, Sartre also engaged in practical criticism. Concretely, besides the two articles on Faulkner's *Sartoris* and *The Sound and the Fury*, he wrote further commentaries on a number of novels written by Dos Passos, Nizan, Mauriac, Nabokov, Camus, etc. Notwithstanding the particular target of these articles (e.g. the problem of freedom in Mauriac and his erroneous technique of being inside and outside his characters at the same time, or Dos Passos' ability to show without comments and instructive explanations, etc.[19]) they all have an explicit phenomenological character: they all *describe* consciousness—of something—and interpret it without the use of such terms as subjective attitude or the inner life. In all these articles, Sartre's principal concern is the writer's technique, his *style*, which he views as conditioned by the writer's *metaphysics*. The determination of each particular writer's metaphysics then becomes Sartre's primary critical task, and on this basis he subsequently tries to understand and explain the writer's style.

This kind of approach was perfected, for example, by 1943 when he criticizes Camus' masterpiece *The Outsider*. He begins with an elucidation of Camus' notion of *the absurd* as it is explained in *The Myth of Sisyphus*, and after a comparison of the style of Camus with that of Hemingway, who had obviously influenced him, Sartre writes: "We are now in a better position to understand the form of his narrative. Each sentence is a present instant. . . . The sentence is sharp, distinct and self-contained. It is separated by a void from the following one. . . . The sentences in *The Outsider* are islands. . . . To the absurd man, this is the one and the only good. And that is why the novelist prefers these short-lived little sparkles, each of which gives a little pleasure to an organized narrative."[20]

Another common characteristic of all these articles is that Sartre seems to be exclusively concerned with the *what* of a writer's metaphysics. The *why* of this metaphysics linked up with the writer's situation is still outside his concerns. This was a period during which he was not particularly interested in the socio-historical aspects of human reality and he was of the opinion that a literary work is an end in itself.[21] At this point, however, we should briefly consider his major philosophical work *Being and Nothingness* (1943), and especially the parts which are essential for an understanding of his literary criticism: his radical doctrine of freedom and his existential psychoanalysis.

b. *Being and Nothingness: Freedom and Existential Psychoanalysis*

In *Being and Nothingness,* Sartre distinguishes between being-in-itself, that is, being which is simply "what it is," and being-for-itself, that is, a being which is not what it is, a being that is "the foundation of itself as a lack of being," namely, consciousness.[22]   He further distinguishes two levels of consciousness:[23] the pre-reflective (non-positional consciousness of itself) and the reflective (positional consciousness of itself, consciousness of consciousness—of something—that is, subjectivity.)[24]   Even so, Sartre explains that "All consciousness is positional in that it transcends itself in order to reach an object, and it exhausts itself in this same positing."[25]

Consciousness, then, in itself is but a nothingness; it merely exists without an essence or a nature of its own.   Transferred on the level of the famous existential formula according to which 'existence precedes essence,' this means that human reality and meaning (essence) can only be achieved on the basis of man's *freedom* to move towards its achievement by going beyond his socio-historical, etc. conditioning.   This, of course, results in Sartre's rejection of the absolutism of all determinism and of a human nature created by God.

The arguments against Sartre's perception of human freedom in *Being and Nothingness* are well-known and there is not any specific reason for their repetition here.   It suffices to mention that the first reaction of the Marxists was its total rejection (and the rejection of *choice* as its essence) as "abstract, forced, totally vacuous and irrationalized . . ." (Lukács), and as uprooted from both "history and knowledge" (Garaudy).[26] Although rushed and overplayed, this early Marxist response (to a philosophy which, intermingled with a certain kind of literature, e.g. *Le Mur, La Nausee,* etc., was in a sense indistinguishable source of knowledge[27]) was well-founded, and as it will be evident later on, Sartre himself subsequently benefited from these individualistic philosophy which regards intuition as a basic source of knowledge[27]) was well-founded, and as it will be evident later on Sartre himself subsequently benefited from these and many other Marxist attacks.[28]   We should also emphasize, that this Sartrean concept of freedom is neither historical nor political, but *philosophical,* and that its meaning is radically different from what might be understood by a first impression.

Sartre points out:

> the formula 'to be free' does not mean to 'obtain what one
> has wished' but rather 'by oneself to determine oneself
> to wish' (in the broad sense of choosing). In other words,
> success is not important to freedom. . . . The technical
> and philosophical concept of freedom, the only one which
> we are considering here, means only the autonomy of
> choice . . . the choice, being identical with acting, supposes
> a commencement of realization in order that the choice
> may be distinguished from the dream and the wish.[29]

Moreover, Sartre, dealing with the relation between freedom
and facticity—freedom's own facticity being that it is not "able
not to be free"[30]—that is, the given, i.e. one's place, body,
past, position, etc., states that the supreme paradox of freedom
is that "there is freedom only in *situation*, and there is a situation only through freedom."[31] How is it so?

Sartre explains that this facticity, this given, is nothing
but "the in-itself nihilated by the for-itself which has to be
it," and that this facticity is discovered by our freedom and
our free choice to create ourselves: "I learn of this knowledge
from all the points of the future which I project; it is from
the standpoint of this chosen future that facticity appears to
me with its characteristics . . ." Hence, "Without facticity freedom would not exist—as a power of nihilation and of choice—
and without freedom facticity would not be discovered and
would not have meaning."[32] Thus, it is evident that genuine
authentic freedom is inseparable from facticity in the situation.
In other words, although it seems that one's freedom is limited
by things, the others, or even by natural forces, in reality man's
freedom is unlimited.

There is nothing capable of imposing a limit to man's
freedom, not even his finitude (i.e. the fact of his death). In
the framework of *Being and Nothingness*, then, the for-itself
leads to a radical perception of man's *responsibility*. Sartre
writes: "Man being condemned to be free carries the weight
of the whole world on his shoulders; he is responsible for the
world and for himself as a way of being."[33]

The Sartrean concept of freedom refers to the individual
praxis, that is, to the individual in *action* by placing full responsibility on him. As Sartre puts it, man always chooses,

even when he does not choose to choose, and he is responsible for his choices by which he ultimately chooses himself.   To choose oneself, however, means *to be*, and this is the only *irreducible* category of human reality, while the other two, namely *to do*, i.e. to make oneself, and *to have*, i.e. to possess, are reducible to the former.   These three cardinal categories of concrete human reality derive from man's *desire* to make and to possess in order to be.   Desire itself—a key concept in *Being and Nothingness*—which is a lack of being, is defined on the one hand by man's striving to become God, that is, "in relation to the In-itself-as-self-cause," and, on the other, in relation "to a brute, concrete existent which we commonly call the object of the desire."[34]

The fact that *Being and Nothingness* does not put any objective limit to man's desire, illuminates further the absolute nature of the Sartrean concept of freedom.   This absolutism is retained even when freedom is related to man's action (always *intentional*, based on *subjective* motives, wishes, passions, etc., which are provoked by *objective* causes,[35] a relationship demonstrating the objective basis of the subjective realm of consciousness) despite Sartre's manifested inability to account for the lack of authenticity on the concrete level of living and acting individuals.

For example, his notion of *bad faith* which expresses the individual's failure to wish or to choose to be free and, even worse than that, which is but a project of self-deception,[36] resulting in one's refusal to exercise his freedom, i.e. to be what he is and not what he is not (cf. Sartre's examples of the waiter in a cafe and of a woman on a date), is unsatisfactory.   This notion cannot explain the gap between the freedom of human consciousness and the bad faith of human praxis; Sartre himself is unable to give examples of authenticity and he just uses this term by-passing.[37]

In all, *Being and Nothingness* leaves open the question of how man is free and yet unable to exercise his freedom. Moreover, the absolutism of Sartrean freedom—besides his underplaying of the real effects of the situation and his ambiguous notion of bad faith—is manifested in the French philosopher's inability to perceive the freedom of the individual in his relation to the freedom of the other, because for the author of *Being and Nothingness* the other is only a mediator to oneself ("the other is the indispensable mediator between myself and me"[38]) and with whose freedom one's own freedom is in *conflict*. Hence, given man's awareness of his responsibilities, *anguish*—this notorious category of existentialism—comes as a logical consequence. However, despite that authenticity seems to be unattainable as long as it depends on the *individual alone* to achieve it, Sartre's emphasis on man's responsibility as well as on the possibility of the attainment of freedom in a situation, can be considered as the precondition of the subsequent transcendence of some of his major shortcomings in *Being and Nothingness*. In any case, we can now see how the latter establishes the foundations of a new method to approach man: *existential psychoanalysis*.

It is in order to grasp man's behavior patterns and desires that Sartre has recourse to existential psychoanalysis which begins from the basic findings of ontology.[39] The exclusive aim of this method is to rediscover an individual's *original choice* of being—which is irreducible—through the study of his concrete existential projects.[40] To make this explicit, we should take a look at Sartre's own account of the distinctive characteristics of his ambitious enterprise.

To begin with, Sartre criticizes empirical psychology because it holds that human desires are "contained" or "dwelling" in consciousness, and also because it considers its investigation as terminated successfully when it arrives at a definition of the ensemble of an individual's desires and drives (through empirical observation). He argues, for example, that to explain Flaubert by merely stating that he was ambitious is not enough, since ambition itself is hardly explained. What the empirical psychologist fails to reach is that *"veritable irreducible"*[41] which alone could reveal the *unity* which is Flaubert.

Sartre maintains that this irreducible is nothing but the *original project*, a fundamental, purely individual and unique initial project which not only discloses the totality that an individual is, but which also expresses an individual's original choice of being. This initial project he proposes to be defined on the basis of comparison of an individual's desires, drives and tendencies, and not by a simple summation of them as the empirical psychologists do. The criterion of success of this comparison is when it is established that irreducibility has been reached, that is, when "the projected end appears as the *very being* of the subject."[42]

The fundamental human project is the project of being

God, but this does not mean that all individuals make identical initial projects which would render Sartre's method useless. The initial projects of all individuals have ultimately an identical meaning, yet they are pursued in various ways: "While the *meaning* of the desire is ultimately the project of being God, the desire is never constituted by this meaning; on the contrary, it always represents a particular discovery of its ends. These ends in fact are pursued in terms of a particular empirical situation, and it is this very pursuit which constitutes the surroundings *as a situation*. The desire of being is always realized as the desire of a mode of being. And this desire as a mode of being expresses itself in turn as the meaning of the myriads of concrete desires which constitute the web of our conscious life."[43] Existential psychoanalysis then searches passionately for the individual's original choice of being, and besides its rejection of *libido* and of the *will to power*, it is nevertheless only partially dependent on the findings of ontology, and it is also largely based on Freudian psychoanalysis, the similarities and differences with which Sartre lists carefully.

In terms of their similarities, both the Freudian and the existential psychoanalysis regard the relationship between the fundamental structures of an individual and the manifestation of these structures, i.e. in the form of specific drives, tendencies, etc. as similar to the relationship between a symbolization and a symbol. Second, they both reject the pre-existence of original data, nature, etc. Third, they both view man as a living, historical process. Fourth, they both try to define an individual's basic attitude—which is prior to all logic: Freudian psychoanalysis seeks to find out an individual's *complex*; existential psychoanalysis seeks to find out his original choice. Finally, they both agree that the subject cannot psychoanalize himself because he cannot possibly go beyond that which he already comprehends.

Freudian psychoanalysis presupposes the existence of an *unconscious psyche* which escapes the subject's intuition, while existential psychoanalysis, which rejects the existence of the unconscious, makes the distinction between consciousness and knowledge: it accepts that an individual's original choice—which is prereflective—is wholly experienced by him and he is conscious of it, but he cannot analyze and conceptualize it; this can only be achieved by another. Sartre points out that both psychoanalyses fail to grasp "the project as it is for itself," because there is "an incompatibility between existence for itself and the objective existence." He adds, however, that even if this was possible, it would not be more than a clarification of the subject's reflection which, taken as knowledge, is but "quasi-knowledge."[44] The last similarity between these two methods is that they are both objective. Even so, they are divided by two irreconcilable differences.

First, empirical psychoanalysis has chosen its own irreducible, libido or the will to power, a priori. Existential psychoanalysis conceives of this irreducible as a choice which is a response to a lack of being. Moreover, in contrast to the very general and abstract categories of libido or the will to power, a choice is always specific and unique because it is made by a particular and unique individual. Therefore, existential psychoanalysis does not go from the complex to libido or to the will to power: it regards the latter two at best as the concrete choices of *some* individuals that cannot be reducible to them. As for the complex itself, it is "the ultimate choice, it is the choice of being and makes itself such,"[45] and it is its uniqueness that existential psychoanalysis purports to reveal.

Second, existential psychoanalysis—which unlike empirical psychoanalysis is concerned about a choice and not a state—opposes the establishment of mechanical relationships between the individual and his environment. Sartre states that the latter can act upon the individual "only to the extent that he comprehends it; that is, transforms it into a situation. Hence, no objective description of this environment could be of any use to us."[46] Thus, Sartre rejects all mechanical causation and objective generalities, and he demands of the investigator to be flexible and prepared to follow the abrupt changes in an individual's choices, keeping constantly in mind that choices are often "recalled." This implies that the specific methodological procedure which existential psychoanalysis uses in one case, should be modified in another, in order to meet the precise demands of its new object, i.e. a different subject, the same subject in another period, etc.

The Sartrean adherence to freedom is here manifested on two levels: on the level of the subject who chooses freely his mode of being, and on the level of the method itself which is by no means bound to a prefabricated, rigid procedure that would deprive it of any real heuristic value. Existential psychoanalysis as an objective approach to the subjective choices

of the beings of individuals should not stop before it has revealed
"being and the mode of being of the being confronting this
being." For this purpose, instead of taking refuge in the stock
of symbols at hand, "it will have to rediscover each time on
the basis of a comparative study of acts and attitudes, a symbol
destined to decipher them." Its success, of course, will be
tested only by a number of facts that the original choice of
being it has discovered is able to explain, which should be compared if possible to the subject's own testimony, but also by
the irreducibility of the latter. In all, "The behavior studies
by this psychoanalysis will include not only dreams, failures,
obsessions and neuroses, but also and especially the thoughts
of waking life, successfully adjusted acts, style, etc. This psychoanalysis has not yet found its Freud."⁴⁷

In his outline of existential psychoanalysis in *Being and
Nothingness*, Sartre bases himself on two erroneous assumptions
both of which he tries to overcome during the long course of
application and gradual improvement of his method from *Baudelaire* to *Saint Genet* and finally to *The Idiot of the Family*.
The first, is his *total* rejection of the Freudian idea of the unconscious, and the second, his *uncompromising* stand towards
the environment's effect on the individual.

Sartre's initial account of this relationship was right and
wrong at the same time, depending on one's point of reference.
He was right to the extent that an individual *makes* his choices
according to his comprehension of his environment. And he
was wrong to the extent that even though an individual chooses
his own choices, he does so within the framework of his conditioning by his environment whether he is aware of it or not.
This became evident to Sartre when—after years of bitter debates
with his critics, as well as self-improvement—he was convinced
that there are definite objective limits to freedom. From a
methodological point of view, this implies the necessity of an
additional analysis of the environment (regardless of the subject's
comprehension of it): an objective kind of analysis the indispensability of which Sartre realized in his Flaubert, i.e. the
objective analysis of Flaubert's epoch.

This early formulation of existential psychoanalysis provided the solid foundation of Sartre's literary criticism both as a
theory and method. Moreover, *Being and Nothingness* (through
which Sartre moved from the study of the consciousness of
something—i.e. in his four phenomenological studies of percep-

tion, imagination and emotions—to that of the consciousness of the other as mediator to oneself, and to a strong emphasis on both man's active freedom to choose oneself according to his fundamental desire to be, and to his responsibility, an idea that Sartre never ceased to develop[48]), opened the way for the construction of his most provocative concept which, mediating between freedom and responsibility, on the one hand, and literary creation, on the other, defines the field of existential literary evaluation: the concept of *commitment*.

c. *Commitment and Literary Evaluation*

Commitment as such is not an original Sartrean notion; it has nevertheless an exclusive Sartrean meaning that is primarily philosophical. Given the methodological orientation of our approach, we can just say that commitment, which according to Sartre is the essence of what is called 'littérature engagée,' is neither a merely descriptive concept, nor a merely evaluative one;[49] neither simply an "outlook on life"[50] nor just the "politically motivated . . . [even though it] remains politically polyvalent so long as it is not reduced to propaganda," opposite and/or alternative to "autonomous" literature;[51] neither just a manner by which a writer addresses the freedom of his readers, nor is it only a moral category instead of an aesthetic one.[52]

Commitment, as the essence of the act of writing is a concept that Sartre never refrained from enriching with meaning alongside his concept of responsibility. Like the act of writing itself, commitment eventually became for Sartre "everything," and ultimately it incorporated within it all its partial and particular meanings, thus acquiring a *total* meaning.[53] Therefore, Mészáros is right in pointing out that "Sartre's conception of commitment in literature" does not "lead to thematic restriction and political illustration, as well as to a paralysis of artistic spontaneity."[54]

Like the writing as the chosen project by which a writer defines and totalizes himself or creates himself while creating literature, commitment, as the concrete engagement of man's uncompromising responsibility in situation, is the mode of the conscious realization of the writer as a human, historical and finite being. As a project and choice of being materialized through writing, then, commitment is the totalization that totalizes the field of the possible of the writer's action, and it results in moral, political, social, aesthetic, descriptive, evaluative, etc. manifestations and functions, each one becoming occasionally predominant according to the existing socio-historical, etc. requirements—e.g. the emphasis on the political aspects of commitment following the years of Resistance and post-Resistance political apathy.

The overall critical function of commitment, however, is of central importance because ever since the time of Socrates men have realized that the unexamined life is not worth living, and it is in this sense that Sartre regards 'littérature engagée' as "a critical mirror,"[55] and determines the task of "The real work of the committed writer . . . to reveal, demonstrate, demystify, and dissolve myths and fetishes in a critical and acid bath."[56]   It seems, that what distinguishes the committed from the uncommitted writer is this critical activity, and M. Adereth underlines correctly the difference between "involvement," which no writer can escape, and "commitment," that is, the conscious planning and undertaking of this unavoidable involvement as a purposeful project.[57]   Sartre states in *What is Literature?*, that "a writer is engaged when he tries to achieve the most lucid and the most complete consciousness of being embarked, that is, when he causes the engagement of immediate spontaneity to advance, for himself and others."[58]

The purpose of the Sartrean-existential literary evaluation is much broader than that of literary evaluation proper. It should be mentioned at this point, that Sartre was initially preferring prose which he considered as a "masculine" kind of writing, to poetry which he regarded as "feminine."[59] However, he eventually changed his stand towards at least one particular kind of contemporary poetry after he read some poems by certain black poets,[60] and this in a sense indicated a modification of his sharp distinction between prose and poetry.[61] But besides this general comparative evaluation or prose versus poetry and the other arts in terms of their particular medium—words, color, sound, etc.—and their specific relationship to communication and commitment, Sartre's existential criticism without failing to evaluate literary works according to established criteria (albeit after they are adapted to his own philosophical premises,[62] i.e. the transmission[63] through literature of certain philosophical messages that challenge the freedom of the reader[64]), evaluates them also according to their *existential significance*: on the basis and to the extent of their accomplishment to reveal being in situation. In *What is Literature?* again he writes: "Each painting, each book, is a recovery of the totality of being."[65]

It is evident then why for Sartre doing reveals being, which implies that one is only what one does, and also why he strongly advocates the shifting from literature of *exis* (passivity) to the creation of the literature of *praxis*. It is because for Sartre, "the world and man reveal themselves by undertaking,"[66] hence, his demand of the writer to create only literature of extreme situations, that is, "literature that unites and reconciles the metaphysical absolute and the relativity of the historical fact."[67]

Regardless of the merits and shortcomings of *What is Literature?* in terms of its specifics, i.e. its author's historical knowledge, one should not fail to view it as the hymn-book of literature, and perhaps even as "exaggerating its importance."[68] Sartre asks of the writer to set as his ideal—attainable perhaps only in a genuine (utopian) socialist society—the creation of *total* literature, that is, literature able to achieve "the synthesis of *praxis* and *exis*, of negativity and construction, of doing, having and being. . . ."[69] The beauty of this literature would not be determined by its form and matter, but rather by "the density of being."[70] But to appreciate fully Sartre's evaluation of literature, we should compare it with that of Nietzsche's, whose own ideas influenced the literature of Europe (e.g. Rilke, Thomas Mann, Shaw, Gide, Malreaux, etc.), that of countries in Europe's backward periphery (i.e. modern Greek literature through one of its most significant representatives, Nikos Kazantzakis), and of course, the existentialist mode of thinking through Jaspers, Heidegger, and Sartre himself.

Concretely, Nietzsche, this great lover of classicism, perceived of art and literature as an ecstasy that falsifies reality and, at the same time, as endowed with an insurmountable healing power, able to save man from mental and emotional stagnation and despair. For this genius, art's ultimate purpose is to celebrate life (the essence of Nietzsche's concept of tragedy being "the exaltation of life in spite of horror"[71]), and to serve life because it alone can bring "the joy of being in *our* world, of being free from the anxiety of the alien."[72] Finally, Nietzsche maintains that the attainment of artistic excellence and greatness is accomplished only by the artist-creator who is able to rise above himself and his art, that is, above his real life.

For Sartre, on the contrary, artistic greatness can be reached neither above nor alongside life; by the same token art does not go beyond the sphere of life, affecting subsequently the latter in such a way as to make it livable and enjoyable. As we have seen, for Sartre art and literature create and reveal being and the world on the basis of man's ultimate ideal to be the in-itself-for-itself. For Sartre, therefore, art in general and literature in particular *is* life, real and conscious. Thus he answers the question 'what is writing' by emphasizing that it is an enterprise, a commitment, a choice, "as this total enterprise of living that each one of us is. . . ."[73]

The central question of Sartre's literary criticism, 'why does one write?' is only partially answered up to this point and so is that of Sartre's literary evaluation. Writing as the ultimate project of being is an answer on one level, albeit the fundamental level. On another level, Sartre maintains that the revealing of being and the world through the act of writing, or the realization of being and the totalization of self in and by writing, is closely connected to our feelings of inessentiality in relation to the thing that is revealed. Consequently, Sartre states that "one of the chief motives of artistic creation is certainly the need of feeling that we are essential in relationship to the world."[74]

The artist feels essential in relation to his creation. Nevertheless, as he himself sets up his own norms of creation, and the created object is always for him a subjective discovery, he can never perceive it from an objective distance. In other words, the artist cannot be both a revealer and a producer. Thus, a peculiar dialectic seems to be at work: "In the perception, the object is given as the essential thing and the subject as the inessential. The latter seeks essentiality in the creation and obtains it, but then it is the object which becomes the inessential."[75] More than anywhere else this dialectic is manifested in literature: for the literary fact to take place, the act of reading is prerequisite. However, since the writer cannot be his own reader—as he can never perceive of his writing as an object—the other as a reader becomes necessarily the writer's indispensable partner. A partner in what? In nothing less than the very act of artistic creation: a totalization that is totalized every time the act of reading takes place and which lasts as long as this act lasts.

There is no doubt that the two co-creators of the literary object perform different tasks. The writer *projects*—"*his* knowledge, *his* will, *his* plans, in short himself . . . his own subjectivity;" the reader *foresees*: he engages himself in constant guesswork awaiting with longing and emotion the confirmation or contradiction of his predictions from his objective distance—"without waiting, without a future, without ignorance, there is no objectivity."[76] Therefore, Sartre concludes, the assumption that one writes for himself is a false assumption. Writing and reading are dialectically related; without both these acts, the literary object cannot be realized. In all, "There is no art except for and by others. Reading seems, in fact, to be the synthesis of perception and creation."[77]

The creative role played by the act of reading, then, and the decisive importance of the reader is one of the themes that Sartre returns to time and again. In *What is Literature?*, he argues that the writer has always gone farther than any reader can possibly go, and in this sense reading is a creation directed by the writer, albeit a new and original creation alike to that of the writer's.[78] As he kept saying many years after he wrote *What is Literature?*, the reader invents the writer, while reading itself can be viewed as a kind of rewriting.[79] And in his Japan lectures (1965), he characterizes the relationship between the reader and the writer as one of non-knowledge, since what the latter communicates is not knowledge but the human condition, being-in-the-world: "When reading a writer's work, the reader is referred back indirectly to his own reality as a singular universal. He realizes himself—both because he enters into the book and does not completely enter into it—as another part of the same whole, as another view-point of the world on itself."[80]

Sartre, of course, does not fail to examine writing and reading as historical phenomena. Further, he maintains that a writer chooses his subject by the mere choice of his readers, that is, his public. It should be noticed at this point that Sartre's notion of the public is different from Taine's notion of the milieu. As he explains, the latter should be rejected because it *produces* and *determines* the writer; "the public, on the contrary, is a waiting, an emptiness to be filled in, an *aspiration*, figuratively and literally. In a word it is the other."[81] In this framework, Sartre distinguishes the public as *actual* or *virtual,* *real* or *ideal.* As for literature, it is "the subjectivity of a society in permanent revolution," which nevertheless does not *act* upon the readers, it only "makes an appeal to their freedom."[8 2] For these reasons, the reading public is a basic factor in Sartre's criticism as it is evident in his major existential biographies.

d. *Sartre and Marxism*

Baudelaire (1947), *Saint Genet* (1952) and *The Idiot of the Family* (I, II—1971; III—1972), written during a period of a quarter of a century—the study of Flaubert remained unfinished—became the testing ground of the methodological validity of existential psychoanalysis and of its underlying assumptions, philosophical or otherwise. Its theoretical outline in *Being and Nothingness* provided only the starting point of a far-reaching process which, fueled by the strong Marxist and other attacks, led to a continuous evolution of the Sartrean thought and to a considerable improvement of his method. The latter, moving progressively away from some of its initial positions, began approaching the Marxist philosophy and method, historical materialism, with mutually beneficial results, but after insistent and laborious effort on Sartre's part.

Concretely, as we have discussed in chapter four of this study, Lukács had realized Marxism's need to incorporate the categories of subjectivity and individuality alongside its main categories, in order to be able to acquire a truly total view of human reality. However, even though Lukács himself did not accept—unlike Merleau-Ponty's generalization which implicitly refers to all Marxist philosophers—that it was possible for Marxism "to express the weight of social reality by situating the dialectic wholly in the object,"[8 3] neither he nor any other Marxist could possibly adopt the Sartrean project toward a theory of consciousness and subjectivity simply because its overall methodological basis was not Marxist but phenomenological. From the Marxists' point of view, the exclusive Sartrean preoccupation was the consciousness of the individual, and it had resulted in extreme individualism, subjectivism and abstract freedom.

Sartre, of course, did respond to the Marxists and his

reply was vigorous. In *Existentialism and Humanism* (1946) and *Materialism and Revolution* (1946), he defended persistently his concern for subjectivity. Moreover, he counterattacked the Marxists and Stalinism insisting that they should accept the primacy of subjectivity. At the same time, he himself indicated his first retreat from his absolutist conception of freedom.[84] His decisive step, however, towards the Marxists on the political level and Marxism on the philosophical and theoretical levels was taken when he wrote his articles known as *The Communists and the Peace* (1952-1953).

In these articles Sartre argued in favor of the CP as the sole legitimate representative of the working class, and also in favor of the Soviet Union as a peaceful power in contrast to a bellicose United States. Above all, he for the first time payed close attention to the relationship between the freedom of the individual and the concrete historical reality by viewing freedom in the light of historical mediations.[85] Yet, despite these efforts towards some reconciliation of Marxism and Existentialism it became evident that almost everything was left to be done.

After the appearance of *The Communists and the Peace*, Merleau-Ponty, in his brilliant critique in *The Adventures of the Dialectic*, pointed out that even with his "Ultrabolshevist" phase,[86] Sartre had failed to bridge the gap between his extreme conception of freedom and Marx's concepts of society and history; that he had not succeeded in integrating the category of subjectivity into the Marxist system; that in fact, he had not gone beyond his initial sharp distinction between the self and the other—a distinction that Marxism had never made; and that the source of all these failures—as the Marxists themselves had already emphasized—remained Sartre's inability to transcend his dualistic conception of reality in *Being and Nothingness* (in-itself, for-itself) and take *systematically* into account the primary role played by certain concrete mediations: "The question is whether, as Sartre says, there are only *men* and *things* or whether there is also the interworld, which we call history, symbolism, truth-to-be-made."[87]

In addition, Merleau-Ponty exposed what he considered as Sartre's dramatic change since the time of *What is Literature?* He underlined, for example, that in contrast to his initial stand, Sartre had eventually introduced the *social* as a criterion of literature; by the same token, the literary act of *unveiling* the world had now become *direct action*; finally, the writer had been replaced by the gaze of the oppressed which "appeals to man's action. It is no longer literature which animates a society in permanent revolution; it is the Party which makes this society."[88]   Consequently, Merleau-Ponty continues, Sartre's initial conception of commitment is abandoned and the latter now becomes an active and political commitment which, as far as literature is concerned, is totally unacceptable because it expresses the meaning of a freedom that has lost its capacity to choose and to judge.   But this freedom is not freedom at all because it has already chose, and this demonstrates that Sartre has adopted an "ideology of choice."   And Merleau-Ponty concludes that "The declared choice is nearly the proof that there has been no choice."[89]

As a piecemeal assessment of Sartre's work in part, Merleau-Ponty's critique, however overstretched, is well-taken.   Yet, it loses much of its significance as an evaluation of that which really matters: the totality of the Sartrean *oeuvre.**   In any case, all failures mentioned by Merleau-Ponty, and particularly the fundamental failure, namely Sartre's relative neglect of the socio-historical mediations, are reflected to a different degree in the two existential biographies produced during the same phase of his development: *Baudelaire* and *Saint Genet*.   The qualitative and methodological differences, though, between these two works reflect also Sartre's attempt to overcome his shortcomings.

Specifically, as he moves from the one study to the other, his awareness and concern for the role played by society and history is progressively increased.   *Saint Genet*, for example, takes account of certain mediations which are barely noticed in *Baudelaire*.   Moreover, it is with *Saint Genet* that Sartre moves decisively towards the transcendence of the opposition between the subjective and the objective—a process that culminates in his *Critique of Dialectical Reason* and its famous preface, *Search for a Method*, published in 1960, the work that among other things laid down the foundation for the placing of the existentialist methodological insights at the service of Marxism. Thus, Sartre must have surprised his critics once more (i.e.

---

*Cf. for example our preceding discussion of the concept of commitment.

Lukács, Merleau-Ponty, Lefebvre, et al), since, by putting their criticisms to his own use, he not only began to overcome his dualism but he also started to work on the subject/object dialectic on two levels: on the level of the investigating subject and that of the investigated object.

e. *From Baudelaire to Saint Genet*

Indicative of Sartre's formidable intellectual development is that when in an interview given more than twenty years after the publication of *Baudelaire* the interviewer mentioned this study, he interjected that this was "A very inadequate, an extremely bad one. . . ."[90] Indeed, besides the various criticisms that were made against *Baudelaire* and especially against Sartre's allegedly subjective reasons for attacking the poet,[91] he himself became eventually concerned about what he considered to be his major drawback: the social and historical mediations which had escaped his attention as he was trying to disclose the poet's original choice and then to relate it to his overall project on the basis of a description of the mode of being of the poet's consciousness. In other words, Sartre became very much annoyed when he realized that he had identified a man's "free choice" with his "destiny,"[92] without the intervention of any mediations, and without any real consideration of all those socio-historical factors that also affect a man's destiny.

In *Saint Genet*, the work that was referred to by its commentators only in terms of superlatives[93] and which revolutionized man's understanding of man, Sartre's method as well as its application manifest an extraordinary improvement. Of course, Sartre is still far away from a thorough consideration of those socio-historical mediations that mediate an individual's life, i.e. his social class, yet it is on the basis of the mediation of the *Other* that Genet is ultimately defined. Thus, faithful to those philosophical principles which support his existential psychoanalytical technique, Sartre commences his phenomenological description of the highly complex totalising process that is Genet, with an initial careful reconstruction of the "original event to which he constantly refers. . . ."[94] His theoretical objective is to underline and transcend the limits of both the deterministic Freudian psychoanalysis which pays no attention whatsoever to society and history, and the objectivist Marxist approach which while concentrating its analytic-synthetic powers on the latter, disregards the individual. Above all, Sartre wishes to demonstrate that freedom is the sufficient and necessary explanatory principle of the totality which is an individual person, and also "to prove that genius is not a gift but the way out that one invents in desperate cases."[95]

A detailed account of Sartre's methodological procedure and step-by-step findings in *Saint Genet* is not a prerequisite here. We can only point out that his method has the advantage of being both progressive and regressive, advancing the understanding of Genet's life and work by means of multiple totalizations, de-totalizations and re-totalizations; that its ceaseless back and forth movements like dense waves sweep, disperse and regroup all those facts, events, desires, feelings, wounds, defenses, vindications, decisions, indecisions, actions, happenings, havings, doings, etc. which totalize a phase of Genet's life-process and at the same time detotalize another, retotalizing simultaneously a new one at another plane, but always within the banks of that torrential river which is the grand totalization of the totality that is Jean Genet; a grand torrential river and a tiny piece of straw at the same time; a tiny piece of straw inside the stormy field of influence of the Other, this powerful mediator of Genet's choices to be a thief, a homosexual, a writer, etc.; this all powerful Other which itself is in turn annihilated. It is in the omnipresence of the Other that Jean Genet is at the same time "the weakest of all and the strongest," all and nothing, "zero and infinity."[96]

The mediation of the Other is a hermaphrodite force both centrifugal and centripetal that results in the fusion of subjectivity and objectivity, in their interpenetration and their interdependence, and which is an inseparable part of the dialectical movement that is Genet's life, during which the objective Other is annihilated and objectified anew in a constant process of objectivization-annihilation. Sartre expresses the three moments of this dialectical movement from oneself to the Other and then back to oneself as follows: "*Thesis*: to be oneself is to be the Other. *Antithesis*: The Other vanishes, the self remains. *Return to the thesis*: This self is no longer anything for *itself*, for it was not aware of itself quo Other; it is again alienated in the Other."[97] The Other is the system of reference of the totalization of the totality that is Genet's life. Sartre is very explicit on this: "It is always against the Other and the Other's intentions that he has chosen to fight in becoming willfully and definitely what the Other obliges him to be. Since he is denied the right to be a man, he will become a woman. . . . But it is not for himself that he wishes to effect this resentful metamorphosis: it is against the Other and in the presence of the Other."[98]

To exemplify how the Other is the mediator to oneself and how this mediation results in a unique fusion of subjectivity and objectivity, as well as in the alienation of oneself, (which by placing emphasis on the object that he is to Others, he neglects the subject that he is to himself), let us see how Sartre—unlike *Baudelaire's* case—accounts for man's destiny in *Saint Genet.* Concretely, Sartre argues that the children who are exposed to persistent social pressures, judgments, prohibitions, prejudices, etc. since very early in their life become totally and definitely alienated. In effect,

> They internalize the objective and external judgments which the collectivity passes on them, and they view themselves in their subjective individuality on the basis of an 'ethnic character,' a 'nature,' an 'essence' which merely express the contempt in which *Others* hold them. . . . They thus allow themselves to be governed by *another*, that is, by a being who has reality only in the eyes of others. Their failings and errors are transformed into a permanent predisposition, that is, into a destiny. Such is the case of the child Genet.[99]

In this framework, man is faced with an extremely serious problem which causes his separation from the other men: the fact that man is an object to another man and a subject to himself but not "both object and subject for each other and by each other."[100] This fact obliges man either to go to the limits of himself as subject or to sink into solitude—a mixture of objectivity and subjectivity when it is experienced as failure, and a negative relationship of oneself to all. Sartre confirms that man's final hope is to reconcile the subject and object within himself—an impossible enterprise indeed under the existing socio-historical conditions. At present, "We spent our time fleeing from the objective into the subjective and from the subjective into objectivity. This game of hide-and-seek will

end only when we have the courage to go to the limits of ourselves in both directions at once. At the present time, we must
bring to light the subject, the guilty one. . . ."[101] In any case,
the thing we should stress here is that once the heavy presence
of mediations to an individual's life is realized, the traditional
opposition between subjectivity and objectivity becomes meaningless. More than a dozen years after the publication of *Saint
Genet*, Sartre states: "As far as I am concerned there is no such
thing as subjectivity: there are only internalization and ex-
teriority."[102]

f. *Search for a Method and Critique of Dialectical Reason*

The fundamental theme of the subjective/objective dialectic
is taken up again in Sartre's momentous introduction to his
Critique, the *Search for a Method*: the subjective is presented
as just a moment of the objective process, as "the internalization
of the external," and the objective as "the externalization
of the internal." Both moments result from man's *praxis*—"a
passage from objective to objective through internalization"—
that takes place according to man's *project*—"the subjective
surpassing of objectivity towards objectivity"—which alone
as the mediator between two moments of objectivity can account
for man's history, actions, creativity, etc. Sartre describes
this difficult-to-be-grasped dialectic, which is a totalization
perpetually flowing out of man's lived reality, as follows:

> In the *lived experience*, the subjectivity turns back upon
> itself and wrenches itself from despair by means of
> *objectification*. Thus the subjective contains within
> itself the objective, which it denies and which it surpasses
> toward a new objectivity; and this new objectivity by
> virtue of *objectification* externalizes the internality of
> the project as an objectified subjectivity. This means
> *both* that the lived as such finds its place in the result
> and that the projected meaning of the action appears in
> the reality of the world that it may get its truth in the
> process of totalization.[103]

On the level of the investigator, the subject/object dialectic takes a broader significance due to Sartre's attempt to re-evaluate and improve by rectification the objectivist Marxist theory of knowledge. Very illuminating for Sartre's own position (and also for his personal relationship as an investigator to his psychoanalytical biographies) is a long footnote in *Saint Genet*, in which while admitting that the critic distorts objectivity to the extent that he perceives his object from his own perspective, he emphasizes that at the same time objectivity is revealed to the extent that all findings are *verified* by the objective facts available. Thus, "A critic's mental attitude and emotional making serve as 'revealers,' prepare the intuition." Sartre's use of the intuitive method, then, appears similar to that of Weber's, since they both ultimately rely on thorough verification on the basis of the objective facts—among them certain "transhistorical" truths which are by no means "eternal." Therefore, according to Sartre, the investigator should aim not at an absolute but at a *situated* objectivity: "In a *good* critical work, we will find a good deal of information about the author who is being criticized and some information about the critic. . . . Man is an object for man; the value of objectivity must be restored in order to dispose of the subjectivist banalities that always try to beg the question."[104] This brings us once more back to the issue of the impossibility of the adoption of the scientific method by the socio-cultural sciences.

In his *Search for a Method*, Sartre makes a frontal attack on this problem but from a position inside the Marxist philosophy which he accepts as the only valid interpretation of history, and in relation to which existentialism is a simple ideology living on its margin. He points out, however, that Marxism is not any longer based on the dialectical unity of theory and praxis, and that by operating on the level of generalities it has lost its analytical power and heuristic value, becoming in the hands of its vulgar practitioners a *"voluntarist idealism,"*[105] as Lukács has very accurately observed. For this coming-to-an-end Marxism, the truth is already known and the knowledge already constituted; the facts are only used ceremoniously, to assert them. For existentialism, on the contrary, truth is always in the becoming, a totalization. Notwithstanding these criticisms, Sartre makes it clear that he is by no means opposing Marxism; he is just trying to revitalize it. In effect, he offers Marxism the *methodological* principle holding that "certitude begins with reflection" which does not contradict Marx's *anthro-*

pological principle "which defines the concrete person by his materiality."

For Sartre, reflection and intuition provide only a point of departure, and he rejects any identification with "idealist subjectivism." Further, he quotes an excerpt from Marx which seems to suggest an objective approach to phenomena, and another from Lenin which refers to consciousness as an approximate reflection of being, and he underlines the need of Marxism to accept the experimenter as "a part of the experimental system." Of course, Sartre is well aware that Marxism itself provides all elements necessary for the construction of a *realistic* epistemology, but he argues that the Marxist practice, following Marx's construction of a complete "system of coordinates," failed to achieve it. Instead, this fundamentally a prioristic Marxism, by ignoring all subjectivity in order to promote strictly objectivistic positions and attitudes, succumbed into idealism, the same idealism one falls into when all objectivity is eliminated in the interest of subjectivity.

A realistic Marxist epistemology, Sartre, maintains, can be constructed only when knowing is situated in the world, and when the contemporary Marxists realize "that subjectivity is neither everything, nor nothing; it represents a moment in the objective process (that in which externality is internalized), and this moment is perpetually eliminated only to be perpetually reborn."[106] In view of the shortcomings of the vulgar Marxist practice, Sartre feels that "everything remains to be done; we must find the method and constitute the science."[107]

One of the chief errors that vulgar Marxists' commit is that they replace particularity by a false (i.e. conceived a priori) and abstract universality; such a practice evidently opposes Marx's own methodological advice that the investigator must move from the "abstract to the concrete." In contrast to vulgar Marxism, Sartre singles out a method developed by Henri Lefebvre in his *Perspectives de Sociologie Rurale*, because it makes possible the integration of the "vertical" complexity of history with the "horizontal" complexity of society. Sartre characterizes this method as "faultless," and he does not hesitate to adopt it on condition that it is adequately modified according to the demands of each specific object of investigation.[108]

For Sartre, vulgar Marxism "lacks any hierarchy of mediations." For example, when it studies particular individuals and their activities, it starts directly with their adulthood, totally neglecting the determining phase of their formative years: their *childhood*. Therefore, in order for vulgar Marxism to come down from the clouds of abstract generality to the concrete reality of particular individuals, it must employ the method of existential psychoanalysis, which is uniquely equipped to deal with the principal mediations of family and childhood. This method will try to account for both the effect of an individual's childhood upon his adulthood and those objective structures and material conditions which affect his life. As for the reason that existential psychoanalysis is interested primarily about extreme situations, i.e. situations in which a man's alienation has been a permanent feature since his childhood, it is because these are the characteristic situations of our exploitative socio-economic system.

Existential psychoanalysis is no more than a mediation which does not contradict any of the basic Marxist principles, simply because it does not offer an alternative explanatory principle. It merely facilitates, or better, it alone achieves the understanding of even some of those aspects of one's behavior that appear to be irrational and which are rooted in childhood. The latter, however, is not conceived as a phase unaffected by the general material and other conditions of an individual's environment, i.e. his class—in which case a basic Marxist principle would have been violated—but as "a particular way of living the general interests of our surroundings."[109]

Another auxiliary discipline, namely, American sociology could be of significant use to Marxism despite its lack of a firm theoretical basis, as it is the case with existential psychoanalysis itself. But for Marxism to be really fruitful it must take systematically into account the vast number of concrete mediations which affect the totality of an individual's life-process. In view then of vulgar Marxism's stubborn contempt for certain Western disciplines, Sartre sets as his primary objective the integration on the methodological level within Marxism of existential psychoanalysis and sociology. The result was his progressive-regressive method: a totalization that totalized within itself not only Sartre's initial conception of existential psychoanalysis in *Being and Nothingness*, but also his negative and positive theoretical findings ever since, those of his long and laborious journey into genuine Marxism and away from its vulgar practices included.

In effect, the abstract conception of freedom is abandoned,

and man's actions and creativity are now being explained on the basis of his *project*. This concept, of course, has been developed alongside Sartre's remarkable intellectual development: it is not any longer based on man's "lack" and "desire," but on his "need" and the "scarcity" that limits his world. This last concept marks Sartre's change from *Being and Nothingness* to his *Critique of Dialectical Reason*, and it depicts the present inability of society to emancipate itself from its needs.

Certainly, Sartre never ceased to regard freedom as the cornerstone of his philosophy. He only rectified the essential meaning of this concept: freedom initially meant an abstract and false probability; now it was signifying a concretely attainable reality, under certain conditions. A time came then when enriched by his own experiences as a Being-in-the-World, Sartre regarded his early statements about freedom as "incredible."[110] Thus, almost a decade after the publication of his *Critique* he formulated his mature stand towards freedom as follows: "I believe that a man can always make something out of what is made of him. This is the limit I would today accord to freedom: the small movement which makes of a totally conditioned social being someone who does not render back completely what his conditioning has given him. Which makes of Genet a poet when he had been rigorously conditioned to be a thief."[111]

Sartre's progressive-regressive method is an improvement over the method of historical materialism which is only progressive, as it is practiced by the Marxists. In addition, it is basically heuristic, and unlike the Marxist method which is mainly concerned with the object and which eliminates "the questioner from the investigation," this advanced Sartrean method focuses equally on both the subject and the object. Sartre writes: "In order for the notions like reification and alienation to assume their full meaning, it would have been necessary for the questioner and the questioned to be made one."[112] We should stress, at this point, that what existentialism questions is not the principles of historical materialism, but only its historical transformation into a mechanistic determinism.

The testing-ground of Sartre's method—which being dialectical through-and-through was actually developed into a method of historical analysis—became a grand critical investigation in two phases: one regressive, on which the intelligibility of sociological knowledge would be based, and the other progressive on the basis of which the intelligibility of historical knowledge would be established. The overall goal of this critical investigation was "to reveal and establish dialectical rationality that is to say, the complex play of *praxis* and totalization" or, in other words, "to establish a structural and historical anthropology."[113]

In contrast to Marxism which proceeds from general and large categories, i.e. the mode and relations of production, social classes, etc. to their internal contradictions and occasionally to the individual, Sartre's critical investigation started moving in the opposite direction: from the individual as he creates himself by his praxis, to historical man, that is, from the individual in all his particularity and uniqueness, to history.

Unfortunately, the progressive moment of Sartre's investigation, that is, his ambitious plan about history, ("to establish that there is *one* human history, with *one* truth and *one* intelligibility"[114]), did not materialize. His *Critique of Dialectical Reason* includes only the regressive moment of his plan: on the one hand, it is an attempt towards the definition and transcendence of the limits of dialectical reason; and on the other, it provides a dialectical account of the individual praxis versus the "practico-inert," (the domain of the "equivalence between alienated *praxis* and worked inertia"[115]), of the human collectives and of the human groups in their variations and transformations. A basic assumption of the *Critique of Dialectical Reason* is that the dialectic—regarded both as a "resultant" and a "totalizing force"—is revealed "only to an observer situated in interiority," and able at the same time to go beyond his individual life, into History: to an observer who can "see his own life as the Whole and the Part, as the bond between the Parts and the Whole, and as the relations between the Parts, in the dialectical movement of (History's) Unification."[116]

g. *The Idiot of the Family*

Sartre's abandonment of the second volume of the *Critique* was also due to his firm commitment to a more urgent task which forced him to discontinue his "theoretical disquisitions" which led to "nowhere": the pressing question that confronted

Sartre, especially after the publication of *Words* (1963), was how a concrete application of his regressive-progressive method, derived from the integration within Marxism of both existential psychoanalysis and American sociology, was possible.[117]   To meet this challenge he undertook another grandiose project: the total study of a "singular individuality," of the "unique adventure" of a particular "being-in-the-world," of a "singular universal":[118]   Gustave Flaubert.

This plan was haunting his mind for years, and *Search for a Method* includes a lengthy outline of the appropriate methodological procedure.   There, Sartre indicated that the investigation should have first to determine the "field of possibles" and the "field of instruments" of Flaubert's period, and it should subsequently try to account for the singular totality of Flaubert's life and activity within the framework of that period, by means of a "differential interpretation."[119]   This "differential" should be considered from the point of view of both the progressive and the regressive movements of the method, and always in respect to Flaubert's biography.

The three published volumes of Sartre's "true novel"[120] about Flaubert, on the one hand, constitute a stupendous attempt towards the application of his complex and multileveled methodological synthesis; on the other, they are the manifestation and relative completion of the spectrum of his evolving change and development, according to the interplay of a multitude of internal and external determinations in a constant process of interiorization and re-exteriorization.   In this sense, *The Idiot of the Family* is the largest totalization of Sartre's lifework which, as Mészáros points out, "can only be comprehended through the dialectic of continuity and discontinuity," or "as increasingly more complex superseding-preservations."[121]

Viewed in this broader perspective, we can disregard at this point the narrow and specific criticisms of this work by the philologists[122]—irrespective of their validity—who do not seem sufficiently qualified to appreciate the existential dimension and significance of the investigator's relationship to the investigated object, and approach *The Idiot of the Family* in terms of its two essential differences from *Being and Nothingness, Saint Genet* and, to some extent, the *Critique.*

The first difference underlines the developing totalization of Sartre's evolving conception of freedom in relation to his advancing apprehension of the problem of mediations, as well as his transcendence of the time-old opposition between the subjective and the objective. This is eloquently depicted in the following self-reflective statement:

> in *L' Etre et le Neant*, what you could call 'subjectivity' is not what it would be for me now, the small margin in an operation whereby an interiorization re-exteriorizes itself in an act. But 'subjectivity' and 'objectivity' seem to me entirely useless notions today, anyway. I might still use the term 'objectivity,' I suppose, but only to emphasize that everything is objective. The individual interiorizes his social determinations: he interiorizes the relations of production, the family of his childhood, the historical past, the contemporary institutions, and he then re-exteriorizes these in acts and options which necessarily refer us back to them. None of this existed in *L' Etre et le Neant*.[123]

In the same erruption of self-criticism, Sartre characterizes *Saint Genet* as "very, very inadequate," because he had failed to examine how and to what degree the various institutions and historical factors had affected Genet's life-process, that is, to show Genet not merely as a freedom mediated by the Other but also as a product of his time.

Such omissions were avoided in *The Idiot of the Family* where Sartre enlarged the field of mediations and expanded systematically his explorations into the vertical realm of history and the horizontal of society—i.e. he paid special attention to Flaubert's relationship to the bourgeoisie—drawing thus the boundaries of Flaubert's freedom. In effect, and regardless of the practical results of Sartre's particular attempt which by themselves cannot be taken as the measure of the validity of his method, one might appreciate the volume of the enterprise he undertook by the magnitude of his objective:

> I would like the reader to feel the presence of Flaubert the whole time; my ideal would be that the reader simultaneously feels, comprehends and knows the personality of Flaubert, totally as an individual and yet totally as an expression of his time. . . . Flaubert can only be understood by his difference from his neighbors. . . . My aim is to try to demonstrate the encounter between

the development of the person, as psychoanalysis has
shown it to us, and the development of history.[124]

There is another difference that can be seen as an example
of the dialectical nature of Sartre's life-project, its ability to
negate its unsuccessful partial totalisations and subsequently
retotalize these transformed elements through negation on a
higher level, and its constant openness to modification and
readjustment.

To begin with, Sartre has admitted that his early work
has been an exercise in rationalism,[125] where the concept
of consciousness that stressed the intentional character of human
praxis held a predominant position, and the Freudian idea of
a causal unconscious has been totally excluded. The uncon-
ditional rejection of the unconscious, however, deprived existential psychoanalysis of certain Freudian insights which it
could not afford to do away with. Sartre eventually realized
for example that his more rationalistic work, *Being and Nothingness*, "in the end . . . becomes an irrationalism, because it cannot account rationally for those processes which are 'below'
consciousness and which are also rational, but lived as irrational."[126]

In his study of Flaubert, Sartre revised his initial stand
as follows: on the one hand, he preserved his opposition to the
Freudian version of the unconscious (as an ambiguous notion
referring to a set of mechanical determinations[127]), and on
the other, he replaced his initial concept of consciousness by
that of the *lived experience*. We should point out right from
the start, however, that this is an ambiguous concept too like
that of the Freudian unconscious the meaning of which it purports to preserve and supersede. As Sartre explains, lived experience,

is neither the precautions of the preconscious, nor the
unconscious, nor consciousness, but the terrain in which
the individual is perpetually overflowed by himself and
his riches and consciousness plays the trick of determining itself by forgetfulness. . . . Lived experience is
always simultaneously present to itself and absent from
itself . . . [and it shows] that every psychic fact involves
an intentionality which aims at something, while among
them a certain number can only exist if they are com-

prehended, but neither named nor known.[128]

Unlike the Freudian unconscious, lived experience, ("a total absence of knowledge but a real comprehension"), is in essence always intentional, susceptible of *comprehension* but not of *intellection*—as these two terms are distinguished in the *Critique*.[129] In this sense, lived experience is a perpetual "totalization which cannot be conscious of what it is . . . [because] one can be conscious of an external totalization, but one cannot be conscious of a totalization which also totalizes consciousness."[130]

h. *Language and Style*

Sartre's partial reconciliation to the Freudian idea of the unconscious was simultaneously a way of coming to terms, to a limited extent, with the ascending intellectual force of the 60's, French structuralism, especially after Levi-Strauss' forceful attack in *The Savage Mind* on Sartre's *Critique*. The main issue was whether social reality could be approached in terms of a conscious subject behaving and acting intentionally, or objectively, that is, in terms of an unconscious linguistic structure, independent of the subject; at the heart of this issue, of course, was the question of the intelligibility of consciousness.

As we have mentioned earlier in this study, for Levi-Strauss, social reality and consequently its most essential structure, language, could not possibly be investigated from the standpoint of the subject: language is completely autonomous, it is its own truth and its own reality and it can only be intelligible by means of an unconscious and objective structure. In *The Savage Mind* he writes: "Linguistics . . . presents us with a dialectical and totalizing entity but one outside (or beneath) consciousness and will. Language, an unreflecting totalization, is human reason which has its reasons and of which man knows nothing."[131]

Levi-Strauss, who attacked both phenomenology and existentialism (i.e. he characterized Sartre a speculative philosopher, a humanist, etc.) took a clearly scientistic position, and he declared that the mission of philosophy, until science is developed enough to take over completely, is "to understand being in relationship to itself and not in relationship to my-self."[132]   In this climate, and after some very interesting de-bates, Sartre's counter-offensive was manifested as an attempt towards a new totalization purporting at the simultaneous preser-vation and overcoming of his initial stand in relation to language and structure.

In an interview given to *Revue d' esthetique* in 1965, Sartre reaffirmed his assessment that language is a practico-inert entity, a means not an end, and always mediated by the writer. The word, he said, is "an artifact—a product of history reworked by myself." Moreover, he repeated his rejection of structuralism and he insisted that man is at the center of social reality.[133]   Also, in his famous Japan lectures, delivered the same year, he dealt with language extensively and systematically, and he referred to it as an autonomously developing practico-inert that mediates between men who in turn mediate between its various aspects.

As a mediated mediation, language is a *signifier* that im-poses itself as a presence; the language contained in a book is a "part of the world" by which the "totality of the world" is manifested.   Sartre points out that as a presence in a given literary work language has the purpose of revealing an absence; the language employed in a specific literary creation is a meaning that its objective is non-meaning; it is a communication that strives to go beyond language: within the confines of a literary work language is the sayable which aims not at the communica-tion of knowledge but at the presentation and revealing of being-in-the-world "as a constitutive and unsayable relationship be-tween everyone and everything, and between each man and all others,"[134] as a relationship between singularity and univer-sality, as *silence*. Sartre writes: "the total unity of the recom-posed work of art is silence—that is to say, the free incarna-tion, through words and beyond words, of being-in-the-world as non-knowledge folding back over a partial but universalizing knowledge."[135]

A writer reaches silence with words—which are both sacri-ficed objects and objective material realities—by means of "his ability to attract the reader's attention to the materiality of any given word." However, this is not a subject upon which we can elaborate here; for our own purposes, we can notice that this silence, this absence to which the signifying content of a literary work points, is but a structure about the importance of which Sartre argues persistently: this, together with his larger interest about language, is indicative of his coming closer to the structuralist standpoint.

In effect, the relative approach of the two positions on language becomes evident if we compare the structuralist thesis, according to which men do not express themselves through language, but language expresses itself through men, with Sartre's statement about the use of ordinary (not technical) language, by which he accepts the latter also as a dynamic system that operates through man. He specifically maintains that when I use common language, "I act in opposition to my own interests. . . . I speak it and, in the same breath, I am, as an other, spoken by it. . . . No sooner have I said: 'Good morning, how are you?' than already I no longer know whether I am making use of language or whether language is making use of me."[136] This means that from the moment a simple word is uttered the totality of language is evoked to participate in the intentional communication between two subjects. The writer, Sartre maintains, fully exploits the dialectical phenomenon of man's use of and of his being used by language, and he makes "his *being-in-language* the expression of his *being-in-the-world*."[137] This is accomplished through the writer's unique manipulation and mediation of language from the standpoint of his singular individuality, that results in his personal *style*.

It has already been said that Sartre always regarded style as the key to the understanding of a writer's metaphysics, and for this reason as literary criticism's primary object of investigation.[138] Since his study of Flaubert, however, his interest in style was broadened to the extent that in an interview that he gave during one of his late visits to Athens in February 1977, he said that he would like to write a book about "NOTHING . . . (because) that which counts in literature is the style and not the subject."[139] This statement sounds like a repetition of that made by Flaubert, and it indicates the influence of the latter on his great biographer. In fact, Sartre identifies with and at the same time goes far beyond the author of *Madame Bovary*: for Flaubert, a certain style simply corresponds to a particular subject, and it can be the means by which the writer's "personality" can be excluded from his writings;[140] for Sartre, on the contrary, the latter is impossible because it is precisely the style that reveals the writer's personality. Therefore, the NOTHING which he referred to in his interview is no less than the writer's life-world.

For Sartre, the principal function of style, e.g. the employment of ambiguous phrases, the playing with words, etc. is not the communion of any knowledge about the writer, but the presentation of his being-in-the-world. In Sartre's own formulation, the function of style is to produce "the singular universal by showing simultaneously language as a generality that produces and wholly conditions the writer in his facticity, and the writer as an adventurer, turning back on his language, and assuming its follies and ambiguities in order to give witness to his practical singularity and imprison his relationship with the world, as lived experience, in the material presence of words."[141]

Style, nevertheless, would be ineffective if the writer fails to transmit specific meanings through his work. Thus, a very complex dialectic seems to operate between a work's style (i.e. the *totality* that remains in the background) and its meaning (i.e. the *part* of the meaningfully used language which is but a quasi-meaning), and between its non signifying elements (the part which is a presence) and the significance (the totality which is an absence) to which it points, the search for which Sartre considers as the contemporary writer's fundamental task. This is a matter of great importance for literary criticism, hence, a longer quotation is required:

> The essential task of the modern writer is to work on the non-signifying element of ordinary language to enable the reader to discover the being-in-the-world of a singular universal. I propose to call this task the search for significance. . . . Such a significance is the presence of the totality in the part. The style of a writer lies in this respect in his interiorization of exteriority. . . . Style constitutes the expression of our invisible conditioning by the world behind us, and meanings constitute the practical efforts of an author thus conditioned to attain through this conditioning the elements of the world in front of him.[142]

This renewed emphasis on language and style was a moment of Sartre's movement to approach structuralism, while in a second moment of the same movement he underlined his difference with it. Thus, the subject's centrality was preserved in spite of the recognition of his being acted upon by a self-developing structure, namely, language: a structure which is absent from the partial totalization of any concrete discourse and invisible to the speakers.

Sartre's insistence that social reality can only be understood in terms of an intentionally acting subject was expressed alongside his realization that the days of naturalism, symbolism and bourgeois realism in literature are gone and language is the principal material of the post World-War-II prose-writer.[143] He also found a similar situation in the post World-War-II theatre which he called 'critical.' Here, three elements, namely, plot, psychological determination and bourgeois realism are completely refused, the theatre's traditional anthropomorphic character is abolished and the subject is totally excluded. What the critical theatre focuses on is but an object: "Language and conversation."[144]

As a playwright himself, Sartre works on the level of myth. But the developing reality of the critical theatre obviously strengthens the position of the structuralists on language, who rightly insist that no theory of consciousness can account for the invisible structures. Sartre's dialectical method can certainly account for the intentional actions of individuals and groups, as well as for the intentionally worked matter, that is, matter consciously mediated by man, yet, those invisible structures are still escaping.

Sartre's partial totalization on the level of the individual, that is, his concept of lived experience which in a sense aimed at the integration of structuralism did not achieve its purpose. In addition, on the social level, his statement that his structure of social facts is the response of the practico-inert "to the agents who work it [or that] structures are created by activity which has no structure, but suffers its results as a structure,"[145] does not provide a satisfactory explanation. Finally, to the specific question of "How can individual acts result in ordered structures," he answers that he had planned to investigate this in the second volume of the *Critique*. The fact, however, that this project did not materialize had a positive connotation: it demonstrated the continuing movement of Sartre's totalizing activity which being open-ended, that is, free, was constantly pointing to the future—until his death.

2. *Towards a Dialectical Critical Enterprise*

Sartre's literary criticism is nothing less than an immense critical enterprise. But, to merely view his accomplishments as an individual achievement is inaccurate as he exploited to the maximum the experience of decades of ongoing collective effort. In this sense, his theoretical and methodological premises constitute a giant totalization, totalizing ceaselessly the available knowledge for an understanding of man by man.

In many respects Sartre seems to be the extention of Lukács, who first opened the road towards a heuristic Marxism. He was able to turn Lukács' path into an avenue by using an enlarged field of intellectual instruments and by integrating sociology and existential psychoanalysis into the dialectical Marxist method. Thus, he advanced from Lukács' concept of dialectical totality to his own concept of dialectical totalization, and from Lukács' mere reference to the category of individuality to the concrete penetration of the singular universal.

The distinctive quality of the dialectical Marxist approaches to literature is their unshakable concern for totality, (Lukács), which, with the rise of existential Marxism, (Sartre), becomes the persistent and exhaustive examination of a continuously expanding totalization which also totalizes its own totalizer. With dialectical Marxism then we go beyond the limits of traditional critical investigations which are often self-restrained by their objectives and priorities.

It is existential-Marxist literary criticism that perhaps makes the task of critical exploration unmanageable for the average (trained in philology alone) critic, and it is Sartre himself who makes an extraordinary demand of him. Marxism demands of the critic to take the point of view of totality. Sartre, the critic, that is, a singular individual who was able to put at his command the combined resources of social science, philosophy and the art of literature, has given an unprecedented example of critical practice.

Speaking from the ramparts of dialectical Marxism, Sartre demands of the contemporary critic to transcend the boundaries of modern specialization, to cross the lines of ideological confinement, and to step outside his object of investigation, while never losing sight of it from within, in order to view it in perspective, and himself, the researcher, as part of his object: as the one who sets up its meaning and his own traps. In addition, points out—that understanding, which includes interpretation and evaluation, is an effective historical relation; that he is the creation and the creator; that he is everything (i.e. the indispensable mediator) and that he is nothing (i.e. his object's existence is independent of his own, while a future approach might render his own obsolete); that he is the relative in the absolute and the absolute in the relative; and that his criticism, any criticism, is a commitment for which he is completely responsible.

To the extent that literary criticism is the critic's project of being-in-the-world, it is unique, and like literature itself it is full of idiosyncratic, irrationalist and personal elements; but to the extent that it is a project about other men's projects of being-in-the-world, it must follow those methodological/theoretical guidelines that account for their individual and collective life in society and history.

Lukács' doctrine of Marxist realism and Sartre's existential exploration of the dialectic between the subjective and the objective, provide literary criticism with a solid base. Lukács' starting point is the product; Sartre begins with the producer. Both, however, expand their critical endeavor, according to their own available field of instruments, to include an examination of the interaction between all four coordinates, namely, the writer, the work, the universe and the audience, to which they add a fifth one: the critic.

It should be noted that besides Lukács who pioneered the way, a multitude of important individuals contributed to the Sartrean achievements through their own projects and critical commentaries: in France alone the *arguments group* and the structuralists, as well as distinguished thinkers and scholars like Maurice Merleau-Ponty, Henri Lefebvre, etc. Sartre's totalization—in the midst of a post-War intellectual fervor centered in France— never ceased integrating the positive results of the individual and collective totalizations of others, and thus, he did succeed in developing a more satisfactory method for the study of man's purposeful literary products. It is to his credit that he was able to apply and keep improving his method through a long and laborious effort, and even to move towards the intellection of the invisible social structures in an attempt to integrate structuralism which had made of the linguistic structure a methodological and theoretical panacea. Sartre demands of the critic to be aware—as Gadamer correctly

In view of Sartre's practice, criticism appears to be both art and science, and as such the adequate training and intellectual preparation of the critic is just the indispensable precondition for the successful undertaking of a critical enterprise. What will ultimately elevate the totalisation of such an activity to the level of a genuine achievement is not just the blind following of some rules. Only the totalization of the dialectical relationship between the objectively established facts and the critic's singular individuality going beyond the statement can reach the level of creative praxis, out of which a new word can spring and blossom.

Regardless of Sartre's victories and defeats—which closely reflect the contemporary state of man's ability to know man-in-the-world—he has given a unique example of an undogmatic and dialectical thinker. A thinker who by going to the limit has ultimately demonstrated some of the possibilities of Marxism for man's self-understanding on the individual, social and historical planes at present. He has also provided a most fruitful and rich example of literary criticism.

Two years before his death Sartre states: "My best book is the one that I haven't written yet, the one that I plan to write and which I might never write."[146]   He did not have a chance to write his future 'best' book, but he has proven more than once by his evolving intellectual maturation the truth of another dialectic: the dialectic between failure and success, which manifests that the 'Loser Wins.'

NOTES

[1] Jean-Paul Sartre, *Critique of Dialectical Reason*, transl. by Alan Sheridan-Smith, ed. by Jonathan Ree (London: NLB, 1976), pp. 45-47.

[2] Cf. István Mészáros, "Jean-Paul Sartre: A Critical Tribute," in Ralph Miliband and John Saville, eds. *The Socialist Register, 1975* (London: The Merlin Press, 1975), p. 10.

[3] Sartre, "The Purposes of Writing," in *Between Existentialism and Marxism, op. cit.*, p. 29.

[4] Benjamin Suhl, *Jean-Paul Sartre: The Philosopher as a Literary*

Critic (New York: Columbia University Press, 1970), p. 268.

[5] Jean-Paul Sartre, *Search for a Method*, transl. by Hazel E. Barnes (New York: Vintage Books, 1968), p. 161.

[6] Jean-Paul Sartre, "Time in the Work of Faulkner," in *Literary and Philosophical Essays*, transl. by A. Michelson (New York: Collier Books, 1970), pp. 84-85.

[7] Cf. Mészáros, "Jean-Paul Sartre: A Critical Tribute," *op. cit.*, pp. 34-38.

[8] Cf. Sartre, "The Itinerary of a Thought," in *Between Existentialism and Marxism, op. cit.*, p. 46.

[9] Jean-Paul Sartre, *The Transcendence of the Ego*, transl. by F. Williams and R. Kirkpatrick (New York: The Noonday Press, 1966), pp. 31, 97.

[10] Jean-Paul Sartre, *Imagination*, transl. by F. Williams (Ann Arbor: The University of Michigan Press, 1962), p. 146.

[11] *Ibid.*, p. 143.

[12] Jean-Paul Sartre, *The Emotions: Outline of the Theory*, transl. by B. Frenchtman (New York: The Wisdom Library, 1948), p. 21.

[13] *Ibid.*, p. 93.

[14] Jean-Paul Sartre, *The Psychology of Imagination*, (New York: The Citadel Press, 1963), p. 16.

[15] *Ibid.*, p. 77.

[16] *Ibid.*, p. 268.

[17] *Ibid.*, p. 274.

[18] *Ibid.*, p. 277.

[19] Sartre, *Literary and Philosophical Essays, op. cit.*, pp. 7-25, 94-103.

[20] *Ibid.*, pp. 41-43.

[21] Mark Poster, *Existential Marxism in Postwar France, op. cit.*, p. 75.

[22] Jean-Paul Sartre, *Being and Nothingness*, transl. by H. E. Barnes (New York: Washington Square Press, 1975), pp. 29, 135.

[23] *Ibid.*, pp. 9-17.

[24] *Ibid.*, p. 23.

[25] *Ibid.*, p. 11.

[26] George Novack, ed. *Existentialism versus Marxism* (New York: A Delta Book, 1966), pp. 152, 156.

[27] Strasser, *op. cit.*, p. 41.

[28] Cf. Poster, *op. cit.*, chap. 4.

[29] Sartre, *Being and Nothingness, op. cit.*, pp. 621-622.

[30] *Ibid.*, p. 625.

[31] *Ibid.*, p. 629.

[32] *Ibid.*, pp. 626, 634, 636-637.

[33] *Ibid.*, p. 707.

[34] *Ibid.*, p. 735.

[35] *Ibid.*, pp. 559, 576-577.

[36] *Ibid.*, p. 88.

[37] *Ibid.*, p. 116 no. 9.

[38] *Ibid.*, p. 302.

[39] *Ibid.*, p. 734.

[40] *Ibid.*, p. 764.

[41] *Ibid.*, p. 716.

[42] *Ibid.*, p. 721.

[43] *Ibid.*, p. 724.

[44] *Ibid.*, p. 730.

[45] *Ibid.*, p. 731.

[46] *Ibid.*, p. 731.

[47] *Ibid.*, p. 734.

[48] Cf. Sartre, "The Itinerary of a Thought," *op. cit.*, p. 34.

[49] Zdenko Skreb, "Littérature Engagée," in Strelka, ed. *Literary Criticism and Sociology, op. cit.*, pp. 203-204.

[50] M. Adereth, *Commitment in Modern French Literature* (London: Victor Gollancz, Ltd., 1967), p. 47.

[51] Theodor Adorno, "Commitment," *New Left Review*, no. 87-88 (September-December 1974), p. 76.

[52] Eugene F. Kaelin, *An Existentialist Aesthetic: The Theories of Sartre and Merleau-Ponty* (Madison: The University of Wisconsin Press, 1966), p. 119.

[53] Sartre, "The Purposes of Writing," *op. cit.*, pp. 13-14.

[54] Mészáros, "Jean-Paul Sartre: A Critical Tribute," *op. cit.*, p. 12.

[55] Sartre, "The Purposes of Writing," *op. cit.*, p. 25.

[56] *Ibid.*, p. 29.

[57] Adereth, *op. cit.*, p. 35.

[58] Sartre, *What is Literature?, op. cit.*, p. 70.

[59] Cf. Joseph Halpern, *Critical Fictions: The Literary Criticism of Jean-Paul Sartre* (New Haven: Yale University Press, 1976), pp. 1-18.

[60] Cf. *Ibid.*, pp. 74-84.

[61] In relation to Sartre's distinction between prose and poetry together with the other arts, cf. for example, George H. Bauer, *Sartre and the Artist* (Chicago: The University of Chicago Press, 1969), pp. 1-11. However, for Sartre's modified view of the relationship between prose and poetry in reference to communication and commitment, cf. Sartre, "The Writer and his Language," in Jean-Paul Sartre, *Politics and Literature*, transl. by John Calder (London: Clader and Boyars, 1973), pp. 97-107.

[62] For Sartre's criteria of good literature, cf. for example, Suhl, *op. cit.*, pp. 265-272.

[63] Cf. Sartre, *What is Literature?*, *op. cit.*, pp. 13-15.

[64] Sartre, "A Plea for Intellectuals," in *Between Existentialism and Marxism*, *op. cit.*, pp. 40-41.

[65] *Ibid.*, p. 51.

[66] *Ibid.*, p. 233.

[67] *Ibid.*, p. 216.

[68] Sartre, "The Purposes of Writing," *op. cit.*, p. 14.

[69] Sartre, *What is Literature?*, *op. cit.*, p. 234.

[70] *Ibid.*, p. 233.

[71] Wellek, *A History of Modern Criticism: 1759-1950*, IV, *op. cit.*, p. 356.

[72] Nietzsche, quoted in *Ibid.*, p. 346.

[73] Sartre, *What is Literature?*, *op. cit.*, p. 29.

[74] *Ibid.*, p. 33.

[75] *Ibid.*, p. 34.

[76] *Ibid.*, pp. 35, 36.

[77] *Ibid.*, p. 37.

[78] *Ibid.*, pp. 38, 39, 48.

[79] Sartre, "The Purposes of Writing," *op. cit.*, pp. 22, 30.

[80] Sartre, "A Plea for Intellecturals," *op. cit.*, p. 277.

[81] Sartre, *What is Literature?*, *op. cit.*, p. 68.

[82] *Ibid.*, p. 153.

[83] Maurice Merleau-Ponty, *Adventures of the Dialectic*, transl. by J. Bien (Evanston: Northwestern University Press, 1973), p. 95.

[84] Sartre, "Materialism and Revolution," in *Literary and Philosophical Essays*, *op. cit.*, pp. 235-246.

[85] Cf. Sartre, *The Communists and the Peace*, transl. by M. Fletcher, J. Kleinschmidt and P. Berk (New York: Brazilier, 1968), p. 80.

[86] Merleau-Ponty, *op. cit.*, p. 100.

[87] *Ibid.*, p. 200.

[88] *Ibid.*, p. 157.

[89] *Ibid.*, p. 198.

[90] Sartre, "The Itinerary of a Thought," *op. cit.*, p. 42.

[91] Cf. for example, Philip Thody, *Jean-Paul Sartre: A Literary and Political Study* (New York: MacMillan, 1960), p. 140.

[92] Jean-Paul Sartre, *Baudelaire*, transl. by M. Turnell (London: Horzon, 1949), p. 185.

[93] Cf. Suhl, *op. cit.*, p. 151.

[94] Jean-Paul Sartre, *Saint Genet: Actor and Martyr* (New York: New American Library, 1971), p. 5.

[95] *Ibid.*, p. 584.

[96] *Ibid.*, pp. 330, 331.

[97] *Ibid.*, p. 337.

[98] *Ibid.*, pp. 292-293.

[99] *Ibid.*, p. 34.

[100] *Ibid.*, p. 590.

[101] *Ibid.*, p. 599.

[102] Jean-Paul Sartre, "The Writer and his Language," *op. cit.*, p. 90.

[103] Sartre, *Search for a Method, op. cit.*, pp. 97, 98. Cf. also n. 4 p. 98.

[104] Sartre, *Saint Genet, op. cit.*, p. 563, n.

[105] Sartre, *Search for a Method, op. cit.*, p. 28.

[106] *Ibid.*, p. 33, n.

[107] *Ibid.*, p. 35.

[108] Sartre's enthusiasm about Lefebvre's method is due to its inclusion of a phenomenological descriptive phase, to its ability for a double movement (progressive and regressive) and to its potential applicability "in all the domains of anthropology." Thus, Sartre quotes approvingly Lefebvre's proposal of "a very simple method employing auxiliary techniques and comprising several phases: a)*Descriptive.* Observation but with a scrutiny guided by experience and by a general theory. . . . b)*Analytico-Regressive.* Analysis of reality. Attempt to *date* it precisely. c)*Historical-Genetic.* Attempt to rediscover the present but elucidated, understood, explained." (*Ibid.*, p. 52, n.)

[109] *Ibid.*, p. 65, n. 5.

[110] Sartre, "The Itinerary of a Thought," *op. cit.*, p. 34.

[111] *Ibid.*, p. 35.

[112] Sartre, *Search for a Method, op. cit.*, pp. 175, 177.

[113] Sartre, *Critique of Dialectical Reason, op. cit.*, pp. 39, 69.

[114] *Ibid.*, p. 69.

[115] *Ibid.*, p. 67.

[116] *Ibid.*, pp. 36, 38, 52.

[117] Sartre, "The Itinerary of a Thought," *op. cit.*, p. 43.

[118] Sartre, "A Plea for Intellectuals," *op. cit.*, p. 275.

[119] Sartre writes: "The meaning of our study here must be a 'differential,' as Merleau-Ponty would call it. It is in fact the *difference* between the 'Common Beliefs' and the concrete idea or attitude of the person studied, the way in which the beliefs are enriched, made concrete, deviated, etc., which, more than anything else, is going to enlighten us with respect to our object. This *difference* constitutes its uniqueness; to the degree that the individual utilizes 'collectives,' he depends—like all the members of his class or his milieu—upon a very general interpretation which already allows the regression to be pushed to material conditions. But to the degree that his behavior demands a differentiated interpretation, it will be necessary for us to form particular hypotheses within the abstract framework of

universal significations . . . what I want to indicate here is that we approach the study of the differential upon the basis of a totalizing demand. . . . It is not a *trait* of the individual; it is the total individual, grasped in his process of objectification." (*Search for a Method, op. cit.*, pp. 137-138.)

[120] Sartre, "The Itinerary of a Thought," *op. cit.*, p. 49.

[121] István Mészáros, "From 'The Legend of Truth' to a 'True Legent: Phases of Sartre's Development," *Telos*, no. 25 (Fall, 1965), p. 119.

[122] Cf. for example, Halpern, *op. cit.*, especially pp. 156-159.

[123] Sartre, "The Itinerary of a Thought," *op. cit.*, p. 35.

[124] *Ibid.*, pp. 43-44.

[125] *Ibid.*, p. 41.

[126] *Ibid.*, p. 42.

[127] *Ibid.*, pp. 37, 38.

[128] *Ibid.*, pp. 39, 42.

[129] Sartre emphasizes that *comprehension* and *intellection* are two forms of certainty not opposed to each other but related as a species (comprehension) to a genus (intellection). Comprehension refers to the *intentional praxis* of an individual or a group. Intellection is a complex way of grasping the source of "actions without an agent, productions without a producer, totalizations without a totalizer, counter-finalities and internal circularities . . . [Also of] . . . multiplicities producing totalized thoughts and acts without reference to the individuals composing them, indeed without their even being aware of it." And he defines these forms as follows: "I shall call any temporalizing dialectical certainty, in so far as it is capable of totalizing *all* practical realities intellection, and reserve the term comprehension for the *totalizing* group or any *praxis* in so far as it is intentionally produced by its author or authors." (*Critique of Dialectical Reason, op. cit.*, p. 76.)

[130] Sartre, "The Itinerary of a Thought," *op. cit.*, p. 41.

[131] Claude Levi-Strauss, *The Savage Mind, op. cit.*, p. 252.

[132] Claude Levi-Strauss, *Tristes Tropiques*, transl. by J. and D. Weightman (London: Jonathan Cape, 1973), p. 58.

[133] Sartre, "The Writer and his Language," *op. cit.*, pp. 77, 93, 125.

[134] Sartre, "A Plea for Intellectuals," *op. cit.*, p. 278.

[135] *Ibid.*, p. 278.

[136] *Ibid.*, p. 279.

[137] *Ibid.*, p. 280.

[138] Cf. for example, *Search for a Method, op. cit.*, p. 141.

[139] Interview by Marlena Politopoulou, *H AYRH*, 27th February, 1977, p. 10, col. 3. (My translation).

[140] Cf. Flaubert, *op. cit.*, p. 91.

[141] Sartre, "A Plea for Intellectuals," *op. cit.*, p. 280.

[142] *Ibid.*, pp. 281, 282.

[143] *Ibid.*, p. 268.

[144] Sartre, "Myth and Reality in the Theatre," in *Politics and Literature, op. cit.*, p. 63.

[145] Sartre, "The Itinerary of a Thought," *op. cit.*, p. 55.

[146] Interview by Marlena Politipoulou, *op. cit.* (My translation).

BIBLIOGRAPHY

Abel, Theodore. "The Operation Called Verstehen." *American Journal of Sociology*, LIV, (1948).

Abrams, M. H. *The Mirror and the Lamp: Romantic Theory and the Critical Tradition*. New York: Oxford, 1971.

—. *A Glossary of Literary Terms*. 3rd ed. New York: Rinehard and Winston, Inc., 1971.

Adams, Hazard, ed. *Critical Theory since Plato*. New York: Harcourt Brace Jovanovich, Inc., 1971.

Adereth, M. *Commitment in Modern French Literature*. London: Victor Collancz, Ltd., 1967.

Adorno, Theodor. "Commitment." *New Left Review*, no. 87-88 (September-December, 1974).

Apel, Karl Otto, et al. ed. *Hermeneutik und Ideologiekritik*. Frankfurt am Main: Suhrkamp Verlag, 1971.

Arvon, Henri. *Marxist Esthetics*. Translated by H. R. Lane. Ithaca: Cornell University Press, 1973.

Bachelard, Gaston. *The Poetics of Space*. Translated by E. Gilson. Boston: Beacon Press, 1970.

Bann, Stephen and Bowlt, John E., eds. *Russian Formalism*. Edinburgh: Scottish Academic Press, 1973.

Barthes, Roland. *On Racine*. New York: Hill and Wang, 1964.

—. *Writing Degree Zero*. Translated by A. Lavers and C. Smith. London: Jonathan Cape, 1967.

—. *S/Z.* Translated by R. Miller. New York: Hill and Wang, 1974.

Bauer, George H. *Sartre and the Artist.* Chicago: The University of Chicago Press, 1969.

Baxandall, Lee. "Marxism and Aesthetics: A Critique of the Contribution of George Plekhanov." *The Journal of Aesthetics and Art Criticism,* XXV, no. 3 (Spring, 1967).

Baxandall, Lee and Morawski, Stephan, eds. *Marx and Engels on Literature and Art: A Selection of Writings.* St. Louis: Telos Press, 1973.

Benedict, Ruth. *Race: Science and Politics.* New York: The Viking Press, 1970.

Benjamin, Walter. *Illuminations.* Edited by Hannah Arendt. New York: Schocken Books, 1969.

Berger, Peter L. and Luckmann, Thomas. *The Social Construction of Reality.* New York: Doubleday and Company, Inc., 1967.

Bergin, T. G. and Fisch, M. H., transl. *The New Science of Giambattista Vico.* Ithaca: Cornell University Press, 1972.

Bodkin, Maud. *Archetypal Patterns in Poetry.* New York: Vintage Books, 1958.

Boon, James A. *From Symbolism to Structuralism.* New York: Harper Torchbooks, 1973.

Bowlt, John E., ed. and transl. *Russian Art of the Avant-Garde: Theory and Criticism, 1902-1934.* New York: The Viking Press, 1976.

Bradbury, John M. *The Fugitives: A Critical Account.* Chapel Hill: The University of North Carolina Press, 1958.

Brang, Peter. "Sociological Methods in Twentieth Century Russian Literary Criticism," in *Literary Criticism and Sociology.* Edited by Joseph P. Strelka.

Brik, Osip M. "Contributions to the Study of Verse Language," in *Readings in Russian Poetics: Formalist and Structuralist Views.* Edited by L.

Matejka and K. Pomorska.

Brill, A. A., transl. and ed. *The Basic Writings of Sigmund Freud*. New York: The Modern Library, 1965.

Broekman, Jan M. *Structuralism*. Dordrecht: D. Reidel Publishing Company, 1974.

Brooks, Cleanth. "Modern Criticism," in *The Achievement of American Criticism*. Edited by Clarence Arthur Brown. New York: The Ronald Press Company, 1954.

—. *The Well Wrought Urn*. London: Dennis Dobson, 1968.

Burke, Edmund. "A Philosophical Inquiry into the Origin of Ideas of the Sublime and Beautiful," in *Critical Theory Since Plato*. Edited by Hazard Adams.

"A Confrontation," in *New Left Review*, no. 62 (July-August, 1970).

Cassirer, Ernest. *An Essay on Man*. New Haven: Yale University Press, 1944.

Christofides, G. C. "Gaston Bachelard's Phenomenology of Imagination," in *The Romanic Review*, vol. 52-53 (February, 1961).

Crews, Frederic C. "Literature and Psychology," in *Relations of Literary Study*. Edited by James Thorpe.

"Crisis in Criticism: The Picard-Barthes Debate," in *T.L.S.* London: Oxford University Press, 1967.

Culler, Jonathan. *Structuralist Poetics*. London: Routledge and Kegan Paul, 1975.

Daiches, David. *Critical Approaches to Literature*. Englewood Cliffs, N.J.: Prentice-Hall, Inc., 1956.

deLaszlo, Violet S., ed. *The Basic Writings of C. G. Jung*. New York: Modern Library, 1959.

della Volpe, Galvano. "Theoretical Issues of a Marxist Poetics," in *Marxism and Art.* Edited by B. Lang and F. Williams.

Demetz, Peter. *Marx, Engels, and the Poets.* Translated by J. L. Sammons. Chicago: The University of Chicago Press, 1967.

"Dialectical Methodology," in *T.L.S.* (March 12, 1970).

Doubrovsky, Serge. *The New Criticism in France.* Translated by D. Coltman. Chicago: The University of Chicago Press, 1973.

Eagleton, Terry. *Marxism and Literary Criticism.* London: Methuen and Co. Ltd., 1976.

Ehrmann, Jacques, ed. *Structuralism.* New York: Anchor Books, 1970.

Ejxenbaum, Boris. "The Theory of Formal Method," in *Readings in Russian Poetics: Formalist and Structuralist Views.* Edited by L. Matejka and K. Pomorska.

Eliot, T. S. *Selected Essays.* New York: Harcourt, Brace and Company, 1950.

—. *The Sacred Wood.* London: Methuen and Co. Ltd., 1964.

Embree, Lester, ed. *Aron Gurwitsch: Phenomenology and the Theory of Science.* Northwestern University Press, 1974.

Engels, Frederick. *Anti-Duhring.* New York: International Publishers, 1939.

—. *Ludwig Feuerbach.* New York: International Publishers, 1941.

English, H. B. and English, A. C. *A Comprehensive Dictionary of Psychological and Psychoanalytical Terms: A Guide to Usage.* New York: David McKay Company, Inc., 1968.

Erlich, Victor. *Russian Formalism: History-Doctrine.* 2nd ed. The Hague: Mouton and Co., 1965.

Escarpit, Robert. *Sociology of Literature.* Translated by E. Pick. Rainesville, Ohio: Lake Erie College Studies, 1965.

Fekete, John. *The Critical Twilight.* London: Routledge and Kegan Paul,

1978.

Fischer, Ernst. *The Necessity of Art.* Translated by A. Bostock. Middlesex: Penguin Books, 1970.

Flaubert, Gustave. "On Realism," in *Documents of Modern Literary Realism.* Edited by J. Becker. Princeton: Princtron University Press, 1963.

Freud, Sigmund. *A General Introduction to Psychoanalysis.* Translated by Joan Riviere. New York: Pocket Books, 1969.

—. "Creative Writers and Daydreaming," in *Critical Theory Since Plato.* Edited by Hazard Adams.

Frye, Northrop. *Anatomy of Criticism.* Princeton: Princeton University Press, 1957.

Gadamer, Hans-Georg. *Truth and Method.* New York: The Seabury Press, 1975.

—. "On the Scope and Function of Hermeneutical Reflection." Translated by G. B. Hess and R. E. Palmer, in *Continuum*, vol. 8, nos. 1 and 2 (Spring and Summer, 1970).

Giglioli, Pier Paolo, ed. *Language and Social Context.* Middlesex: Penguin Books, 1972.

Glover, Edward. *Freud or Jung?* Cleveland: World, 1965.

Glucksmann, Miriam. "Lucien Goldmann: Humanist or Marxist?" *New Left Review*, no. 56 (July-August, 1969).

—. *Structuralist Analysis in Contemorary Social Thought.* London: Routledge and Kegan Paul, 1974.

Goldmann, Lucien. "The Sociology of Literature: Status and Problems of Method," in *International Social Science Journal*, XIX, no. 4 (1967).

—. "The Early Writings of Georg Luk'acs," in *Triquarterly*, no. 9 (Spring, 1967).

—. "Criticism and Dogmatism in Literature," in *The Dialectics of Liberation*. Edited by D. Cooper. London: Penguin Books, 1968.

—. *The Hidden God*. Translated by P. Thody. London: Routledge and Kegan Paul, 1970.

—. *Marxisme et Sciences Humaines*. Paris: Gallimard, 1970.

—. *La Creation Culturelle Dans la Societe Moderne*. Paris: Denoel/Gonthier, 1971.

—. *Immanuel Kant*. Translated by Robert Black. London: NLB, 1971.

—. *Racine*. Cambridge: Rivres Press, 1972.

—. "Genetic-Structuralist Method in History and Literature," in *Marxism and Art*. Edited by Berrel Lang and Forrest Williams.

—. "Reflections on History and Class Consciousness," in *Aspects of History and Class Consciousness*. Edited by István Mészáros. New York: Herder and Herder, 1972.

—. *The Human Sciences and Philosophy*. London: Cape Editions, 1973.

—. "Dialectical Materialism and Literary History." *New Left Review*, no. 92 (July-August, 1975).

—. *Towards a Sociology of the Novel*. London: Tavistock Publications, 1975.

Gramsci, Antonio. *The Modern Prince and Other Writings*. New York: International Publishers, 1967.

Grooten, J. and G. Jo Steenbergen. *New Encyclopedia of Philosophy*. New York: Philosophical Library, 1972.

Guerard, Albert. *Literature and Society*. Boston: Lothrop, Lee and Shepard Company, 1935.

Habermas, Jürgen. "Summation and Response," in *Continuum*, vol. 8, nos. 1 and 2 (Spring and Summer, 1970).

Halpern, Joseph. *Critical Fictions: The Literary Criticism of Jean-Paul Sartre*. New Haven: Yale University Press, 1976.

Hamilton, Peter. *Knowledge and Social Structure*. London: Routledge and Kegan Paul, 1974.

Handy, William J. *Kant and the Southern New Critics*. Austin: University of Texas Press, 1963.

—. ed. *A Symposium on Formalist Criticism*. Texas: The University of Texas Press, 1965.

Hauser, Arnold. *The Philosophy of Art History*. London: Routledge and Kegan Paul, 1959.

Hawthorn, Jeremy. *Identity and Relationship*. London: Lawrence and Wishart, 1973.

Hegel, G. W. F. *Encyclopedia of Philosophy*. Translated by Gustav Emil Mueller. New York: Philosophical Library, 1959.

—. *Aesthetics: Lectures on Fine Art*. Translated by T. M. Knox. London: Oxford University Press, 1975.

Heidegger, Martin. *Being and Time*. Translated by J. Macquarrie and E. Robinson. New York: Harper and Row, Publ., 1962.

Heiss, Robert. *Hegel, Kierkegaard, Marx*. Translated by E. Garside. Delacorte Press/Seymour Lawrence, 1975.

Hughes, H. Stuart. *Consciousness and Society*. New York: Vintage Books, 1961.

Hulme, T. E. "Romanticism and Classicism," in *Critical Theory Since Plato*. Edited by Hazard Adams.

Hyman, Stanley Edgar. *The Armed Vision*. New York: Vintage Books, 1955.

Huxley, Aldous. *Tomorrow and Tomorrow and Tomorrow and Other Essays*. New York: Harper, 1956.

I'll Take My Stand: The South and the Agrarian Tradition, by Twelve Southerners. New York: 1930.

Jacobi, Jolande, ed. *C. G. Jung: Psychological Reflections*. Princeton: Princeton University Press, 1970.

Jakobson, Roman. "The Dominant," in *Readings in Russian Poetics: Formalist and Structuralist Views*. Edited by L. Matejka and K. Pomorska.

Jameson, Frederic. *Marxism and Form*. Princeton: Princeton University Press, 1971.

—. *The Prison-House of Language*. Princeton: Princeton University Press, 1972.

Jung, C. G. *Four Archetypes*. Translated by R. F. C. Hull. Princeton: Princeton University Press, 1973.

—. "On the Relation of Analytical Psychology to Poetry," in *Critical Theory Since Plato*. Edited by Hazard Adams.

—. "The Problem of Types in Poetry," in *Psychological Types; or The Psychology of Individuation*. Translated by H. Godwin Barnes. New York: Harcourt, Brace and Company, Inc., 1923.

—. *Modern Man in Search of a Soul*. Translated by W. S. Dell and Cary F. Baynes. New York: Harcourt, Brace and Co., 1933.

Kaelin, Eugene F. *An Existentialist Aesthetic: The Theories of Sartre and Merleau-Ponty*. Madison: The University of Wisconsin Press, 1966.

Kant, Immanuel. *The Critique of Judgement*. Translated by J. C. Meredith. London: Oxford University Press, 1961.

Kaplan, Morton and Kloss, Robert. *The Unspoken Motive*. New York: The Free Press, 1973.

Kaufmann, Fritz. "Art and Phenomenology," in *Essays in Phenomenology*. Edited by Maurice Natanson.

Kiralyfalvi, Bela. *The Aesthetics of Gyorgy Lukács*. Princeton: Princeton

University Press, 1975

Kockelmans, Joseph J., ed. *Phenomenology*. New York: Doubleday and Company, Inc., 1967.

Kristeva, Julia. "The Ruin of a Poetics," in *Russian Formalism*. Edited by Stephen Bann and John E. Bowlt.

Lang, Berrel and Williams, Forest, eds. *Marxism and Art*. New York: David Mckay Company, Inc., 1972.

Laurenson, Diana and Swingewood, Alan. *The Sociology of Literature*. London: MacGibbon and Kee, 1972.

Lefebvre, Henry. *Dialectical Materialism*. Translated by J. Sturrock. London: Jonathan Cape, 1974.

Leff, Gordon. *The Tyranny of Concepts: a Critique of Marxism*. London: The Merlin Press, 1969.

Lemon, T. and Reiss, Marion J., transl. *Russian Formalist Criticism: Four Essays*. Lincoln: University of Nebraska Press, 1965.

Lenin, V. I. *On Literature and Art*. Moscow: Progress Publishers, 1970.

LeRoy, G. C. and Beitz, U., eds. *Preserve and Create*. New York: Humanities Press, 1973.

Levi-Strauss, Claude. *Structural Anthropology*. Translated by C. Jakobson and B. G. Schoept. New York: Basic Books, 1963.

—. *The Savage Mind*. Chicago: The University of Chicago Press, 1966.

—. *The Raw and the Cooked*. Translated by J. and D. Weightman. New York: Harper Torchbooks, 1969.

—. *Tristes Tropiques*. Translated by J. and D. Weightman. London: Jonathan Cape, 1973.

Lifshitz, Mikhail. *The Philosophy of Art of Karl Marx*. Translated by R. B. Winn. Bristol: Pluto Press Limited, 1973.

Lindauer, Martin S. *The Psychological Study of Literature*. Chicago: Nelson Hall, 1974.

Lukács, Georg. "Appearance and Essence," in *Preserve and Create*. Edited by G. C. LeRoy and U. Beitz.

—. *Studies in European Realism*. New York: Grosset and Dunlap, 1964.

—. *Writer and Critic and Other Essays*. Edited and translated by A. D. Kahn. New York: Grosset and Dunlap, 1970.

—. *The Theory of the Novel*. Translated by Anna Bostock. Cambridge, Massachusetts: the M.I.T. Press, 1971.

—. *Realism in Our Time*. New York: Harper and Row, Publishers, 1971.

—. *History and Class Consciousness*. Translated by R. Livingstone. Cambridge, Massachusetts: The M.I.T. Press, 1973.

Lukes, Steves. "Methodological Individualism Reconsidered," in *The Philosophy of Social Explanation*. Edited by Alan Ryan. London: Oxford University Press, 1973.

Macksey, Richard and Donato, Eugenio, eds. *The Language of Criticism and the Sciences of Man: The Structuralist Controversy*. Baltimore: The John Hopkins Press, 1970.

Margolis, Joseph, ed. *Philosophy looks at the Arts*. New York: Scribner's, 1962.

Marković, Mihailo. "The Problem of Reification and the Verstehen-Erklären Controversy," in *ACTA SOCIOLOGICA*, vol. 15 (1972).

Marx, Karl. *Theories of Surplus Value*, Part I.

—. *A Contribution to the Critique of Political Economy*. Moscow: Progress Publishers, 1970.

—. *Grundrisse*. Translated by M. Nicolaus. Middlesex: Penguin Books, 1973.

—. *Capital*. I. Moscow: Progress Publishers, n.d.

Marx, Karl and Engels, Frederick. *The German Ideology.* Edited by C. J. Arthur. New York: International Publishers, 1973.

Matejka, L. and Pomorska, K., eds. *Readings in Russian Poetics: Formalist and Structuralist Views.* Cambridge, Massachusetts: The M.I.T. Press, 1971.

Mayrl, Williams. "Introduction," in Lucien Goldmann. *Cultural Creation in Modern Society.* St. Louis: Telos Press, 1976.

—. "Genetic Structuralism and the Analysis of Social Consciousness," in *Theory and Society*, vol. 5, no. 1 (January, 1978).

McIlwain, Charles. *The Growth of Political Thought in the West.* New York: MacMillan Company, 1932.

Merleau-Ponty, Maurice. *Adventures of the Dialectic.* Translated by J. Bien. Evanston: Northwestern University Press, 1973.

Mészáros, István. *Marx's Theory of Alienation.* 3rd ed. London: Merlin Press, 1972.

—. "Ideology and Social Science," in *The Socialist Register, 1972.* Edited by Ralph Miliband and John Saville. London: The Merlin Press, 1972.

—. *Lukács' Concept of Dialectic.* London: The Merlin Press, 1972.

—. "Jean-Paul Sartre: A Critical Tribute," in *The Socialist Register, 1975.* Edited by Ralph Miliband and John Saville. London: The Merlin Press, 1975.

—. "From 'The Legend of Truth' to a 'True Legend': Phases of Sartre's Development," in *Telos*, no. 25 (Fall, 1975).

Miller, J. Hillis. "The Literary Criticism of Georges Poulet," in *MLN*, vol. 78 (December, 1963).

Morawski, Stephan. "The Aesthetic Views of Marx and Engels," in *The Journal of Aesthetics and Art Criticism*, XXVIII, no. 3 (Spring, 1970).

Mukarovsky, Jan. "Standard Language and Poetic Language," in *Critical Theory Since Plato.* Edited by Hazard Adams.

Mulhern, Francis. "Introduction to Goldmann," in *New Left Review*, no. 92 (July-August, 1975).

Natanson, Maurice, ed. *Essays in Phenomenology.* The Hague: Martinus Nijhoff, 1960.

—. ed. *Phenomenology and the Social Sciences.* Evanston: Northwestern University Press, 1973.

Novack, George, ed. *Existentialism versus Marxism.* New York: A Delta Book. 1966.

—. *An Introduction to the Logic of Marxism.* New York: Pathfinder Press, 1973.

Palmer, Leonard R. *Descriptive and Comparative Linguistics.* London: Faber and Faber, 1972.

Parkinson, G. H. R., ed. *Georg Lukács: The Man, his Work and his Ideas.* London: Weidenfeld and Nicolson, 1970.

Parsons, Talcott. *The Structure of Social Action.* New York: The Free Press of Glencoe, 1961.

—. Max Weber: *The Theory of Social and Economic Organization.* New York: The Free Press, 1964.

Pei, Mario. *Invitation to Linguistics.* New York: Doubleday and Company, Inc., 1965.

Philipson, Morris. *Outline of a Jungian Aesthetics.* Northwestern University Press, 1963.

Pinkus, Theo, ed. *Conversations with Lukács.* Cambridge, Massachusetts: The M.I.T. Press, 1975.

Planty-Bonjour, Guy. *The Categories of Dialectical Materialism.* New York: Frederick A. Praeger, Inc., Publishers, 1967.

Plekhanov, George V. *Fundamental Problems of Marxism.* Moscow: Progress Publishers, 1962.

—. *Art and Society*. New York: Oriole Editions, 1974.

Pomorska, K. "Russian Formalism in Retrospect," in *Readings in Russian Poetics: Formalist and Structuralist Views*. Edited by L. Matejka and K. Pomorska.

Poster, Mark. *Existential Marxism in Postwar France*. Princeton: Princeton University Press, 1975.

Poulet, Georges. "Criticism and the Experience of Interiority," in *The Language of Criticism and the Sciences of Man: The Structuralist Controversy*. Edited by R. Macksey and E. Donato.

Propp, Vladimir. "Morphology of the Folktale," in *International Journal of American Linguistics*, vol. 24, no. 4.

Radcliffe-Brown, A. R. *Structure and Function in Primitive Society*. London: Cohen and West, 1952.

Ransom, J. C. *The New Criticism*. Norfolk, Connecticut: New Directions, 1941.

—. *Poems and Essays*. New York: Vintage Books, 1955.

—. *The World's Body*. Port Washington, New York: Kennikat Press, Inc., 1964.

—. *God Without Thunder: An Unorthodox Defense of Orthodoxy*. Hamden, Connecticut: Archon Books, 1965.

Richard, Jean-Pierre. *Poésie et profondeur*. Paris, 1953.

—. *Littérature et sensation*. Paris, 1954.

Richards, I. A. *Principles of Literary Criticism*. 4th ed. London: Kegan Paul, Trench, Trubner and Co. LTD., 1930.

—. *Coleridge on Imagination*. 3rd ed. London: Routledge and Kegan Paul, LTD., 1962.

—. *Practical Criticism*. New York: Harcourt, Brace and Company, 1964.

—. *Poetries and Sciences*. London: Routledge and Kegan Paul, 1970.

Rieff, Phillip. *Freud: The Mind of the Moralist*. New York: The Viking Press, 1950.

Riley, M. W. *Sociological Research*. New York: Harcourt, Brace and World, Inc., 1964.

Robey, David, ed. *Structuralism: An Introduction*. London: Oxford University Press, 1973.

Rockwell, Joan. *Fact in Fiction*. London: Routledge and Kegan Paul, 1974.

Rodriguez, Ilena and Zimmerman, Marc. "Lucien Goldmann: Cultural Creation in Modern Soceity," in *Telos*, no. 28 (Summer, 1976).

Runciman, G. W. *A Critique of Max Weber's Philosophy of Social Sciences*. Cambridge University Press, 1972.

Sartre, Jean-Paul. *The Emotions: Outline of the Theory*. Translated by B. Frenchtman. New York: The Wisdom Library, 1948.

—. *Baudelaire*. Translated by M. Turnell. London: Horizon, 1949.

—. *Imagination*. Translated by F. Williams. Ann Arbor: The University of Michigan Press, 1962.

—. *The Psychology of Imagination*. New York: The Citadel Press, 1963.

—. *What is Literature?* Translated by W. Fowlie. New York: Harper Colophon Books, 1965.

—. *The Transcendence of the Ego*. Translated by F. Williams and R. Kirkpatrick. New York: The Noonday Press, 1966.

—. *The Communists and the Peace*. Translated by M. Fletcher, J. Kleinschmidt and P. Berk. New York: Brazilier, 1968.

—. *Search for a Method*. Translated by Hazel E. Barnes. New York: Vintage Books, 1968.

—. *Literary and Philosophical Essays*. Translated by A. Michelson. New

York: Collier Books, 1970.

—. *Saint Genet: Actor and Martyr.* New York: New American Library, 1971.

—. *Politics and Literature.* Translated by J. Underwood and J. Calder. London: Calder and Boyars, 1973.

—. *Between Existentialism and Marxism.* Translated by John Matthews. London: NLB, 1974.

—. *Being and Nothingness.* Translated by H. E. Barnes. New York: Washington Square Press, 1975.

—. *Critique of Dialectical Reason.* Translated by Alan Sheridan-Smith. Edited by Jonathan Ree. London: NLB, 1976.

—. Interview by Marlena Politopoulou, *H AYRH*, February 27, 1977.

Saussure, Ferdinand de, *Course in General Linguistics.* Edited by C. Bally and A. Sechhaye in collaboration with A. Reidlinger. Translated by Wade Baskin. London: Peter Owen, 1964.

Scholes, Robert. *Structuralism in Literature.* New Haven: Yale University Press, 1974.

Schucking, Levin L. *The Sociology of Literary Taste.* London: The University of Chicago Press, 1966.

Schuetz, Alfred. "Phenomenology and the Social Sciences," in *Phenomenology.* Edited by Joseph J. Kockelmans.

Sherwood, Richard. "Victor Scklovsky and the Development of Early Formalist Theory on Prose Literature," in *Russian Formalism.* Edited by Stephen Bann and John E. Bowlt.

Shils, Edward A. and Finch, Henry A., eds. *Max Weber: The Methodology of the Social Sciences.* New York: The Free Press, 1968.

Shipley, Joseph T., ed. *Dictionary of World Literary Terms.* Boston: The Writer, Inc., 1970.

Shklovsky, Victor. "The Resurrection of the Word," in *Russian Formalism*. Edited by S. Bann and J. Bowlt.

—. "The Connection Between Devices of Syuzhet Construction and General Stylistic Devices," in *Russian Formalism*. Edited by S. Bann and J. Bowlt.

—. "Art as Technique," in *Russian Formalist Criticism: Four Essays*. Translated by T. Lemon and Marion J. Reiss.

Siegel, Paul N., ed. *Leon Trotsky on Literature and Art*. 2nd ed. New York: Pathfinder Press, Inc., 1972.

Skreb, Zdenko. "Littérature Engagée," in *Literary Criticism and Sociology*. Edited by Joseph P. Strelka.

Slockower, Harry. "The Psychoanalytic Approach to Literature: Some Pitfalls and Promises." *Literature and Psychology*, XXI, no. 2 (1971).

Spector, Jack J. *The Aesthetics of Freud*. New York: McGraw-Hill Book Company, 1974.

Spiegelberg, Herbert. *The Phenomenological Movement: A Historical Introduction*. 2 vols. The Hague: Martinus Nijhoff, 1960.

—. *Doing Phenomenology*. The Hague: Martinus Nijhoff, 1975.

Stacy, R. H. *Russian Literary Criticism: A Short History*. Syracuse: Syracuse University Press, 1974.

Strasser, Stephan. *Phenomenology and the Human Sciences*. Pittsburgh: Duquesne University Press, 1974.

Strelka, Joseph, ed. *Problems of Literary Evaluation*. University Park and London: The Pennsylvania State University Press, 1969.

—. ed. *Literary Criticism and Sociology*. University Park: The Pennsylvania State University Press, 1973.

Suhl, Benjamin. *Jean-Paul Sartre: The Philosopher as a Literary Critic*. New York: Columbia University Press, 1970.

Sutton, Walter. *Modern American Criticism*. New Jersey: Prentice-Hall, Inc., 1963.

Taine, Hippolyte A. *Balzac: A Critical Study*. New York: Haskell House Publishers, LTD., 1973.

Tate, Allen. "Literature as Knowledge," in *Essays of Four Decades*. Chicago: The Swallow Press, Inc., 1968.

Tennenhouse, Leonard, ed. *The Practice of Psychoanalytic Criticism*. Detroit: Wayne State University, 1976.

Theodorson, George A. and Theodorson, Achilles G., *Modern Dictionary of Sociology*. New York: Apollo Editions, 1970.

Thody, Philip. *Jean-Paul Sartre: A Literary and Political Study*. New York: MacMillan, 1960.

Thompson, Ewa M. *Russian Formalism and Anglo-American New Criticism*. The Hague: Mouton, 1971.

Thorpe, James, ed. *Relations of Literary Study*. New York: Modern Language Association of America, 1967.

Todorov, Tzvetan. *Poetique de la prose*. Paris: Seuil, 1971.

Trotsky, Leon. *Literature and Revolution*. Translated by Rose Strunsky. Ann Arbor: The University of Michigan Press, 1971.

Trudgill, Peter. *Sociolinguistics: An Introduction*. Middlesex: Penguin Books, 1974.

Tynjanov, Jurij and Jakobson, Roman. "Problems in the Study of Literature and Language," in *Readings in Russian Poetics: Formalist and Structuralist Views*. Edited by L. Matejka and K. Pomorska.

Tynjanov, Jurij. "Rhythm as the Constructive Factor in Verse," in *Readings in Russian Poetics: Formalist and Structuralist Views*. Edited by L. Matejka and K. Pomorska.

Ullman, Stephan. *Meaning and Style*. New York: Barnes and Noble, 1973.

Vasquez, Adolfo Sanchez. *Art and Society: Essays in Marxist Aesthetics.* Translated by M. Riofrancos. New York: Monthly Review Press, 1973.

Vivas, Eliseo. "The Object of the Poem," in *Critical Theory Since Plato.* Edited by Hazard Adams.

—. "Philosphy of Culture, Aesthetics and Criticism: Some Problems," in *A Symposium on Formalist Criticism.* Edited by William J. Handy.

Volosinov, V. N. *Marxism and the Philosophy of Language.* Translated by L. Matejka and I. R. Titunik. New York: Seminar Press, 1973.

Vygotsky, Lev Semenovich. *The Psychology of Art.* Cambridge, Massachusetts: The M.I.T. Press, 1971.

Wagner, Helmut R., ed. *Alfred Schutz on Phenomenology and Social Relations.* Chicago: The University of Chicago Press, 1970.

Wellek, Rene. *A History of Modern Criticism: 1750-1950.* 4 vols. New Haven: Yale University Press, 1955.

—. *Concepts of Criticism.* Edited by Stephen G. Nichols, Jr. New Haven and London: Yale University Press, 1964.

Wellek, Rene and Warren, Austin. *Theory of Literature.* 3rd ed. London: Jonathan Cape, 1966.

Williams, Raymond. "Introduction," in *Racine.* By Lucien Goldmann.

—. "Base and Superstructure," in *New Left Review,* no. 82 (November-December, 1973).

Wilson, Edmund. *The Triple Thinkers.* New York: Oxford University Press, 1948.

Witt-Hansen, J. *Historical Materialism, The Method, The Theories. Book One: The Method.* Copenhagen: Munksgaard, 1960.

Wolff, Janet. *Hermeneutic Philosophy and the Sociology of Art.* London: Routledge and Kegan Paul, 1975.

Zimmerman, Marc. "Lucien Goldmann: From Dialectical Theory to Genetic Structuralism." *Berkeley Journal of Sociology*, vol. XXIII (1978-1979).

Zis, Avner. *Foundations of Marxist Aesthetics*. Moscow: Progress Publishers, 1977.

Zordan, Z. A. *The Evolution of Dialectical Materialism*. New York: St. Martin Press, 1967.

INDEX